Taking the Lead:

The Management Revolution

2ND EDITION

Contributing Authors:

Paul Sonnenburg
and
John Allman

Prepared by:

IN·TELE·COM
INTELLIGENT TELECOMMUNICATIONS

For use with:

Management

Meeting and Exceeding Customer Expectations

Plunkett and Attner, 6th Edition

SOUTH-WESTERN College Publishing

An International Thomson Publishing Company

Editor-in-Chief: Valerie A. Ashton
Acquisitions Editor: Randy G. Haubner
Production Editor: Shelley Brewer
Production: Judy Sullivan/INTELECOM
Manufacturing Coordinator: Sue Disselkamp
Marketing Manager: Stephen E. Momper

Taking the Lead: The Management Revolution is a television-based course produced by

1 2 3 4 5 Cl 1 0 9 8 7

Printed in the United States of America

ISBN: 0-538-86311-0

ITP
International Thomson Publishing
South-Western College Publishing is an ITP Company. The ITP trademark is used under license.

Contents

Introduction

M A N A G E M E N T   T O D A Y

As we approach the 21st century, it is daunting just to describe the world's problems let alone devise solutions. Surely never in human history have we faced such an array of perils and opportunity. Certainly never has the need for wise and forceful action been more immediate and compelling.

And where, you may ask, shall we find wise and forceful action? As P.T. Barnum said, "Right before your very eyes!" As you watch *Taking the Lead's* 26 episodes, and read Warren Plunkett's and Raymond Attner's *Introduction to Management*, you will meet a formidable array of knowledgeable and energetic men and women. These are people who have sought out today's challenges and persuaded others to collaborate in solving them, people who truly enjoy their work, and who eagerly share their knowledge and experience.

The people you are about to meet are genuinely distinguished leaders in their respective fields. Some are legends, some will be. Some are merely extraordinarily competent and articulate. But each eagerly accepted the invitation to participate in creating *Taking the Lead*. They made time in busy schedules for conferences and video taping sessions, and they graciously welcomed our writers, directors, researchers, and camera crews into their workplaces. These executives, consultants, academics, scientists, engineers, doctors, lawyers, and historians – managers all – typify the colleagues you will encounter in your own career. And we share them with you now in the same spirit of discovery they extended to us.

What is to be discovered in studying management? Surprisingly, only in this century have we attempted to systematically survey the elements that go into running organizations. Writing in 1941 in *The Managerial Revolution*, scholar J. Burnham said: "The theory of managerial revolu-

v

tion asserts that modern society has been organized through a set of major economic, social, and political institutions which we call capitalist. Now these institutions are undergoing transformation; within the new social structure, a different social group – the managers – will be the dominant class."

Fifteen years later Peter F. Drucker (*The Practice of Management*, New York Harper & Row, 1954 [HarperBusiness, 1993]) confirmed Burnham's judgement:

> *The emergence of management as an essential, a distinct and a leading institution is a pivotal event in social history. Rarely, if ever, has a new basic institution proven indispensable so quickly; and even less often has a new institution arrived with so little opposition, so little disturbance, so little controversy.*
>
> *Management will remain a basic and dominant institution perhaps as long as Western civilization itself survives. For management is not only grounded in the nature of the modern industrial system and in the needs off the modern business enterprise to which an industrial system must entrust its productive resources – both human and material. Management also expresses basic beliefs of modern Western society. It expresses the belief that economic change can be made into the most powerful engine for human betterment and social justice – that as Jonathan Swift first overstated it two hundred and fifty years ago, whoever makes two blades of grass grow where only one grew before deserves better of mankind than any speculative philosopher or metaphysical system builder.*

Drucker offers this caution: "[Management] is in fact indispensable – and this explains why, once begotten, it grew so fast and with so little opposition. . . . Only superior management competence and continuously improved management performance can keep us progressing . . ."

THE MANAGER AND READING

Someone certainly is reading the latest books on management. Many someones, including you. Your reading colleagues all around the world are managers eager to expand their knowledge, to discover more about their job, their company, the competition, the trends and developments and ideas that place management among one of the most dynamic and compelling arenas of modern endeavor. One reason for management's authentic energy and interest is that a great many intelligent and interesting people write about it all the time. From grizzled scholars, gurus, and seasoned journalists to managers on the front, these diversely opinionated and informed experts constantly pour out written material. From classic statements of theory and practice to impassioned "how to" books and supercharged hype for the latest salvation, a manager's challenge is to separate the stimulating, entertaining, and relevant from the mundane.

Perhaps the best advice is to cultivate a healthy skepticism. A skeptic is "one who instinctively or habitually doubts, questions, or disagrees with assertions or generally accepted conclusions." Test what you read against your own good sense. Demand solid evidence, good and sensible argument. Explore widely and in depth before deciding about important issues. Look and decide for yourself, exercising independence of mind and spirit. The surest defense against the mediocre and the false is to read widely. Make the time to explore history, economics, politics, the sciences. Consider not only current material, but the best that has been offered. Fernand Claudel, Michel Montaigne, Will and Ariel Durant, George Steiner, Daniel Boorstin, Patrick Moynihan, David Starr, David Halberstam, Joel Kotkin, and many others. Nor should the good manager's reading exclude fiction, poetry, or drama. Few non-fiction books can offer more about the ideas shaping management today than George Eliot's *Middlemarch*, or the novels of C.P. Snow, or even Ayn Rand.

The able manager is a well-informed person who welcomes every opportunity to access the ideas and facts discovered and shared by colleagues worldwide. Management crosses borders with fluent ease. The shared language of management transcends its jargon to achieve a broader language of its own that reflects its camaraderie and shared esprit that helps to make the able manager a contributor to many activities. The manger is a thoughtful person, a person with commitment to the world of ideas. Managers are constantly learning, they have duties, obligations to themselves, to their colleagues and employees, to their communities, and to the life of the mind.

You should consider the reading lists at the back of this guide and in Plunkett & Attner as invitations. During your involvement in this course, endeavor to spend some time each week perusing the recommended. They will vastly enhance your pleasure in every aspect of your studies.

THE STUDY GUIDE

As a telecourse that explores the ideas and practices of contemporary management, *Taking the Lead* includes four complementary elements in addition to your campus instructor: (1) the series of 26 half-hour video programs; (2) the new and wholly revised fifth edition of a popular textbook, An Introduction to Management, by Warren R. Plunkett and Raymond F. Attner; (3) this Telecourse Study Guide; and (4) sustained concurrent reading of appropriate books and periodicals.

Each lesson includes

- **Learning Objectives** that identify the lesson's core facts, ideas, and processes as presented in the text and video materials.

- An **Overview** of the lesson's subject material intended to establish a sense of context for specific elements and to suggest their orderly relationship within the lesson and to the course as a whole.

- **Assignments** that link the video lesson with the immediately applicable portions of the textbook and suggest a process for accomplishing the related learning activities.

- A list of **Key Terms** and definitions. Mastery of a discipline requires intimate familiarity with its specialized language. Much of management's vocabulary consists of technical jargon and conventional terms and phrases narrowly construed. For convenient access and reinforcement, we have repeated from the textbook the applicable glossary entries in each lesson.

- **Video Viewing Questions** invite your concurrent analysis of some of the central ideas taken up in the video program and serve as a nucleus for post-viewing review.

- The **Self-Test** provides a convenient check on your progress in assimilating the material.

- The **Expanded Analysis** encourages you to probe the meaning and utility of the lesson's concepts by considering their applications to wide-ranging management settings.

1 Management at Work: The Managerial World

Upon completing this lesson, you should be familiar with the facts, ideas, and processes contained in this lesson, and be able to:

- Recognize that management is a universal part of every organization and a function of everyday life.

- Define management in its human, technical, and conceptual dimensions, and specify why management is necessary.

- Describe in general terms the functions of management and the manager's principal roles and responsibilities.

- Differentiate myths and realities of a manager's job.

- Explain the management pyramid.

- Compare and contrast the skills needed for supervisory, mid-level, and top-level management positions.

- Discuss the multiple demands placed upon a manager both from within and from outside the organization; suggest ways to establish priorities and balance competing demands.

O V E R V I E W

The Universal Manager

Even while intensively pursuing individual agendas, people are social creatures. Given a choice between isolation and belonging to a group, almost without exception we choose to live and work within the supportive convenience of other humans. People work together in part because personal effort succeeds best in the context of orderly and purposeful systems called organizations.

Organizations vary in size, form, resources, membership, and purpose; but their goals nearly always include making and sharing goods and services for their members or outsiders. Because society requires organizations in order to operate, and organizations cannot function without managers to direct the activity of people, the manager has been instrumental in shaping human achievement from the early days of tribal activity.

Every kind of organization needs managers, all of whom share certain basic responsibilities and functions. Managers coordinate work toward common objectives, make decisions, and commit the organization's resources to the accomplishment of its goals.

The Substance of Management

During the last 150 years, knowledge about management has been expanded and refined into a dynamic body of theory and practice. Tested ideas and proven systems allow today's managers to solve contemporary problems at every level, from those of small companies to mammoth global enterprises. Management is the process of setting and achieving goals through five basic functions: planning, organizing, staffing, leading, and controlling. Working through the organization's staff, managers make decisions to set and attain the group's goals by applying human, financial, material, and information resources.

The Manager's Layered Universe

In most organizations, managers can be found at three different levels. At the top are the chief executive officer or president, and immediate subordinates – the people who handle overall management. They establish broad objectives and operating policies and direct most of the company's dealings with the external environment. Middle managers implement top management's objectives and policies; their subordinates are other managers. First-line managers or supervisors direct the company's accomplishment of work at the operating level. Manager titles vary with the organization and the specific job. Identification of managers by their areas of topical responsibility – marketing, operations, finance, and human resources, among others – is also a common practice.

Management Functions

In setting and achieving goals by applying resources, managers undertake the five basic functions of management – simultaneous elements of a process that requires coordination and integration. As managers identify goals and ways to accomplish them, their **planning** initiates the other four functions. **Organizing** determines how personnel and other resources will be structured. **Staffing** obtains needed people and trains them to accomplish the desired tasks. **Leading**, or directing, develops the organizational environment in which work is to be accomplished. And **controlling** establishes standards against which to measure progress toward objectives developed during planning so that corrections can be made if necessary.

The time and effort each manager devotes to particular functions varies with his or her level in the organization. In planning, for example, top-level managers are concerned with long-term plans while people at the lower management levels concentrate on more immediate needs – next week's schedule, today's deadline. With flexibility and adaptability, competent managers consistently strive to coordinate their own activities with the activities of managers at other levels in the organization. They also take outside influences into account, adapting their work to conditions and events in the real world.

In planning, managers establish and determine how to achieve objectives; in organizing, they develop the structures that facilitate accomplishing the objectives. Flexibility affects this function, too. Changes inside and outside the organization often call for new plans and organizational units.

Through the management function called staffing, managers analyze and project their organization's personnel needs, including the skills and experience needed and the number of people required. They recruit and hire suitable job candidates, and orient them to the company environment. And they provide ongoing training to help employees develop skills and accomplish their assignments effectively.

When leading, the manager provides leadership. Able managers systematically develop a personal method to achieve goals through people. They provide coaching and guidance, involve people in decision making, and build work teams that integrate members' unique abilities.

Planning, staffing, and leading require a mechanism to ensure smooth and successful operation; this is called controlling. Managers promote success and prevent failure by providing the means to monitor the performance of individuals and work units. Sound controls encourage the early discovery of problems and timely corrective action.

Management Roles

In observing companies like Hybritech, Patagonia, Apple, and others, it is evident that the manager must fill various roles at different times throughout the workday. Among the many "hats" a manager wears are:

- figurehead, leader, and liaison officer – interpersonal roles;
- monitor, disseminator, and spokesperson – informational roles;
- entrepreneur, disturbance handler, resource allocator, and negotiator – decisional roles.

In playing such roles, managers accomplish their managerial functions. The planning and organizing functions require the manager to perform the decisional role of resource allocator. In staffing, the manager plays the interpersonal leadership role by providing subordinates with feedback on performance. In leading, the manager acts as disseminator, entrepreneur, and disturbance handler; the manager serves as monitor in performing the controlling function.

Management Skills

Managerial skills are often classified as technical, human, and conceptual. **Technical skills** include the knowledge of and the ability to use specialized processes. **Human skills** embrace the ability to interact and communicate effectively with other persons. **Conceptual skills** – conceiving ideas and abstract relationships – let the manager see things as a whole and how parts relate to one another. A manager's level in the organization determines the relative importance of possessing each of these three skills.

Myths & Realities

While the five management functions remain important, sweeping changes in the business environment have pushed three pivotal issues to the forefront. The first is internationalization, in which transnational firms do business worldwide. The second development is the growing demand that corporations be responsible for their actions and act ethically. The third is the global emphasis on quality. Developments in each of these areas will demand a manager's time and focus.

Studies show that modern managers work differently than commonly thought. Instead of being able to reflect and work systematically, managers often work in fragmented, crisis-oriented bursts of activity. Instead of serenely delegating work to others, managers have extensive regular duties to perform. And in place of relying upon analytic procedures, managers appear to lean heavily on intuition and experience.

Today's managers deal with both routine tasks and the complex challenges caused by technological and social changes around the globe. Among such challenges are immigration, racial tensions, drug addiction, and the AIDS virus. Managers must prepare for the future needs of their staff and the larger community.

Changes in approach to management fundamentals requires time, effort, and a genuine commitment to creating an environment in which trust and teamwork are valued and communication is open. Creating such an environment may be the manager's most critical task.

ASSIGNMENTS

- Read the Overview, familiarize yourself with the Learning Objectives, and peruse the Key Terms below. Then turn to Plunkett & Attner, *Introduction to Management*, and read Chapter 1, "Management: An Overview," pages 3–30.

- Next, scan the Video Viewing Questions and watch the video program for Lesson 1, "Management at Work: The Managerial World."

- After watching the video, answer the viewing questions and assess your learning with the Self-Test.

- Familiarize yourself with the Review Questions, Discussion Questions for Critical Thinking, and Skill-Building Exercises on page 32 of Plunkett & Attner.

- Strengthen your understanding of the lesson's ideas and issues by undertaking the Expanded Analysis.

KEY TERMS

conceptual skills The ability to view the organization as a whole and see how its parts relate and depend on one another; and to deal with ideas and abstractions.

first-line, or supervisory management The lowest level of management; subordinates are non-management workers.

human skills The ability to interact and communicate with other people successfully; to understand, work with, and relate to individuals and groups.

management The process of setting and achieving goals through the execution of five basic management functions that use human, financial, material, and informational resources.

management hierarchy The pyramid arrangement of the several levels of management.

managers People who direct the activities of others.

middle management Managers below the rank of vice-president but above the supervisory level.

organization A group of two or more people that exists and operates to achieve common objectives.

role A set of expectations for a manager's behavior.

technical skills The ability to use the processes, practices, techniques, and tools of the specialty area a manager supervises.

top management Managers responsible for the overall management of the organization, for establishing organizational or company-wide objectives or goals and operating policies, and for directing the company in its relationships with its external environment.

VIDEO VIEWING QUESTIONS

1. How does the CEO's management style seem to influence the operations of Patagonia and Virgin?

2. Why is Total Quality Management considered such an important management idea?

3. How do the various management skills relate to different levels of management?

4. How does the recent tendency toward "flatter" organizations affect the middle manager?

5. What is a "technological gate keeper?"

6. What are the significant differences between management and leadership? How do management and leadership relate?

S E L F - T E S T

1. Which statement most accurately describes management? Management is essential

   a. only in large, complex groups.
   b. primarily in new organizations until activities are put in motion.
   c. to all organizations throughout their lives.
   d. only for organizations that lack clear objectives.

2. In large organizations, management typically takes place in three levels. These levels

   a. commonly fluctuate, with proportionate distribution of managers shifting as needs change.
   b. concentrate managers at the mid-level, with comparatively few at top or bottom.
   c. usually take the shape of a pyramid, with the greatest number at the bottom, fewest at the top.
   d. should include approximately equal numbers of managers.

3. Planning is sometimes considered the primary management function, probably because

   a. planning is usually done by first-line supervisors.
   b. planning is the only function that affects the other four.
   c. planning lays the groundwork for the other functions.
   d. planning requires the most skill of all management tasks.

4. Which statement best describes the relationship between the five management functions and the three management levels?

   a. Managers at each level perform different functions.
   b. Managers at all levels perform all five functions, but in different proportions.
   c. Functions are assigned to managers regardless of level according to their particular skills.
   d. Controlling is accomplished by first-line supervisors, while other functions are handled at middle and top levels.

5. At various times, managers may fill any of several different roles. The most effective manager will probably

   a. discover which roles he or she fills best and concentrate on those roles.
   b. concentrate on two or three roles and delegate work in other areas to qualified colleagues.
   c. move easily from one role to another as changing circumstances require.
   d. master one role at a time before moving on to the next.

6. An organization is

   a. any company large enough to include the three levels of management.
   b. any group of two or more persons that function together to accomplish common objectives.
   c. a group established to manage resources for profit.
   d. any group large enough to require a professional manager.

7. Leadership is defined as the ability to

   a. achieve stated goals.
   b. allocate and oversee the use of resources.
   c. ensure that things go according to plan.
   d. get people to follow voluntarily.

8. The management skills needed to properly execute the management functions are

   a. technical, human, and conceptual.
   b. interpersonal, informational, and decisional.
   c. planning, organizing, staffing, leading, and controlling.
   d. planning, organizing, and monitoring.

9. A first-line manager's staffing responsibilities

   a. conclude when a suitable candidate has been hired for a position.
   b. are best delegated to the human resources manager who possesses the necessary specialized training.
   c. are open-ended, including each subordinates' growth and development.
   d. end when an employee has mastered the skills of the assigned position.

10. Which of the following groups includes what most experts consider to be the primary management functions?

    a. Planning, acquiring, implementing, allocating
    b. Planning, organizing, staffing, leading, controlling
    c. Planning, monitoring, leading, controlling, scheduling
    d. Planning, staffing, coordinating, negotiating, monitoring

EXPANDED ANALYSIS

1. Are there kinds of organizations in which the personal styles of management employed at Patagonia and Virgin might not be effective? Why or why not?

2. Do you think the primary management functions apply to the U.S. Federal government? How does the President's job differ from that of the CEO at a multinational corporation?

3. Evaluate Richard Branson's statement: "I think that anybody running any company must realize that the most important asset he has is his people." Do you agree? Why?

4. How have developments such as huge increases in global competition, a flood of computer-driven information, public demand for quality and added value, and dwindling job security affected management function and managerial roles?

2

In Transition:
The Changing, Challenging
Environment of Management

L E A R N I N G   O B J E C T I V E S

Upon completing this lesson, you should be familiar with the facts, ideas, and processes contained in this lesson, and be able to:

- Compare management today with that of earlier periods; and assess the impact of the prevailing political/social/economic climate on management theory and practice.

- Explain why businesses today are considered open systems.

- Recognize changes in management today resulting from:
  a. increased government regulation
  b. environmental concerns
  c. the cultural and social diversity of the workforce
  d. multinational markets and competition
  e. demand for ethical and social responsiveness
  f. economic climate
  g. technological advancements

- Identify the elements and forces, internal and external to the organization, that directly or indirectly affect its operation.

O V E R V I E W

The History and Theory of Management

While the process of management begins with human history, modern practice has developed from theory that originated with the Industrial Revolution and the invention of reliable steam-powered machinery. Two schools of management thought emerged in Britain, the United States, and Europe: the **classical scientific school** that focused on manufacturing and work process; and the **classical administrative school** that emphasized the flow of information and how organizations should operate.

Classical Management Theory

Classical scientific school pioneers include Britain's Charles Babbage (1792–1871), who demonstrated, in the 1830s, that widely useful management principles could be established through observation and experience. Babbage advocated dividing work into processes that could be mastered by individual workers. In America, Frederick Taylor (1856–1915) approached factory problems systematically and developed cornerstone ideas that still influence management thinking. In promoting the science of management, he urged his colleagues to select, educate, and train workers scientifically, and to create cooperation between management and labor. Two other Americans, Frank (1868–1924) and Lillian (1878–1972) Gilbreth, added to Taylor's findings by concentrating on actual work processes, particularly through time and motion studies of worker activity. Their studies accelerated improvements in worker efficiency and reduction of fatigue. Henry Metcalf (1847–1917) focused on administration and information flow. Managers, he felt, should record their observations and experiences for their colleagues to advance practical study of the science of administration. Henry Gantt (1861–1919), who worked with Henry Taylor on several projects, emphasized the value of motivated workers, relating efficiency to compensation, and arguing that improved methodsbenefit from worker support. In many ways, Gantt pioneered the idea of a manager's social responsibility. He also devised a practical tool, the Gantt chart, that facilitates work planning for complex jobs and is still widely used.

Context for Modern Management

Early in the 20th century, the accepted organizational model was the hierarchical pyramid, with layers of authority emanating from the top. Employees were considered an extension of top management, who alone would do the thinking. This approach to management, and the design of increasingly sophisticated machinery, led to mass manufacturing and the emergence of large companies where top managers assumed total responsibility for the enterprise. The process was greatly accelerated by World War I, when the industrializing world discovered that swift production of enormous quantities of manufactured goods influenced the course of victory on the battlefield.

One effect that accompanied growth in company size was expansion of the management pyramid. As companies grew and top management became removed from workers, middle management arose to fill the gap. These bureaucracies, with their many departments and layers, were often compared to well-oiled machines. Every manager's role and rank were clearly defined, all the parts fit together, and the system – through two world wars and America's prosperity of the 1950s – churned out previously unimaginable amounts of work.

Classical Administrative Thought

Where classical scientific thought centered on rigorous planning and organization, and the control of work and staff, classical administrative thought, by contrast, emphasized efficiency and productivity. Administration of complex organizations required coherent principles, it was argued. The French humanist Henri Fayol (1841–1925) identified the five basic management functions of planning, organizing, staffing directing, and controlling, and refined a set of 14 general principles – from work specialization to worker harmony – that remain compelling today. Fayol's thorough, compassionate analysis places him among the most important contributors to the discipline of management.

The distinguished German sociologist Max Weber (1864–1920) characterized the bureaucracy as an "ideal" form of organization and projected three kinds of authority within organizations: rational, traditional, and charismatic. The American political scientist Mary Parker Follett (1868–1933) explored how organizations cope with conflict, defined the social context of work, and advocated training for management as a serious profession. U.S. communications industry executive and teacher Chester Barnard (1886–1961) probed the sociological nature of the organization. He urged managers to enlist employee acceptance of managers' authority or risk degrading that authority. Barnard's best-known work, the 1938 *Functions of the Executive*, projected with remarkable accuracy today's corporate needs for flexibility, bold planning, and internal cooperation.

Behavioral and Quantitative Schools

In **behavioral management theory**, employees were recognized as persons and as valuable assets. In the early 19th century, Scotland's pioneer manager Robert Owen (1771–1858) asserted that conditions both on and off the job influenced workers' output. Only with Follett in the 1920s did the individual worker again receive scholarly attention. Psychologist Elton Mayo's (1880–1949) studies in the mid-1920s also emphasized the behavioral aspects of workers. His studies at the Western Electric Hawthorne plant in Chicago suggested that when management showed genuine concern for workers' dignity and well-being, commitment and productivity rose, and that worker peer pressure also influenced performance.

American psychologist Abraham Maslow's needs-based theory (published in 1943) postulated five basic needs underlying human behaviors: physiological, security, social or affiliation, esteem, and self-actualization. Maslow's theory provided the basis for a reexamination of management practice. In 1960, Douglas McGregor asserted that managers operated with one of two assumptions about human behavior: Theory X – workers are lazy and must be coerced and controlled; and Theory Y (McGregor's own view) – workers willingly accept responsibility and will show ingenuity and creativity with suitable incentives.

Management science, closely linked to operations research and quantitative analysis, relies upon measurement and mathematics. **Quantitative management theory**, begun by U.S. research teams in the early 1940s, emphasizes mathematical approaches. Formal studies utilize procedures from the physical, mathematical, and behavioral sciences to strengthen the basis for decision making.

Systems, Contingency, and Quality Theory

Contemporary management grows from historical roots, and the current emphasis on quality has especially drawn upon systems and contingency theories. However elaborate and sophisticated the work of its academicians and theorists, management thrives on practical reality. The laboratory for testing management ideas operates day and night around the world in countless enterprises of every size and kind. The millions of decisions and transactions that take place every day provide limitless opportunities to observe and assess, in real time and under every conceivable circumstance, the precise utility of ideas and processes.

Contemporary managers use this laboratory of daily operations as their functional environment. Among the defining characteristics of the manager's environment is the fact that the individual parts of the operation affect one another. That irrefutable interrelationship is the keystone of the contemporary management theory known as the **systems theory**. In addition, there are **contingency** theorists who emphasize the fact that no two situations are identical. Managers must look for solutions in their experience and what has been learned by those who have gone before. They need to blend, to borrow, and to be flexible.

Business Systems and Management Environments

The manager's basic working environment is the organization. Organizations function as systems made up of subsystems – dynamic parts that interact to achieve goals according to a plan. Because active subsystems affect one another, managers and company units cannot function independently, but operate as open systems. Their components are linked to one another as well as to the constantly changing external environment.

An organization's **internal environment** includes its mission, leadership style, management philosophy, formal structure, policies, culture and climate, and available resources. The **external environment** embraces all the factors that directly or indirectly influence the organization's people, processes, and systems. Successful businesses structure an internal environment compatible with the world outside – the external environment. Vital to the process are **stakeholders**, the groups directly or indirectly affected by the ways in which business is conducted and managers conduct themselves. Stakeholders include owners, employees, customers, suppliers, and society at large.

The External Environment

Interaction with the exterior environment commonly occurs among the organization's managers, owners, customers, suppliers and other partners, competitors, the labor force, and government regulators. Managers and some other organizational members (typically the sales staff, recruiters, planning specialists, buyers, and purchasing agents) maintain regular contacts with members of these outside groups.

The manager must recognize and understand the elements of the external environment that indirectly interact with the organization – economic, technological, legal and political, sociocultural, natural, and international factors. These factors must be anticipated and their possible impact on the organization appreciated.

As communities grow more culturally diverse and reflect people's varying ethnic and national backgrounds, languages, religious beliefs, life styles, and even age groups, such changes affect the workplace. The percentage of women in the labor force has doubled since 1970, for example, and some regions are changing profoundly with an influx of immigrants from Asia, the Caribbean, and Latin America. Newly diverse communities challenge managers and every institution in society, especially the schools.

Local and global economic forces influence management and management systems, as do government regulations affecting a wide range of activity, from employment practices to international trade. These regulations often dictate business procedures and managers' actions. While its scope and implementation continue to be debated, regulation to protect broad public interests is clearly needed, particularly in such areas as environmental protection, mining, transportation, finance and banking, communications, and labor relations.

Local and regional economies – as well as global trade – increasingly reflect the growing international influences. Economic, political, socio-cultural, technological, and natural forces throughout the world shape managers' decision making and the capacity of companies to reach their goals. These forces require that managers constantly scan their internal and external environments to anticipate changes and adapt with speed and intelligence.

Today's managers realize that without committed men and women empowered to examine their own output and to take responsibility for their actions, no meaningful change can be achieved in productivity or quality. The idea of specialization prized in the classical school has been modified, for example, to include such ideas as cross training and job rotation in order to avoid the physical and psychological hazards of boring, repetitive work. The successful modern business depends on innovation, imagination, and creativity from dedicated workers backed up by managers who fulfill their roles not as commanders but as teachers, coaches, and servants to the people entrusted to their care.

ASSIGNMENTS

- Read the Overview, familiarize yourself with the Learning Objectives, and peruse the Key Terms below. Then turn to Plunkett & Attner, *Introduction to Management*, and read Chapter 2, "Management Thought: Past and Present," pages 34–58; and Chapter 4, "The Manager's Environments," pages 92–111.

  Some instructors may place a greater emphasis on the evolution of management theories (Chapter 2); others will concentrate on the forces that influence today's organizations and their managers (Chapter 4). Check with your instructor, or the course syllabus, for guidance.

- Next, scan the Video Viewing Questions and watch the video program for Lesson 2, "In Transition: The Changing, Challenging Environment of Management."

- After watching the video, answer the viewing questions and assess your learning with the Self-Test.

- Familiarize yourself with the Review Questions, Discussion Questions for Critical Thinking, and Skill-Building Exercises on pages 60 and 112 of Plunkett & Attner.

■ Strengthen your understanding of the lesson's ideas and issues by undertaking the Expanded Analysis.

K E Y   T E R M S

behavioral school The management theory that focuses on people as individuals with needs, as members of work groups and of a larger society; managers view subordinates as assets to be developed.

boundary spanning Manager's surveillance of external environments to identify what is happening or likely to happen, and how those events may influence one's plans, forecasts, and organization.

bureaucracy An administrative system marked by diffusion of authority through a hierarchy of clearly defined positions held by career people and subject to the rigid rules of operation.

classical administrative school The branch of classical management theory that emphasized the flow of information and how organizations should operate in all phases of running factories and businesses.

classical management theory The first school of management thought; pursued the one best way to perform tasks and sought to apply general principles to management functions. Developed two schools: classical administrative and classical scientific.

classical scientific school The branch of classical management theory that focused on the manufacturing environment and work on the factory floor; emphasized the division of labor among specialists and application of scientific methods to management.

competitors Those firms that offer similar products or services to an organization's customers.

contingency school The branch of management theory based on the premise that managers should act on the facts and variables of each unique situation they face; draws freely on other schools to seek most effective solutions.

customers Those individuals and groups that use or purchase the various outputs of an organization, whether inside or outside the organization.

economic forces Those conditions in an economy that indirectly influence management decisions and the costs and availability of an organization's resources.

external environment All the forces outside an organization's boundaries that interact directly or indirectly with it.

internal environment All the elements within an organization's boundaries which help to make it unique and that are to some extent under the control of management.

kaizen A Japanese term used in the business setting to mean incremental, continuous improvement.

labor force The people in the geographically accessible community from which an organization can recruit qualified candidates for its jobs and positions.

legal and political forces The general framework of statutes and case law that apply to all segments of communities at large and businesses in particular; includes the specific regulations imposed by all levels of government.

management information system (MIS) The coordinated arrangement of gathering, collating, and distributing information needed for management decision making; often applied to computer systems specifically designed for work units and the organization at large.

management science The study of complex systems of people, money, equipment, and procedures to understand how they function, in order to improve their efficiency and effectiveness.

mission The verbal expression of an organization's central and common purpose, its reason for existing; also sometimes called "vision."

natural forces Climate and weather, geography and geology that affect an organization.

open system A system in which an individual or organization must interact with various and constantly changing components in both the external and internal environments.

operations management The practice of applying management science tools and techniques to all aspects of manufacturing and service industries, particularly

operations research The application of model building, simulation, game theory, break-even analysis, queuing theory and other analytical tools to ongoing processes and functions to optimize performance.

quantitative school The branch of management thought that emphasizes mathematical approaches and measurability to management functions.

sociocultural forces Pressures on managers and organizations that come from individuals, groups, and communities to respond to their needs and desires.

stakeholders Those groups that are directly or indirectly affected by the ways in which business is conducted and managers conduct themselves; include owners, employees, customers, suppliers, and society.

suppliers Those individuals and groups that provide the resources an organization needs to produce goods or services whether inside or outside the organization.

synergy The increased effectiveness produced through combined action or cooperation, when elements together produce greater results than they could separately.

system A group of interacting, interrelated, or interdependent elements forming a complex whole.

technological forces The combined effects of scientific discoveries, engineering applications, and inventions that result in new materials, products, systems, opportunities, and problems for organizations and individuals.

VIDEO VIEWING QUESTIONS

1. When and under what historical circumstances does thinking about management as an identifiable discipline begin?

2. How do the two world wars appear to have influenced the development of management thought?

3. What factors caused middle management to develop?

4. What are some of the positive aspects of bureaucracy? What are some negatives?

5. How has global competition changed the conduct of management?

6. How do modern views of management hierarchy differ from those of the classical period of management thought?

7. In what ways has the increasing diversity of the workforce challenged managers? In what ways has the push toward more socially responsible corporate behavior challenged managers?

8. At the conclusion of the video, USC's Warren Bennis says: "We're really going to go from macho to maestro." What does he mean?

SELF-TEST

1. Which of these statement best reflects the history of management?

   a. The formal study of management began among American technical teams coping with the logistical difficulties of World War II.
   b. Although management practice began with the Industrial Revolution, the formal study of management is far older.
   c. Management practice begins with human history, but the origins of management as a formal discipline coincide roughly with the rise of mass production at the beginning of World War I.
   d. Formal management studies have been largely confined to the academic setting.

2. Which statement most accurately states the effect of the Industrial Revolution on classical management thought?

   a. The Industrial Revolution launched new research in all academic disciplines, including management.
   b. During the late 19th century, new technology, complex organizations, and the need for greater productivity all contributed to surging interest in coherent principles for management.
   c. Awareness of workers' needs, a central concern of classical management, peaked during the Industrial Revolution.
   d. Extensive European colonization required improved techniques to handle overseas administrative tasks.

3. The foundation of modern management practice and administrative structure are based on the 14 principles of management developed by

   a. Robert Owen.
   b. Frederick W. Taylor.
   c. Henri Fayol.
   d. Henry Metcalf.

4. Which of the following statements is inconsistent with Henri Fayol's principles of management?

   a. Managers should promote harmony among employees.
   b. High employee turnover is advantageous because the lower wages paid to new workers helps keep costs down.
   c. Employees should report to only one supervisor.
   d. The interest of one person or group should be subordinated to the group's requirements.

5. Which management pioneer is **not** associated with classical scientific management ideas?

   a. Frederick Taylor
   b. Henry Metcalf
   c. Charles Babbage
   d. Abraham Maslow

6. With which of the following statements would a behavioral management theorist be most likely to **disagree**?

   a. The social environment and the work environment influence employee productivity about equally.
   b. For most workers, recognition is more important than any job benefits.
   c. Though workers are motivated by many factors on and off the job, the quickest way to increase productivity is to increase workers' pay.
   d. The assumptions a manager make about his/her employees – whether positive or negative – will determine the behavior of those employees.

7. Elton Mayo's experiments at Western Electric suggested that workers' productivity was most influenced by

   a. financial reward.
   b. levels of illumination.
   c. fringe benefits.
   d. recognition.

8. In the present era of intense competition, corporate management's responsibilities are best summarized by which statement:

   a. Management's primary duty is to protect and maximize the inestment of stockholders.
   b. Management must first and foremost protect the welfare of the firm's employees.
   c. Management bears multiple responsibilities to a wide range of stakeholders.
   d. Management's preeminent duty is to protect the environment.

Match the persons with the appropriate management idea or event.

  a. Charles Babbage
  b. Henri Fayol
  c. Frederick Taylor
  d. Abraham Maslow
  e. Mary Parker Follett
  f. Frank & Lillian Gilbreth
  g. Max Weber

9. Analysis of bureaucracy

10. Identified the five basic management functions

11. Human needs as behavior motivation

12. Analysis of work with time and motion studies

13. Early British advocate of general management principles

14. American proponent of professional management training

15. Introduced work breaks and the piece-rate system for worker play

EXPANDED ANALYSIS

1. Which of the pioneer thinkers do you think has had the most significant effect on contemporary management?

2. If a U.S. company is operating in a labor market in which a significant portion of otherwise qualified workers do not speak English, what policies would you recommend regarding recruitment and training?

3. You are the owner of a chain of five profitable retail outlets scattered throughout the city of Los Angeles, California, in April 1992. Your two stores that employed six managers and thirty-five workers in South Central Los Angeles are looted and destroyed during the riots there. What elements in your company's internal environment, and forces in your external environment, must you consider before making a decision to rebuild these stores?

3 Setting the Stage: The Planning Process

Upon completing this lesson, you should be familiar with the facts, ideas, and processes contained in this lesson, and be able to:

- Explain why planning is critical for managers and to the organization's mission and goals.

- Describe the relationships between and among an organization's mission statement, plans, goals, and objectives.

- Summarize the steps in the formal planning process.

- Discuss major barriers to effective planning and how they can be minimized or eliminated.

- Describe contingency planning and the general conditions in which it is important.

- Articulate the importance of communication in the planning process.

O V E R V I E W

Importance of Planning

To introduce the notion of planning, business consultant Steven Cerri says: "Corporations that don't have a sense of who they are, or where they want to go, or how they want to get there, tend to meander through their business life and get buffeted by whatever environmental issue is the most powerful." In today's unforgiving business universe, few such companies sustain "business life" long enough to "meander" much further than bankruptcy court. Indeed, Mr. Cerri's description of an ineffective corporation could have been the inspiration for a video parody circulated among animators some years ago. It was called "Bambi Meets Godzilla." As the two-minute scene unfolds in a golden meadow, the ageless fawn blithely frolics while Disney bluebirds twitter and swoop. Suddenly a shadow blots out the sunshine. An enormous reptilian leg descends in a ground-shivering footfall that reduces Bambi to a furry postage stamp, before lurching off. The End.

The clip might have been titled, "The Company Without a Plan." Aimless and ignorant, such a company could accomplish nothing, and during a brief career would be utterly vulnerable to an indifferent world. With good reason, most managers regard planning as the primary management function because everything they accomplish derives from it.

Planning Defined and Located

The rank of planning as first among management functions becomes immediately clear as we define the idea and explore its contexts. A plan is a program, an intended set of actions worked out beforehand, for the accomplishment of objectives. That working-out process begins with six questions about the enterprise: what, when, where, who, how, and how much. The managers' best answers to these questions serve as the nucleus of planning, which in turn creates both the foundation and blueprint for organizing, staffing, directing, and controlling. Only after planning is begun can the organization actually do anything. And so, with negligible imprecision and the merest apology to Rene Descartes, managers can say about the organization, "We plan, therefore it acts."

During the process of systematically preparing for the future – planning – managers develop a firm's direction and purpose. At each management level, they devise objectives and guidelines to allocate resources, and specify actions to achieve the objectives. With competent planning, managers acquire a formidable edge: they are prepared not merely to react to change, but to embrace it.

The Mission

Management's initial task is to determine the organization's fundamental purposes, its mission. This task belongs to senior managers, who invest a great deal of time and thought in creating a mission statement.

A sense of mission is critical for any organization, regardless of its focus. It is the foundation upon which planning relies. If an organization is not clear about the business it wants to be in, then forecasting and all other aspects of planning become blurred and ineffectual.

Once the mission is established, planners can project a future for their business; anticipate opportunities and hazards; and assess the likely influences of economic, political, technological, or social trends. After analyzing the anticipated future environment, within and outside the organization, specific goals, objectives, and strategies can be developed. When communicated throughout the company, this concise summary of the corporate vision should guide everyone in the organization.

Few organizations can treat the matter of mission as a task that is over and done with once the enterprise is up and running. The planning that led to the Los Angeles Music Center's birth in 1964, for instance, is now directed toward an uncertain future. The rapid population growth and increasing cultural diversity of the Los Angeles area, combined with cutbacks in educational and social services and other economic adversity, are making it more difficult to carry out the mission upon which the organization was founded.

The Planning Process

Even in today's "flatter" organizations, responsibility for varous aspects of the planning process tend to follow hierarchal patterns. Based upon the formal mission, top management generally devises strategic (long-range) objectives and plans; middle managers set the major sub-units' tactical (medium-range) objectives and plans; and first-level managers refine operational objectives and detailed plans to secure the results expected from work groups and individuals. Managers ensure that all elements support one another and the ultimate mission.

Plan Types and Levels

Strategic plans address overall objectives, define primary organizational activities and allocate the human and financial resources, facilities, and equipment needed to achieve the strategic objectives, often for five years or longer. The most effective strategic plans provide ample guidance and at the same time, are adaptable. Says the Los Angeles Center Theater Group's director, Gordon Davidson, "We've had numerous five year plans over the years, and every time you make a five-year plan, no sooner are you a year or two into it, than you have to revise it because times change, economic conditions change, the tone and tenor of society changes."

Tactical plans are projected for shorter time frames and have a narrower scope. A series of tactical plans built on each other achieves the strategic plan. First-line supervisors guide daily, weekly, and monthly work with two kinds of operational plans: single-use and standing. The most common single-use plan may be the budget, employed to project sources and amounts of income and to allocate expenditures, usually for one-year periods. Standing plans address continuing or recurring matters like running payroll or granting credit to customers. Most policies, procedures, and rules fit this category.

The Basic Planning Process

Mission statements, objectives, and plans come together in the planning process. As with the other functions, there is latitude for variation in planning. But, no matter the organization or the manager's preferred approach, the systematic accomplishment of core tasks is the surest way to build effective plans. The generally accepted formal elements of planning are included in this seven-step summary:

Step 1: Analyze and Evaluate the Environment Include the present position and resources available to achieve objectives.

Step 2: Set Objectives Establish targets for the short- or long-range future.

Step 3: Determine Alternatives List possible courses of action that lead to goals.

Step 4: Evaluate the Alternatives List and consider advantages and disadvantages of each possible course of action.

Step 5: Select the Best Solution Choose the course of action with the most advantages and the fewest serious disadvantages.

Step 6: Implement the Plan Determine the people and resources to be assigned, how the plan will be evaluated, and reporting procedure.

Step 7: Control and Evaluate Results Ensure that the plan proceeds as anticipated; adjust.

Defeating Barriers to Planning

To increase prospects for success, managers should work to overcome potential barriers to successful planning and use the best available planning tools and techniques. Knowing them in advance allows managers to avoid or overcome these seven common barriers to planning:

1. Inability to plan

2. Inadequate planning process

3. Lack of commitment to the planning process

4. Inferior information

5. Lack of focus on the future

6. Overreliance on the planning department

7. Overemphasis on controllable variables

Contingency Planning

Experienced managers recognize that forecasting future events is an uncertain exercise. They build margins into their plans, and strive for flexibility in operations whenever possible. They recognize that environmental factors can shift dramatically and swiftly. Preparing to respond effectively should circumstances suddenly change and render the company's original plans useless, prudent managers develop and maintain contingency plans.

Planning Aids

Throughout the planning process, managers ensure the quality of planning as they continuously exchange information, ideas, and feedback, making the best use of three generic planning aids: (1) dynamic communication; (2) quality information; and (3) involvement of others inside and from outside the company.

Planning Tools and Techniques

Management practitioners continue to devise approaches and techniques that will strengthen or refine the planning process. Three proven techniques are:

- **Management by objectives (MBO),** a perennially popular approach introduced by Peter Drucker in the 1950s, in which manager and subordinate collaborate to develop appropriate objectives and implement their fulfillment.

- **Forecasting,** which applies the best available data to develop predictions as the basis for planning; many operations depend upon good sales forecasting as a planning baseline.

- **Linear programming,** in which quantified operational data (profit margins, costs, staff availability, and the like) are entered into simple equations whose solutions suggest practical planning options.

A S S I G N M E N T S

- Read the Overview, familiarize yourself with the Learning Objectives, and peruse the Key Terms below. Then turn to Plunkett & Attner, *Introduction to Management*, and read Chapter 5, "Organizational Planning," pages 114–142.

- Next, scan the Video Viewing Questions and watch the video program for Lesson 3, "Setting the Stage: The Planning Process."

- After watching the video, answer the viewing questions and assess your learning with the Self-Test.

- Familiarize yourself with the Review Questions, Discussion Questions for Critical Thinking, and Skill-Building Exercises on page 144 of Plunkett & Attner.

- Strengthen your understanding of the lesson's ideas and issues by undertaking the Expanded Analysis.

K E Y   T E R M S

budget A single-use plan for predicting sources and amounts of income and how it is to be used.

contingency planning The development of plans to be put in place if circumstances change so drastically as to make the preferred plan unfeasible.

forecasting A planning technique used to develop predictions about the future, which become the basis of plans.

linear programming A planning technique used to determine the optimum combination of resources and activities.

management by objectives (MBO) A planning technique that emphasizes collaborative goal-setting by managers and their subordinates.

mission statement The formal written statement of the organization's purpose.

objective The desired outcome or target that an individual or an organization intends to achieve through planning and plans.

operational objectives The specific results expected from first-level managers, work groups, and individuals.

operational plan Plans developed by first-level supervisors as the means to achieve operational objectives and in support of tactical plans.

plan A scheme, program, or method worked out beforehand for the accomplishment of an objective.

planning Determining the objectives of an organization or work group and developing the overall strategies to achieve them in the uncertain future.

policy Broad guidelines to aid workers in making decisions about recurring situations or functions.

procedure The set of step-by-step directions that describe how to carry out an activity or a task.

program A single-use plan for solving a problem or accomplishing a group of related activities needed to reach a goal.

rule A plan that aims to control human behavior or conduct at work.

single-use plan Plans that apply to activities that do not recur or repeat.

standing plan Plans that are usually made once and retain their value over years, although they may be revised.

strategic goals Long-term goals that relate where the organization wants to be in the future, set by top managers.

strategic plan The steps by which the organization intends to achieve its strategic goals.

tactical objective Goals set by middle managers that describe what the subunits must do in order for the strategic goals to be achieved.

tactical plan The steps by which the major units in the organization will achieve tactical objectives and help achieve the strategic plan.

VIDEO VIEWING QUESTIONS

1. How does planning to operate the Los Angeles Music Center today differ from the planning needed to build the Music Center complex in the 1960s?

2. Identify four ways in which the social, economic, and cultural character of Southern California appear to influence the planning process at a cultural enterprise like the Los Angeles Music Center.

3. How does planning for a fixed-location, live entertainment center seem to differ from the planning associated with a franchise restaurant chain like McDonald's?

4. Compare the planning process of the Music Center Operating Company with the planning process of its individual resident artistic groups.

5. How do planners at the Music Center appear to be adapting to changes in the external environment? What elements in the center's planning relate particularly to the long-term future?

6. How do the Music Center's educational programs relate to the organization's strategic plan?

S E L F - T E S T

1. A mission statement

   a. needs to be prepared only when the company is launched or during times of financial difficulty.
   b. should include a few impossibly demanding elements so that employees are challenged to their utmost performance.
   c. should be primarily a guide for the planning of top managers.
   d. should be frequently reviewed and modified to meet changing conditions.

2. Among the three categories of mission-based plans,

   a. operational plans are the most important because they guide the organization's actual front-line work.
   b. coordination is essential so all plans support the mission.
   c. strategic plans should concentrate on profitability.
   d. tactical plans may be fairly general so long as they do not conflict with the mission statement.

3. Of the following activities, the one **least** suited to the development of a standing plan is

   a. personnel selection.
   b. equipment maintenance.
   c. department budgeting.
   d. emergency evacuation.

4. In order to be useful for planning and decision making, information must be

   a. quantifiable.
   b. consistent with all prior relevant data.
   c. gathered from outside sources in order to be free of departmental bias.
   d. unambiguous.

5. Top management's planning work is most likely to focus on

   a. strategic plans.
   b. data gathering.
   c. data analysis.
   d. tactical plans.

6. Management by objectives is

   a. a planning technique that focuses on factual data in order to avoid making decisions based on subjective criteria.
   b. the first step in the formal planning process.
   c. a collaboration between manager and subordinate centered on negotiated goals and implementation.
   d. a planning system used primarily by first-line supervisors.

7. Select the statement which best characterizes planning.

   a. Planning is an innate skill and cannot be taught to people who don't have the knack.
   b. The best possible plans should be devised on an annual basis, then put in place and given the year to achieve their goals.
   c. Unscheduled changes in plans suggest poor management.
   d. In developing alternatives, a manager should try to create as many roads to the objective as is practical.

8. Which characteristic is **not** an effective planning objective?

   a. Specific and measurable.
   b. Focused on key result areas.
   c. Open-ended.
   d. Reward performance.

9. To which category does TWA's objective of having every flight depart on time belong?

   a. Strategic
   b. Tactical
   c. Operational

Match the items below with the proper definition which follows.

- a. Effective objectives
- b. Operational objectives
- c. Budgets
- d. Forecasting
- e. Standing Plan
- f. Single-use plan
- g. Policies
- h. Rule
- i. Mission Statement
- j. Procedure

10. An ongoing, specific plan for guiding behavior in the workplace.

11. Most policies, procedures, and rules.

12. Typical single-use plan.

13. Largely a responsibility of first-line management.

14. Broad guideline for dealing with key decision making.

15. Plan to modify a city's street corner curbs with ramps for wheel-chairs.

16. A task for the board of directors and top managers.

17. Used to make predictions as basis for planning.

18. A set of step-by-step directions.

19. Must be specific and measurable.

EXPANDED ANALYSIS

1. Compare and contrast the external factors that influence planning at a public institution like the Los Angeles Music Center and a large private company.

2. What do you see as the primary barriers today to planning faced by the mayor of a major city? Of a state or provincial college system?

3. Draft a mission statement for a real or imaginary company of your choice. Sketch core strategic, tactical, and operational plans for the company's next five years.

4 The Game Plan: Strategic-, Business-, and Department-level Planning

---

Upon completing this lesson, you should be familiar with the facts, ideas, and processes contained in this lesson, and be able to:

- Differentiate types of plans at various levels of the organizational hierarchy.

- Discuss the importance of internal assessment and environmental analysis in strategic planning for today's complex business environment.

- Describe the kinds of information required in the development of strategic plans.

- Differentiate growth, integration, diversification, and retrenchment strategies.

- Describe business planning and how it relates to strategic planning.

- Discuss the development of department (functional) plans in marketing, production, human resource, and financial management.

- Specify problems that may result if departmental plans are created independently of each other.

O V E R V I E W

The Nature and Importance of Strategic Planning

Among the three types of planning, we have found strategic plans to be primarily the responsibility of top management, tactical plans largely the province of mid-level managers, and operational plans principally discharged by first-line supervisors. The interdependence of the three types and levels of plans begins with management's initial decisions about the organization's purposes and direction. Ongoing analysis of its internal and external environments leads the organization to develop strategic objectives and strategic plans – a task that will determine the company's future.

While imaginative analysis and strategizing have always marked successful companies, the process in the 1990s has acquired a fateful cast. Today the business community finds itself under greater pressure than at any time in recent memory. Any organization that does not plan strategically risks "the corporate junk heap." Today's perilous urgency correlates directly to the rise of contemporary competition.

Technology is a primary accelerator of competition, and its profound effects confront managers everywhere. Lightning advances in microchip design and manufacture, for example, created an entire industry in little more than a decade. Every company in the business races at breakneck speed to avoid being overcome by the new chip on the block. In the book publishing industry, long dominated by a sedate group of stable companies, desktop publishing technology and computerized marketing have turned the bookmaking and bookselling universe inside out. Among car builders, steel makers, and retailers, to name only an obvious few industries, bold and intelligent strategy is the essential first step in coping with relentless competition.

The other engine driving competition is globalization. No matter where they may be located, companies today confront increasingly assertive rivals not merely throughout their own local and national regions, but from anyplace on Earth. As worldwide communications and transport grow ever more accessible and efficient, every firm enjoys enormously expanded opportunity and unlimited competition – from down the street and from across the ocean.

Strategy and Environment Assessment

In analyzing their firm's actual and ideal market positions, managers examine both trends and changes affecting the marketplace and the best means to achieve their company's objectives. Elements for strategy decisions include these:

- scope – how much area, range, or size of market and product to pursue;
- resource deployment – how to allocate people, plant, and money;
- distinctive competitive advantage – identifying what unique strengths the company may possess or can pursue; and
- synergy – how the firm's parts can produce a joint effort greater than if they act independently.

Formulating strategy is one activity, carrying it out another. In formulating, managers assess internal and external environments and devise objectives and plans. To implement strategy, they execute the strategic plan through communication, incentives, structural changes, and new technology.

Planning Levels and Types

Managers must address corporate, business, and functional strategy levels. Corporate-level strategy charts the course of business for the entire organization. Business-level strategy focuses on how each product-line or strategic business unit (SBU) in the organization competes for the customer. Functional level strategy develops the best department support for the business level.

The Strategic Planning Process

Six steps characterize strategic planning throughout the organization:

1. evaluate the current mission, objectives, and strategies;
2. analyze internal and external environments;
3. reassess mission and objectives;
4. formulate strategies to accomplish the objectives;
5. implement the strategy; and
6. monitor and evaluate performance.

Environment Analysis: Information and Process

Guided by a clear mission, managers probe external and internal environments for strengths, weaknesses, opportunities, and threats (SWOT). Meaningful assessment depends upon quality information about inside and outside environments. Such information is obtainable from essentially limitless sources that range from books and periodical literature to on-line computer services and government reports to customer surveys and expert consultants. The analysis of the external opportunities and threats and the internal strengths and weaknesses is never treated as an isolated exercise. It gives managers the chance to verify the current mission, objectives, and strategies, and to continuously rethink prior assumptions in light of new observations. A company that pursues this sort of constant analysis and adapts its strategy accordingly, is far better equipped to both avoid ugly surprises and stay ahead of the competition.

Corporate and Business-level Strategies

The formulation and implementation of corporate, business unit, and functional level strategies are guided by the organization's mission and objectives. At the corporate level, recent experience offers tested strategy both for companies with a single or a few highly related markets and those with divisions that differ among one another. A company may choose among five so-called grand strategies:

- In a **growth strategy**, the company seeks to significantly expand one or more operations or business units – internally by investment or externally by acquiring additional units.

- An **integration strategy** may be chosen when managers see a need (1) to stabilize supply lines or reduce costs, or (2) to consolidate competition.

- With a **diversification strategy**, the firm opts to move into new products or markets, commonly by acquiring other businesses.

- A **retrenchment strategy** allows the firm to trim by area or eliminate entire businesses.

- The company wishing to maintain its status quo adopts a **strategy of stability**.

Next, managers of single-product firms or individual SBUs must choose a business strategy that defines how the enterprise will compete. (Within their grand strategy, a diversified company must mix SBUs and product lines to generate maximum competitive advantage. This mix of options is called their **portfolio strategy**.) Business strategies may be classified as either adaptive strategies or competitive strategies.

In **adaptive strategies**, the company matches its particular internal characteristics to the external environment in one of four strategy styles. The **prospector strategy** favors innovatively seeking opportunities and expanding; its opposite, the defender strategy, seeks merely to retain current market share or even retrench. The analyzer strategy aims to maintain current market share while perhaps innovating in some markets. The reactor mode implies no strategy at all. The **competitive strategies** of differentiation, cost leadership, and focus rely upon a firm's internal skills, resources, and philosophy.

Functional-level Strategy

The company's major functional departments devise action plans to support the accomplishment of business-level strategies for marketing, production, human resources finance, and research and development. Marketing strategy at the functional level focuses on pricing, promotion, packaging, and distribution. Functional-level production strategy includes plant location, inventory control, technology, commitment to quality and productivity, and subcontracting. Because overall strategic success ultimately relies upon people, human resources managers must develop effective support strategy for staffing, training and development, compensation, and recruiting. The functional-level strategy for finance addresses capital investment, how additional funds are raised, and the handling of profit and debt. In companies for which research and development is a significant factor, functional strategies seek to integrate new technology with the firm's other departments and outside sources for maximum effect.

Strategy Implementation, Culture, and Leadership

Implementation – converting strategy from optimistic conjecture into productive operations – is tough and essential, and it requires a quality match between the strategy and the firm's culture. Apple Computer's senior vice president Kevin Sullivan might have spoken for senior management at any contemporary company when he said: "The goal is to make sure that we have a direction and a strategy that people can get aligned and committed behind."

In implementing strategies, culture, leadership, and organizational structure come into play. Managers must persuade others in the organization to adopt the behaviors or accept the new values necessary to put the strategy into action. In addition to involving mid- and lower-level managers in the strategy formulation process, implementation may be assisted by adjusting the structure of the organization. By changing reporting relationships, creating new departments or work units, and facilitating independent decision-making, the implementation of new strategies can be facilitated.

ASSIGNMENTS

- Read the Overview, familiarize yourself with the Learning Objectives, and peruse the Key Terms below. Then turn to Plunkett & Attner, *Introduction to Management*, and read Chapter 6, "Strategic Planning and Strategic Management," pages 146–172.

- Next, scan the Video Viewing Questions and watch the video program for Lesson 4, "The Game Plan: Strategic-, Business-, and Department-level Planning."

- After watching the video, answer the viewing questions and assess your learning with the Self-Test.

- Familiarize yourself with the Review Questions, Discussion Questions for Critical Thinking, and Skill-Building Exercises on page 174 of Plunkett & Attner.

- Strengthen your understanding of the lesson's ideas and issues by undertaking the Expanded Analysis.

K E Y   T E R M S

analyzer A business-level strategy based on maintaining the current market share while innovating in some markets.

BCG Matrix A planning tool that logically groups strategic business units into categories based on market growth rate and market share.

business-level strategy The kind of plan that focuses on how each product-line or business unit within the organization competes.

corporate-level strategy The kind of plan that charts the course of business for the entire organization.

cost leadership A business-level strategy that focuses on keeping costs as low as possible through efficient operations and tight controls.

defender A business-level strategy based on holding the current market share or even retrenching.

differentiation A business-level strategy that attempts to set the organization's products or services apart from those of other companies.

distinctive competitive advantage An element of strategy that identifies the unique position the organization has in relationship to its competition.

diversification strategy A corporate-level strategy that allows the company to move into new products or markets.

focus strategy A business-level strategy in which an organization targets a specific market.

functional-level strategy The kind of plan that details the activities of the organization's major functional departments.

grand strategy The overall framework or plan of action developed at the corporate level to achieve an organization's objectives.

growth strategy A corporate-level strategy adopted when the organization wants to create high levels of growth.

horizontal integration A strategy to consolidate competition by acquiring similar products or services.

integration strategy A corporate-level strategy adopted when a business sees a need to stabilize its supply lines or reduce costs, or consolidate competition.

portfolio strategy A strategy focused on determining the proper mix of business units and product lines that fit together in a logical way to provide a maximum competitive advantage for the corporation.

prospector A business-level strategy based on innovation, taking risks, seeking out opportunities, and expansion.

reactor A business-level approach in which a business does not adopt a strategy, but responds to environmental threats randomly.

resource deployment An element of strategy that defines how a company intends to allocate its resources to achieve its objectives.

retrenchment strategy A corporate-level strategy adopted when the organization wants to reduce the size or scope of its activities.

scope An element of strategy that specifies the size or position the firm wants to have within its environment.

situation analysis A search for an organization's strengths, weaknesses, opportunities, and threats (SWOT) that forms part of the strategic planning process.

stability strategy A corporate-level strategy adopted when the organization wants to remain the same or maintain its status quo.

strategic business unit An autonomous business division operating within the umbrella of the corporation with its own competitors, market, and product line.

strategic management Top-level management's responsibility for defining the firm's position, formulating strategies, and guiding long-term organizational activities.

strategic planning The decision making and planning processes that chart an organization's long-term course of action.

strategy formulation The processes associated with the planning and decision-making that goes into developing the company's strategic objectives and strategic plans.

strategy implementation The processes associated with executing the strategic plan.

vertical integration A strategy focused on gaining ownership of resources, supplies, or distributive systems that relate to a company's business.

VIDEO VIEWING QUESTIONS

1. Describe the early steps in developing corporate strategy and the key questions managers must ask themselves before they can begin to actually strategize.

2. What elements in a firm's macro environment should especially interest strategic planners?

3. CEO Les McCraw of Fluor Daniel talks about Fluor's strategy of diversification in the early 1980s. Assess management's assumptions about the external environment which led to their particular acquisition choice.

4. How does Fluor Daniel's diversification program in the 1990s differ from that of the 1980s?

5. Describe Apple Computer's changed strategy of PC pricing.

6. What is an action plan? How does such a plan relate to a grand strategy?

SELF-TEST

1. Managers begin the strategic planning process by

   a. gathering information about all aspects of the firm's internal and external environments.
   b. analyzing strategies adopted by competing firms.
   c. assessing available financial resources.
   d. soliciting representative input from managers at all levels.

2. The element **not** normally included among the four elements upon which strategy is said to rest is

   a. distinct competitive advantage.
   b. resource deployment.
   c. synergy.
   d. profitability.

3. The question "How do we compete?" should be asked at which level of strategic planning?

   a. The functional level.
   b. The corporate level
   c. The business level.

4. Sears Roebuck Company's recent actions to close its catalog operation and sell several operating units are part of a strategy of

   a. diversification.
   b. stability.
   c. integration
   d. retrenchment.

5. A portfolio strategy is commonly employed by

   a. financial service companies.
   b. companies hoping to diversify.
   c. companies that operate several independent units.
   d. large companies in the investment of cash reserves.

6. At the business level competitive strategies would **not** include

   a. the defender strategy.
   b. differentiation strategy.
   c. cost-leadership strategy.
   d. focus strategy.

7. The factor **not** usually included among factors critical to strategy implementation is

   a. human resources.
   b. organizational structure.
   c. leadership.
   d. maturity of the organization.

8. Functional strategy relies upon action plans for each of the following activity groupings, **except**

   a. pricing, promotion, packaging, and distribution.
   b. staffing, training and development, compensation.
   c. plant location, use of subcontractors, automation.
   d. mission development, capital generation, liquidation.

9. Successful strategic managers are **least** likely to exhibit which of the following characteristics?

   a. Skilled organizational politics
   b. Rigorous consistency
   c. Well informed
   d. Skilled in time management

10. Which strategy best characterizes Apple Computer's decision to lower prices on its PC line of products?

    a. Diversification
    b. Retrenchment
    c. Integration
    d. Growth

EXPANDED ANALYSIS

1. Because of the end of the Cold War, U.S. defense spending is expected to drop sharply in the 1990s. Merle Aleshire, division planning director at General Dynamics, says because of the difficulty other defense-dependent firms have found in trying to shift from defense production to commercial business, his firm will continue "to focus on what we know best." Do you think this is the best decision? Why or why not?

2. Because of widespread disarray in the U.S. aerospace and airline industries, President Bill Clinton and Congress appointed a federal commission to investigate and recommend ways to restore the industries to health. Do you think faulty strategic planning might be part of the cause of the present problem? What suggestions would you make to the commission?

5 Calling the Shots: Decision Making

Upon completing this lesson, you should be familiar with the facts, ideas, and processes contained in this lesson, and be able to:

- Recognize that decision making is a management function at all levels.

- Indicate the range and types of decisions a manager is asked to make.

- Describe the steps in the decision-making process.

- Compare the decision-making process under conditions of certainty, risk, and uncertainty.

- Compare formal and informal decision making.

- Summarize quantitative approaches to decision making.

- Indicate when and where it is appropriate to apply quantitative approaches of management science to decision making.

- Examine the factors that tend to limit managerial options in the decision-making process.

- Suggest strategies a manager can use to create an effective decision-making atmosphere.

O V E R V I E W

Decision Making, The Universal Management Tool

No matter who they may be, no matter what their organization, if you observe managers at work for even short periods of time will, you will see them making decisions. A **decision** is a judgment reached after consideration, a choice made from available alternatives. In the course of their careers, managers face widely diverse decisions, from utterly inconsequential to epic.

Making decisions is a rational process that can be learned and mastered. Successful managers not only possess decision-making skills, they also have the confidence to use them.

Decision Making Process

Managers make decisions to prevent or solve problems and to seize opportunities. In the course of planning, organizing, staffing, directing, and controlling at all levels, managers are called upon to make decisions. Circumstances generally dictate whether the decision should be programmed or nonprogrammed. **Programmed** (or **deterministic**) **decisions** apply to problems and situations that have occurred often enough to render both the circumstances and solutions predictable. Managers simply apply previously established procedures when the familiar and planned-for situation arises.

But when complex and significant situations arise, and there is no clear cut solution managers tend to use a more formal decision-making process – termed **nonprogrammed** – built upon the accumulated experience of thousands of managers. That experience is condensed in this seven-step process of decision making.

<u>**Step 1: Define the Problem or Opportunity**</u> Effective decision making, about even the most daunting problem, begins by separating the matter into manageable parts. Such analysis facilitates a clear definition of the problem or opportunity, and those areas in which more information is required.

<u>**Step 2: Identify Limiting Factors**</u> After defining the problem, the manager must identify factors that rule out certain alternative solutions. Typically, limiting factors are related to a lack of resources: people, money, or facilities and equipment.

<u>**Step 3: Develop Potential Alternatives**</u> The manager develops alternatives that can potentially solve the problem or capture the opportunity. These alternatives may be derived from task forces or focus groups, or may be drawn from personal experience.

<u>**Step 4: Analyze the Alternatives**</u> Each alternative must be evaluated, in terms of the limiting factors already identified and the consequences that would result from its use.

<u>**Step 5: Select the Best Alternative**</u> The best choice (sometimes combining elements of several alternatives) will offer the fewest serious disadvantages and the most advantages.

<u>**Step 6: Implement the Decision**</u> Unimplemented decisions don't count. People who carry out the decision must know exactly what to do, how to do it, why, and when. If numbers of staff members participate in the decision-making process, and a rational approach is used, the decision should also enjoy genuine commitment throughout the organization.

<u>**Step 7: Establish a Control and Evaluation System**</u> The decision must be controlled and evaluated, and ongoing actions monitored.

The systematic accomplishment of these seven steps allows the manager to proceed with confidence that no vital factor has been neglected, and that the prospect for an effective decision is favorable.

Environmental Influences on Decision Making

Decision making may be categorized by the environment in which it occurs: certainty, risk, and uncertainty. In an environment of certainty, the manager has perfect knowledge of the situation because the circumstances have occurred before, the alternatives are known, and each alternative is fully understood. The manager picks the best known alternative. In the second environment, that of risk, the manager knows the problem and the alternatives, but not the alternatives' consequences; and each probable outcome poses some risk.

In the third and most difficult environment – uncertainty – a manager confronts the unknown. Because of too many variables or too few facts, exact outcomes of available alternatives are difficult to determine or assess. Sometimes, the manager cannot even identify all possible alternatives. In such conditions, managers may make decisions by drawing on experience, judgment, or intuition – factors sometimes referred to as nonquantitative. Although this approach is relatively subjective, it is neither whimsical nor arbitrary. To succeed, it requires extraordinary amounts of skill and understanding.

Limited Resources

Because they do not possess the limitless information, time, personnel, equipment, and supplies needed to make perfect decisions, real-world managers **satisfice**. This means they decide on a course of action that will at least meet the situation's minimum requirements, given the available information, time, and other resources.

The Internal Environment

Because decisions are useless if not supported, managers endeavor to create an atmosphere that promotes support from superiors, subordinates, and the firm's organizational system. Management style plays a strong role in ensuring support, as does the objective quality of the decision that was reached, and the degree to which it is accepted by subordinates. Decisions reached through the formal seven-step process will almost certainly qualify as objective. To gain broad acceptance, managers may invite the participation of those affected. The organizational system – represented by policies, procedures, programs, and rules – may also affect a manager's decision-making and should be factored into the process.

A number of techniques have been developed to facilitate group participation in the decision-making process. These include:

- **brainstorming**, a method of shared problem solving in which group members spontaneously contribute ideas focused on the subject problem or opportunity;
- **nominal groups**, which provide structured opportunities for equal participation by all members; and
- the **Delphi technique**, which also provides structure, leads to consensus, and emphasizes equal participation.

Such systems can be valuable aids for managers in creating an effective decision making atmosphere.

Managerial style transcends the question of collegial and organizational support. Managerial style embraces a manager's unique approach to managing in its entirety, from personal attitudes to specific skills. Although managers approach decisions in many ways, three approaches are commonly favored:

- the **rational/logical** decision model that prefers facts and logic to intuitive judgments;
- the **nonrational/intuitive** decision model favored by "gut decision makers" who rely on their feelings about the situation; and
- the **predisposed** decision model of managers who decide on a solution and then gather the material to support the decision.

Quantitative Decision Making Techniques

To assist in improving the overall quality of decisions, managers may choose from among several quantitative techniques: decision trees, payback analysis, and simulations. **Decision trees** allow managers to visually display alternative decision paths so that potential action outcomes and their relationships to future events can be observed. In a **payback analysis**, managers can assess the viability of various capital equipment purchases by determining how long it takes to pay back the initial cost of each item and choosing the alternative that generates the quickest payback. With **simulation techniques**, which range from elaborate computer constructs to queuing or waiting line models and game theory, managers can economically and effectively test decision alternatives.

Creating an Environment for Effective Decision Making

Competent managers must create an effective decision-making environment for themselves and their organizations. What will facilitate a positive environment? Consider the following: provide adequate time for decisions to be made; nurture self-confidence and courage; encourage others to make decisions; learn from past decisions; recognize differences in decision-making situations; recognize the importance of quality information; make the tough decisions; know when to hold off; be ready to try things; and be ready to ask for help.

A S S I G N M E N T S

- Read the Overview, familiarize yourself with the Learning Objectives, and peruse the Key Terms below. Then turn to Plunkett & Attner, *Introduction to Management*, and read Chapter 7, "Making Decisions," pages 176–206.

- Next, scan the Video Viewing Questions and watch the video program for Lesson 5, "Calling the Shots: Decision Making."

- After watching the video, answer the viewing questions and assess your learning with the Self-Test.

- Familiarize yourself with the Review Questions, Discussion Questions for Critical Thinking, and Skill-Building Exercises on page 208 of Plunkett & Attner.

- Strengthen your understanding of the lesson's ideas and issues by undertaking the Expanded Analysis.

K E Y   T E R M S

alternative A potential course of action that is likely to eliminate, correct, or neutralize the cause of a problem or maximize an opportunity.

brainstorming a method of shared problem solving in which all members of a group spontaneously contribute ideas focused on the subject problem or opportunity.

decision A judgement reached after consideration; a choice made from among available alternatives.

decision making The process of identifying problems and opportunities, developing alternative solutions, choosing an alternative, and implementing it.

decision tree A graphic representation of the actions a manager can take and how these actions relate to further events.

Delphi technique A group decision-making technique in which equal participation is structured by the use of written questionnaires.

game theory A mathematical simulation model in which a competitive situation is analyzed to determine the optimal course of action for an interested party; attempts to predict how people or organizations will behave in competitive situations; allows managers to devise strategies to counter competitors' behavior.

groupthink A phenomenon associated with group decision making in which members so commit to the group that they become reluctant to disagree with other members; can compromise decision making.

limiting factors Constraints that rule out potential alternatives.

management science The school of management thought that focuses on development of mathematical and statistical methods to improve efficiency.

managerial style The individual way a manager goes about managing; includes personal attributes and decision-making approach.

maximize Make the best possible decision; requires ideal resources – information, time, personnel, equipment, and supplies. (See satisfice.)

nominal group A group decision-making technique that creates a structure to provide for equal participation in the decision-making process by all members.

nonprogrammed decision A decision made in response to a situation exhibiting unique circumstances, unpredictable results, and important consequences for the company.

opportunity A good chance for progress or advancement whose realization requires that a decision be made.

payback analysis Evaluation of investment alternatives by comparing the length of time necessary to pay back their initial costs.

problem Any question raised for solution, answer, or decision; the difference between a current condition and a desired or preferred condition.

programmed decision A decision in which the problems or situations have occurred often enough that both the circumstances and solutions are predictable.

queuing or waiting line model A simulation model used to help managers decide what length of waiting line or queue would be preferable.

satisfice To make a decision that meets the minimum requirements necessary to achieve a particular goal with available time, information, and other resources.

simulation A model of a real activity or process.

stochastic An environment or situation involving random variables; may be characterized by conjecture.

symptom A signal that indicates something is wrong, that a problem is present.

VIDEO VIEWING QUESTIONS

1. Describe some ways in which computers can be used in the decision making process. What is a decision support system? An expert system?

2. Contrast deterministic and stochastic decision environments.

3. What are some of the components of "intuitive" decision making? From the perspective of decision making, what are some advantages of breaking problems down into components?

4. Contrast the decision-making environments of the news director at Cable News Network and the head librarian at an urban college.

5. How do policy, procedures, and guidelines appear to affect decision making at CNN?

6. Compare and contrast decision making in vertical hierarchies and flatter organizations such as Mercy Hospital. What are the primary reasons to concentrate decision making at lower organizational levels?

S E L F - T E S T

1. "What is" and "What should be" are often two different states or conditions. The difference can be called

   a. the critical information gap.
   b. a limiting factor.
   c. uncertainty.
   d. a problem.

2. While accomplishing their five management functions of planning, organizing, staffing, controlling, and leading, managers will find decision making most concentrated in
   a. planning and organizing.
   b. planning and staffing.
   c. no single function, but continuously across them all.
   d. planning.

3. A manager prefers to have all relevant information in hand before making a decision. Since that ideal is seldom possible and managers must often make the best decision given the time and information available, managers must make

   a. optimizing decisions.
   b. intuitive decisions.
   c. maximizing decisions.
   d. satisficing decisions.

4. Which of the following abilities is probably **least** important in determining a manager's success in decision making?

   a. The ability to set priorities when many decisions are pending.
   b. The ability to make decisions without relying upon other people.
   c. The ability to strategically select the time of implementation.
   d. The skill to assess the effectiveness of decisions.

5. Although there are many standards for judging the quality of decision making, the success of any decision is likely to be judged primarily on

   a. the results produced.
   b. the degree of a manager's reliance upon rational rather than intuitive approaches to the problem.
   c. the perceived motivation of the decision maker.
   d. its consistency with the company's primary goals.

6. Many elements contribute to sound decisions. Among the following, which element is most likely to determine a quality decision?

   a. Focus on the immediate issue at hand.
   b. Not deciding until all the applicable information has been ascertained.
   c. Rigorously defining the problem or question needing a decision.
   d. Thorough analysis of available alternatives.

7. Although managers make decisions for many reasons, typically a manager makes a decision because

   a. strategic planning determines that it is time to make a particular decision.
   b. a specific need or problem has arisen.
   c. he or she is the only person aware of the problem.
   d. decision making is an expected managerial duty.

8. A significant advantage of group decision making is

   a. that it frees the manager's time for more important tasks.
   b. that by sharing responsibility, it reduces the risk of blame for poor decisions.
   c. that it can improve the level of group support for decisions.
   d. that it provides a broader base of information for better decisions.

9. Effective decision makers

   a. seldom make decisions without complete information.
   b. rely upon their initial impressions of a problem and treat the views of subordinates with great caution.
   c. wait until a problem becomes serious enough to warrant a decision before investing their time on the matter.
   d. know that sometimes no decision at all may be the best decision.

10. Of the following statements about models and simulations, which is the **least** accurate?

   a. Simulations allow experiments or training without inconveniencing customers and tying up line equipment or facilities.
   b. They can save time and financial expense.
   c. With them, managers can perform experiments and tests uninterrupted by actual operations.
   d. In periods of intense competition, managers should rely on data from the real world, not the artificial one of models and simulation.

EXPANDED ANALYSIS

1. Before managers in a traditionally hierarchical company make a commitment to decentralized decision making, what kinds of advance or simultaneous preparation should they undertake in their organization?

2. In the Mercy Hospital shared governance system shown in the video program for this lesson, decision making is largely described from an administrative perspective. Speculate on the possible views of the hospital's physicians and surgeons, lab technicians and housekeeping staff, during the transition from the traditional hierarchy to shared governance. Do you think their attitudes would be similar or different, and why?

6 Putting it Together: The Principles of Organizing

Upon completing this lesson, you should be familiar with the facts, ideas, and processes contained in this lesson, and be able to:

■ Differentiate various types of organizational structures and patterns.

■ Define each of these organizing concepts and principles:
   a. unity of command
   b. job descriptions and specifications
   c. authority flows
   d. assignment of responsibility
   e. delegation of authority
   f. span of control

■ Describe the relationship between organizational design and staffing.

■ Differentiate the formal and informal organization.

O V E R V I E W

The Formal Organization

If corporate plans may be compared to the genetic coding which determines an organism's form and behavior, then a company's formal organization can be seen as the emergent form of the corporation itself. The link between a company's planning and the arrangement of its people, ideas, and resources into the orderly pattern of its formal organization is essential to the long-term success of the organization.

In organizing, managers determine what work is needed, then assign tasks and arrange them into a decision-making framework – an organizational structure. In fulfilling this organizing function, managers undertake five activities. They: (1) review plans and goals, (2) determine work activities needed to achieve organizational objectives, (3) classify needed work and group it into work units, (4) assign work to individuals and delegate authority to decision makers, and (5) design a decision-making hierarchy. Taken together, these steps in the organizing process produce an organization whose unified parts function harmoniously to achieve goals.

With plans and goals in place and a clear idea of the nature and scope of the work needed to accomplish the goals, the first phase of the organizing function begins – the design of work units. Work classification and work unit design for most companies results in more or less traditional departments according to one or more common patterns.

- **Departmentalization by function** consolidates similar activities, simplifies training, and allows specialization.

- **Geographical departmentalization** links activities and responsibilities for one department according to territory.

- **Product departmentalization assembles the activities of creating,** producing, and marketing each product into a separate department.

- **Customer departmentalization groups activities and responsibilities** in departments organized around the needs of specific customer groups.

With the primary structures laid out, management assigns to individuals and units both work activities and the authority needed to accomplish them. Each department's substance, purpose, and anticipated performance determine the kind and amount of authority it needs.

In the final step of organizing – the design of a decision-making hierarchy – managers link the organization's components in coordinated vertical and horizontal operating relationships. Vertical structuring produces a hierarchy relating task responsibility, specialty areas, levels of management (including the chain of command), and the organization as a whole. Horizontal structuring defines the working relationships between operating departments and delineates managerial spans of control – the number of subordinates under the direction of each manager.

Organizational structure should be treated as a flexible management tool to fulfill plans; as plans change, the structure should be responsive.

The completed organizational structure can be displayed on an **organization chart.** Even in companies where frequent changes suggest the use of pencil not ink, such charts can be surprisingly helpful in preventing and solving various kinds of problems. At a glance the charts show chain of command, spans of control, channels of formal communication, departmentalization, work allocated to each job position, the decision making hierarchy, and line/staff authority relationships.

For all the formality, the process has as its primary goal to allow the organization to function effectively. Apple Computer senior vice president Kevin Sullivan provides this perspective: "I think organizing is simply trying to get the right resources grouped in the right way to support what you're trying to achieve. It's a continual evaluation of, 'Do we have the right focus, the right resources, the right interconnects within the organization, that meet the customer and market needs?' "

Major Organizational Concepts

The organizing process draws its force from tested concepts and principles that managers use to develop powerful systems. The concepts are: authority, unity of command, power, delegation, span of control, and centralization/decentralization.

Managers hold degrees of **authority** – the formal and legitimate right to make decisions, give orders, and allocate resources – based on their level and position. Differing relationships between individuals and between departments result in three types of authority.

- **Line authority** – the authority associated with the power to command – flows directly down from superior to subordinate.

- **Staff authority,** held by managers assigned to advise or give technical assistance, routinely flows upward and laterally, and does not include direct control.

- **Functional authority** permits managers to make decisions relating to specific activities performed by personnel within other departments and routinely flows across departmental lines.

The labels "line" and "staff" apply to two categories of departments as well as the parallel types of authority. **Line departments** (the core activities of production, marketing, and finance) are headed by line managers. **Staff departments** (human resources, computer services, legal services, public relations, and medical services, for example) generally advise and assist the line departments.

Unity of Command

Most organizational principles derive from common sense and experience, none more obviously than the principle of **unity of command** – the idea that each person in the company should take orders from and report to only one person. With rare and limited exceptions, each person should have only one boss. **Delegation**, the downward transfer of formal authority from one person to another, is another idea that springs from necessity; the reality that no one person can do it all. Managers delegate so they may focus on critical concerns and still ensure that all needed work is accomplished.

The delegation process depends upon two other core principles, responsibility and accountability, that are usually activated in a four-step sequence: (1) The manager assigns work to a subordinate, (2) the manager delegates to the subordinate necessary and sufficient authority to accomplish the assignment, (3) the subordinate accepts responsibility, the obligation to do the assigned work to the best of one's ability, (4) By accepting responsibility, the subordinate accepts accountability to the manager. Delegation, however, does not relieve the manager of ultimate responsibility and accountability.

Span of Control

The number of subordinates a manager directly supervises – the **span of control** – should rank high in the minds of managers designing the organizational structure. Their guidelines are straightforward: the more complex their jobs, the fewer employees should report to a manager. The more routine their work, the greater number of people one manager can effectively control. As a result, companies usually have narrow spans at the top and wider ones below – the familiar management pyramid.

Whether the setting is an international airline or the makers of high tech computers or designer clothing, decisions about span of control influence managerial effectiveness. When managers supervise too many people, subordinates cannot gain prompt access to their boss. Plans, decisions, and actions are delayed or compromised, time is wasted, and people are unhappy. When managers supervise too few, the result may be overwork or over-supervision and more unhappy people. In general, at lower levels control spans can be wider when the company's staff is more competent – well-trained, experienced, and committed. At mid-level and up, task complexity limits spans of control.

A manager's potential span of control may also be influenced by the company's preference for centralization or decentralization in decision making (matters we shall examine more closely in Lesson 8), which influences control spans for lower and middle managers as well as the number of levels in an organization.

The Informal Organization

Within the formal organization designed by management, there inevitably thrives another dynamic system of social relationships – the informal organization – that no competent manager will ignore. The **informal organization**, a network of personal and social relationships that arise spontaneously among people in the work environment, knows no boundaries – certainly not the boxes on the organization chart.

The informal organization emphasizes people and their relationships, while the formal organization emphasizes official organizational positions. (Elements of power and influence shape the interactions of people within and between formal and informal organizations; elements to be explored in Lesson 8.) Related to the operation of the informal organization, as well as to people's inevitable personal idiosyncrasies, managers discover that employee beliefs, attitudes, and behaviors may differ significantly from what the organization expects of them.

Because the informal organization can affect the formal organization significantly, for good or ill, managers should recognize the existence of informal groups, identify the roles members play within these groups, and use knowledge of the groups to work effectively with them. The informal organization can help to make the total system effective, providing support to management, stability in the environment, useful communication channels, and encouraging better management. But at the same time, the informal organization can present several potential problems for the manager: pressure on group members to conform, potential conflict between expectations of the informal group and the formal organization, possible resistance to change desired by management, the generation of false information or rumors, and possible frustration for inexperienced managers.

ASSIGNMENTS

- Read the Overview, familiarize yourself with the Learning Objectives, and peruse the Key Terms below. Then turn to Plunkett & Attner, *Introduction to Management*, and read Chapter 8, "Organizing Principles," pages 210–247.

- Next, scan the Video Viewing Questions and watch the video program for Lesson 6, "Putting it Together: The Principles of Organizing."

- After watching the video, answer the viewing questions and assess your learning with the Self-Test.

- Familiarize yourself with the Review Questions, Discussion Questions for Critical Thinking, and Skill Building Exercises on page 246 of Plunkett & Attner.

- Strengthen your understanding of the lesson's ideas and issues by undertaking the Expanded Analysis.

KEY TERMS

accountability Being answerable for the results of one's actions.

authority The formal legitimate right of a manager to make decisions, give orders, and allocate resources.

centralization A philosophy of organizing that concentrates authority within an organizational structure.

chain of command The unbroken line of reporting relationships from the bottom to the top of the organization that defines the formal decision-making structure.

cohesion The measure of a group's solidarity – the degree to which the members share the group's ideas and cooperate.

customer departmentalization Creation of departments in response to the needs of specific customer groups.

decentralization A philosophy of organizing and management that disperses authority within an organizational structure.

delegation The downward transfer of formal authority from one person to another.

departmentalization The creation of groups, subdivisions, or departments that will execute and oversee the various tasks that management considers essential.

formal organization The official organizational structure that top management conceives and builds.

functional authority Authority to make decisions about specific activities that are undertaken by personnel in other departments.

functional definition The organizing principle stating that in the process of establishing departments, the nature, purposes, tasks, and performance of the department must first be determined as a basis for authority.

functional departmentalization Creation of departments on the basis of the specialized activities of the business.

geographical departmentalization Creation of departments according to territory.

informal organization A network of personal and social relationships that arises spontaneously as people associate with one another in the work environment.

line authority Direct supervisory authority from superior to subordinate.

line departments Core work units established to meet the major objectives of the organization and directly influence the success of the business.

norms Any standard of conduct, code, or pattern of behavior perceived by a group to be important for its members to honor or conform to.

organization chart A visual representation of the structure of an organization and how its parts fit together.

organizing The management function that establishes the relationships between activity and authority.

power A person's ability to exert influence.

product departmentalization Creation of departments to allow creating, producing, and marketing each product in one work unit.

responsibility The obligation to carry out one's assigned duties to the best of one's ability.

sanctions Rewards or penalties used by informal groups to persuade members to conform to norms.

span of control The principle of organizing concerned with the number of subordinates each manager directs.

specialization or division of labor The degree to which organizational tasks are subdivided into separate jobs.

staff authority Authority to serve in an advisory capacity; authority to advise.

staff departments Work units that assist all departments in meeting the objectives of the organization through advice or technical assistance.

unity of command The organizing principle that states that each person in an organization should take orders from and report to only one person.

unity of direction The organizing principle that states that each group of activities having the same objective should have one head.

VIDEO VIEWING QUESTIONS

1. Compare Northwest Airlines "rule of sevens" with the span of control viewpoints expressed by top managers at Apple and at Patagonia. Do the concerns about span of control seem to differ between the two manufacturing companies and the airline?

2. Identify two potential disadvantages of functional organizational structures.

3. Describe two variations on the divisional structure pattern.

4. Discuss the operation of a matrix organizational structure in light of the principle of unity of command.

5. Contrast the organizational needs of Apple Computer Company during its first few years and at the present time.

6. Based upon the description provided by Apple Computer senior vice president Kevin Sullivan of his company's current organizational structure, see if you can diagram the relationship of Apple Computer's work units in a simple organization chart.

SELF-TEST

1. Which of the following would **not** be considered a critical step in the organizing process?

   a. Reviewing plans and goals
   b. Recruiting qualified staff
   c. Grouping activities into manageable units
   d. Delegating authority

2. The most basic organizational structure is

   a. functional organization
   b. unity of command
   c. the management pyramid
   d. matrix organization

3. Which of the following statements is most accurate? The organizing process is vitally important

   a. in service companies with extensive interaction between line employees and the public.
   b. during a firm's start-up phase, and less thereafter.
   c. in all companies throughout their lifetimes.
   d. in large, multi-division firms.

Match the definitions with the correct terms (a through h). A term may be used once, more than once, or not at all.

   a. accountability
   b. unity of command
   c. line authority
   d. chain of command
   e. functional authority
   f. span of control
   g. delegation
   h. responsibility

4. The number of subordinates a manager directly supervises.

5. The unbroken line of reporting relationships from the bottom to the top of the organization.

6. The obligation to carry out assigned tasks to the best of one's ability.

7. The idea that each person in an organization should take orders from and report to only one person.

8. Taking the consequences, either credit or blame, for one's actions.

9. The right to oversee specific projects or activities performed by personnel in another department.

10. The downward transfer of formal authority from one person to another.

EXPANDED ANALYSIS

1. Since the riots in Los Angeles, California, in April 1992, considerable national attention has been focused on various actions to "Rebuild L.A." Assume that a commission made up of representatives from government and the private sector were to make available a one-time investment of $500 million for the establishment and operation of a public corporation for the general purpose of "significantly improving the quality of life in those portions of Los Angeles

directly affected by the riots." You are asked to head the corporation for its first year. Narrate in some detail what you would do during your year in charge of the corporation. Include a description of the structure of your proposed organization.

7 Laying the Groundwork: Organizational Design

LEARNING OBJECTIVES

Upon completing this lesson, you should be familiar with the facts, ideas, and processes contained in this lesson, and be able to:

- Explain how planning strategies and organizational structure relate, and why organizing is important.

- Indicate how its age, size, and technology tend to affect an organization's structures.

- Relate various organizational strategies to situations in which each has been used effectively.

- Describe the impact of organizational design on the individual employee.

- Recognize that organizations evolve and change over time and must be restructured to cope with these changes.

O V E R V I E W

Designing Organizational Structures

Most businesses constantly reevaluate their structure and reorganize in response to changing conditions that occur in their environment, new production technology, or organizational growth. Utilizing the tool of organizational structure, managers manipulate the elements of departmentalization, decentralization, and chain of command into the organizational design best suited to achieve the specific goals and objectives determined during planning.

Organizational Design Defined

Organizational design is the creation of an organization's structure, including the overall array of positions and departments and their interrelationships. Such structures are not static, but dynamic and dependent upon the people whose activity they guide.

To operate, organizations rely upon such abstract ideas as the acceptance of authority. They create operating units, and they utilize such devices as line and staff positions and departments. But no two companies generate exactly the same organizational structure. Some prefer functional departmentalization; others choose product groups. Some centralize decision-making while others decentralize. Some have narrow spans of control; others have developed wide spans. Organizations evolve to suit their unique operational requirements.

Objectives of Organizational Design

In order to thrive, companies must first be structured according to some suitable and viable organizational premise. Then they must be able to respond to changes in competition, technology, the economy, and other aspects of the corporate environment. Organizational designers try to position their companies to respond to change by adapting their existing elements and integrating new ones as appropriate. When new positions and departments are brought online, designers attempt to maintain collaboration across department lines so that functions and people adapt harmoniously in new relationships. They also strive to build in the flexibility necessary to respond to change.

Organizational Structures, Tight or Flexible

Depending on how managers handle their organizational building blocks (chains of command, centralization versus decentralization, formal authority, and so on) they can create either tight, mechanistic organizations or flexible, organic ones. **Mechanistic organizations** are characterized by rigidly defined tasks, formalization, many rules and regulations, centralized decision making, and communication primarily up and down the chain. Organic organizations, on the other hand, have comparatively few rules, decentralized decision making, and communication across the network.

Because of the accelerating pace of large-scale change, contemporary corporations appear to favor more flexible, decentralized organizational structures. But the choice of structure tends to depend upon the organization's strategy, size, age, environment, and technology.

Organizational Design Influences

Confirming again the inseparability of management functions, organizational design follows planning. When strategy changes, so must structure. A strategy requiring the firm to innovate, seek new markets, grow, and take risks calls for the flexibility and decentralization implicit in organic structures. Conversely, a strategy requiring the firm to protect its present markets, may benefit from the tight control, stability, efficiency, and centralization that mark mechanistic structures.

The organizational needs of small and large organizations (as gauged by their comparative numbers of employees) clearly differ. Small companies with few people and little specialization tend to favor loose, organic systems. Big, complex companies that employ thousands of specialists, by contrast, tend with age to drift into the formality and standardization typical of mechanistic structures. As companies evolve through the stages of a life cycle – birth, youth, midlife, and maturity – imaginative managers will deliberately adapt their firm's structural design so that the organization remains meaningfully responsive to changed circumstances.

Environmental stability and predictability affect a firm's structure. The more stable the environment, the more suitable will be reasonably mechanistic designs. Uncertainty favors organic structures that emphasize flexibility, coordination, and less formal procedure. Similarly, the sort of technology (small batch, mass production, continuous process) used by a company to convert its inputs into outputs directly influences organizational structure. The structure of a small company in New York and Paris whose half-dozen experts broker insurance for art museums will differ markedly from that of the trans-global builder of supertankers with thousands of diversely skilled employees in several huge shipyards.

Organizational Structure Options

Over time, five common organizational options have emerged from which managers often choose (or mix and match as appropriate). These structure options combine elements from both the mechanistic and organic categories.

- **The functional structure** groups jobs into departments based on use of similar skills, expertise, and resources under the familiar headings of finance, production, marketing, and human resources.

- **The divisional structure** centers on self-contained strategic business units (SBUs) that each produce a single product. For each division, the functional departments are brought together to accomplish division objectives. Divisional structures can also be operated according to customer type or by geographical region.

- **The matrix structure utilizes functional and divisional chains of command** simultaneously in the same part of the organization, commonly for major projects. The matrix combines functional specialization with the focus and accountability of the divisional structure and employs a dual chain of command. The overlay of function and project authority yields a grid, or matrix.

- **The team structure** organizes separate functions into a group based on one overall objective. The traditional organizational hierarchy is flattened.

- **The network structure** utilizes a small central organization that relies on other organizations to perform manufacturing, marketing, engineering, or other core functions on a contract basis.

A S S I G N M E N T S

- Read the Overview, familiarize yourself with the Learning Objectives, and peruse the Key Terms below. Then turn to Plunkett & Attner, *Introduction to Management*, and read Chapter 9, "Organizational Design," pages 248–275.

- Next, scan the Video Viewing Questions and watch the video program for Lesson 7, "Laying the Groundwork: Organizational Design."

- After watching the video, answer the viewing questions and assess your learning with the Self-Test.

- Familiarize yourself with the Review Questions, Discussion Questions for Critical Thinking, and Skill-Building Exercises on page 274 of Plunkett & Attner.

- Strengthen your understanding of the lesson's ideas and issues by undertaking the Expanded Analysis.

K E Y   T E R M S

continuous-process production A technology in which the entire conversion process is completed through a series of mechanical or chemical processes. Employees are not a part of the actual production.

divisional structure An organizational design option in which people are grouped based on organizational outputs (products), geography, or customers.

functional structure An organizational design option that groups positions into departments based on similar skills, expertise, and resources used.

large batch or mass production A type of technology that produces a large volume of standardized products.

matrix structure An organizational design option which utilizes the functional and divisional chains of commands simultaneously in the same part of an organization.

mechanistic structure A tight organizational structure characterized by rigidly defined tasks, formalization, many rules and regulations, and centralized decision making.

network structure An organizational design option in which a small central organization relies on other organizations to perform manufacturing, engineering, or other critical functions on a contract basis.

organic structure A flexible, free flowing organizational structure that has few rules and regulations; decentralizes decision making right down to the employees performing the job.

organizational design The creation of or change to an organization's structure.

organizational life cycle The observable and predictable stages of an organization's evolution.

small batch or unit production A type of technology that produces goods in small amounts designed to customer specification.

team structure An organizational design option that places separate functions into a group based on one overall objective.

technology The knowledge, machinery, work procedures, and materials that transform the inputs into outputs.

VIDEO VIEWING QUESTIONS

1. Compare and contrast "hierarchical and pyramidal" and "flat" organizational structures. Identify some strengths and some weaknesses of each.

2. Describe Mercy Hospital's "Care 2000" program in terms of organizational design. How does the physical location of work units affect the operation of the structure?

3. Describe the process Mercy Hospital used to create and implement its "Care 2000" program.

4. What are the major advantages of the network organizational structure currently utilized by the Fluor Daniel Corporation?

5. Describe the role of Fluor Daniels' "functional leaders." What other changes to its human resources practices do you think the company has had to make during its shift from a narrow-focus maker of oil refineries to its present structure?

SELF-TEST

1. The element **not** likely to be considered a primary component of organizational design is

   a. span of control.
   b. recruitment.
   c. departmentalization.
   d. decentralization.

2. A tight, mechanistic organization structure is likely to

   a. utilize extensive communication across the network.
   b. be young and comparatively small size.
   c. rely significantly on centralized decision making.
   d. rely significantly on decentralized decision making.

3. The contingency factor **least** likely to affect management's choice of mechanistic or organic organization designs is

   a. the firm's operating environment.
   b. the company's age.
   c. the organization's current strategy
   d. the current "popularity" of organic organizations among respected business leaders.

4. Select the statement which most accurately describes a company's choice of optimum organizational structure.

   a. Managers may select any structure that fits their perceived combination of contingency factors.
   b. Current research suggests that the network structure is the preferred approach for today's rapidly changing business environment.
   c. Small, young companies should stick with a straightforward functional structure until they grow large enough for more complex designs.
   d. As soon as the company is large enough, managers should adopt the divisional structure because it is flexible and responsive to change.

5. Analysts describe an organizational life cycle in which companies progress through four stages. To which stage would you probably assign a company that has developed a fairly comprehensive set of personnel manuals, is modestly decentralized, subcontracts its legal and public relations tasks, and maintains a company-wide computer payroll system.

   a. Birth stage
   b. Maturity stage
   c. Midlife stage
   d. Youth stage

6. Which of the following is **not** an advantage of the functional structure?

   a. Centralized decision making
   b. Efficient access to technical expertise
   c. Simplified training
   d. Improved identification of profit centers

7. A firm's dominant technology is an important contingency factor affecting its organizational design. A large manufacturing company that uses flexible manufacturing technology and has the capability to accomplish both small batch and mass production in the same facility should probably utilize which type of organizational structure?

   a. mechanistic
   b. organic
   c. divisional

8. In a functional structure, positions are grouped into departments based upon similar skills, expertise, and resources. The "traditional" functional departments are

   a. finance, production, marketing, and human resources
   b. advertising, public relations, legal services
   c. purchasing, maintenance, inventory control
   d. research and development, sales, accounting

9. Which of the following characteristics will **not** be found with a matrix organizational structure?

   a. High motivation of participants
   b. Wide ranging training in both specific skills and management perspectives
   c. Unambiguous lines of authority
   d. Efficient use of technical resources

10. A company's formal organizational structure

    a. should serve as its anchor, the one stable element over which management has genuine control.
    b. normally will shift from a functional approach to a geographic approach.
    c. will grow increasingly decentralized as the firm expands.
    d. should be adaptable to shifting customer, market, and other environmental needs.

EXPANDED ANALYSIS

1. Several U.S. airlines in the early 1990s, including the industry's largest carrier, American Airlines, utilize the functional organizational design. In recent years the industry's fiscal performance has been so poor (only Southwest Airlines posted a 1992 profit, and most of the others sustained record losses) that the President and Congress in April 1993 appointed a special commission to recommend steps to turn things around. Consider the many functions of a modern airline, then suggest what you believe might be the most effective organization structure (functional, divisional, matrix, team, network, or combination) for a large carrier serving cities throughout the continental U.S. and several major destinations overseas. Include these activities in your assessment: airplane fleet selection, sales and marketing, use of travel agents, computer marketing, fleet maintenance, purchasing, crew training, other staff training, accounting, interline relations, compliance with U.S. and foreign gov-

ernment regulations, airport terminal facilities, labor relations, catering, reservations, cargo facilities, noise complaints from homeowner groups near airports, etc.

8 Running the Show: Influence, Power, and Authority

L E A R N I N G   O B J E C T I V E S

Upon completing this lesson, you should be familiar with the facts, ideas, and processes contained in this lesson, and be able to:

- Define the concepts of power, influence, and authority.

- Identify the bases of power in an organization.

- Distinguish between line and staff positions; centralized vs. decentralized organization.

- Discuss the importance of delegation in organizations and how delegation can be handled effectively.

- Identify sources of power within an organization.

- Describe the relationship between formal and informal leadership, and how they can influence one another.

- Explain how informal leaders emerge with an organization, and how group cohesiveness develops.

- Articulate the importance of effective communication in maintaining authority.

O V E R V I E W

Authority and Power: Useful Tools

Each day in the workplace, managers routinely apply the organizational concepts and principles we have explored thus far. The abstract notions of authority, influence, power, unity of command, delegation, span of control, and centralization vs. decentralization are regularly applied in developing systems for running businesses.

Although their subtleties have long intrigued scholars, power, influence, and authority are among the less theoretical abstractions managers utilize every day. Early in the organizing process, as they assign work and implement chains of command, managers rely upon power, influence, and authority to insure that people get things done. The effective manager understands how authority relates to power.

Basically, **authority** is the formal and legitimate right to make decisions, give orders, and allocate resources. Each job description sets forth the formal authority held by the person occupying the position. Managers with line authority give direct orders, evaluate performance, and reward or punish those employees who work for them. More limited staff authority belongs to managers of departments that provide advice or technical assistance, and who serve in an advisory capacity to other departments and managers. Within their own departments, however, such managers do exercise line authority.

As with the line or staff authority granted to managers, there are two primary categories of work units (departments) in most businesses. Line departments, under line managers, accomplish the firm's fundamental core work – production, marketing, and finance. Staff departments, under staff managers, assist line departments and one another. They contribute "indirectly" through advice, service, and assistance, in such areas as human resources, computer services, public relations, and legal services.

When acting with staff authority, managers have no direct control over the departments they advise. Line department managers also often assist one another's departments, acting with staff authority. Using limited functional authority, staff managers may direct specific work done by people in other departments, but this must be done tactfully and with care to avoid compromising the principle of unity of command.

New managers quickly discover that in business, authority by itself is insufficient. Getting things done also requires **power** – the ability to exert influence in the organization beyond authority – which is derived from position. Power belongs to persons and comes from three diverse sources. Legitimate, or position power confers the right to use power based on one's position within the organization. Referent power derives from an individual's personality and its perception by others. Expert power belongs to people with proven superior skills and knowledge.

Delegation: Getting Work Done

With delegation, formal authority is transferred downward from one person to another, effectively multiplying the organization's ability to perform. Superiors who delegate authority to subordinates preserve their time and energy to focus on critical concerns, and the ability to delegate effectively can determine a manager's success or failure. The idea of delegating embraces responsibility and accountability: in assigning tasks, the manager delegates authority, while the employee accepts responsibility and becomes accountable for fulfilling the delegated assignments. The manager, of course, remains responsible and accountable for the use of his or her authority, as well as for the subordinate's performance.

UCLA's William Ouchi emphasizes a crucial element of delegation – that the delegator have confidence that people to whom authority is delegated will make sound decisions. Ouchi urges managers to develop clear objectives by which to measure decisions and to confirm a shared philosophy of management throughout the organization. In this way, when the subordinate encounters a difficult situation, he or she will be able to rely upon a set of well-defined management principles.

Centralization Versus Decentralization

Depending on their management philosophy, senior managers may choose either to concentrate authority for decision making in the hands of a few people (centralization) or to push it down the organization structure into the hands of many (decentralization). To be efficient, authority for each decision should be decentralized to the lowest possible level. Centralized decision making produces narrow spans of control and more levels of management. With centralized management, top-level managers delegate little authority and must closely supervise those who report to them.

The Informal Organization

Managers soon find through experience that not everything in an organization fits within the squares of the organization chart. Along with the formal organization that includes department structure, designated leaders (managers), and decision-making guidelines, there functions a second system of social relationships that collectively make up the informal organization. Because it profoundly influences the productivity and job satisfaction of all members of the organization, managers must understand and utilize this informal organization.

The Informal Organization and Informal Leaders

A company's informal organization is an unruly and complex aggregate of people within the formal design structure that results from personal and social relationships. This thriving network of casual connections powerfully influences a company's affairs. While in the formal organization a person's authority comes from her or his position, **informal power** is given by group members directly to the person regardless of job assignment. Because it depends upon how people feel about each other, informal power is less stable than authority and may change rapidly. Most managers possess some informal power along with their formal authority, but often no more than others in the group. The "manager" and "informal leader" roles are often played by two different people.

Even within large, formal enterprises, informal organizations tend to stay small because relationships are personal. Hundreds of small informal organizations generally flourish within very large companies.

Worker behavior and attitudes within the informal organization may differ drastically from official company policy or expectations. If the employees as a group accept these values or attitudes as standards of behavior, they achieve the status of norms – guidelines for members' behavior that may or may not support the formal organization's objectives. Workers may begin to display cohesion, sharing the informal group's objectives and cooperating among themselves. The manager must monitor two sets of behaviors – the one required by the formal organization and that which develops as people interact informally.

Even though membership in the informal organizations continuously shifts, identifiable leaders and followers emerge. A person may lead in one group and follow in another. People become informal group leaders for diverse reasons, including seniority, age, charisma, work location, or expertise. Any of these attributes can confer status depending upon what group members value. The employee with the most status in the informal organization emerges as its informal leader and may possess great informal power. Able mangers recognize the existence of informal groups, identify members' roles in the group, and learn to use available information so they may work with the informal group, ideally with its leaders, to facilitate overall managerial goals.

If they fit well, the formal and informal organizations can reinforce one another. The informal organization can fill in gaps in the manager's knowledge through advice and even actually doing needed work. By helping to stabilize the work environment, informal organizations can enhance employee acceptance. And they can provide a useful communication channel. However, the informal organization tends to resist change, to propagate rumors, and to amplify managers' weaknesses. And in some instances, by creating an alternative set of roles and expectations, the informal organization may generate confusion and conflict.

While seasoned managers can recognize and utilize the workings of the informal organization, less practiced managers may be frustrated by them.

ASSIGNMENTS

- Read the Overview, familiarize yourself with the Learning Objectives, and peruse the Key Terms below. Then turn to Plunkett & Attner, *Introduction to Management,* and reread Chapter 8, "Organizing Principles," pages 224–244; and Chapter 14, "Leadership," pages 438–454.

- Next, scan the Video Viewing Questions and watch the video program for Lesson 8, "Running the Show: Influence, Power, and Authority."

- After watching the video, answer the viewing questions and assess your learning with the Self-Test.

- Familiarize yourself with the Review Questions, Discussion Questions for Critical Thinking, and Skill-Building Exercises on pages 246 and 460 of Plunkett & Attner.

- Strengthen your understanding of the lesson's ideas and issues by undertaking the Expanded Analysis.

KEY TERMS

accountability Being answerable for the results of one's actions.

authority The formal legitimate right of a manager to make decisions, give orders, and allocate resources.

centralization A philosophy of organizing that concentrates authority within an organizational structure.

chain of command The unbroken line of reporting relationships from the bottom to the top of the organization that defines the formal decision-making structure.

cohesion The measure of a group's solidarity – the degree to which the members share the group's ideas and cooperate.

decentralization A philosophy of organizing and management that disperses authority within an organizational structure.

delegation The downward transfer of formal authority from one person to another.

expert power Influence possessed by a manager due to abilities, skills, knowledge, or experience.

formal organization The official organizational structure that top management conceives and builds.

functional authority Authority to make decisions about specific activities that are undertaken by personnel in other departments.

influence The ability [of a person] to inspire others, to sway them to subject their wills to [the person's].

informal organization A network of personal and social relationships that arises spontaneously as people associate with one another in the work environment.

interaction chart A diagram that shows the informal organization.

legitimate power Authority possessed by managers and derived from the positions they occupy in the formal organization.

line authority Direct supervisory authority from superior to subordinate.

line departments Core work units established to meet the major objectives of the organization and directly influence the success of the business.

norms Any standard of conduct, code, or pattern of behavior perceived by a group to be important for its members to honor or to conform to.

organization chart A visual representation of the structure of an organization and how its parts fit together.

power A person's ability to exert influence.

referent power Influence that comes to people because of the kinds of persons they are – their traits, personalities, and attractiveness to others.

responsibility The obligation to carry out one's assigned duties to the best of one's ability.

sanctions Rewards or penalties used by informal groups to persuade members to conform to norms.

staff authority Authority to serve in an advisory capacity; authority to advise.

unity of command The organizing principle that states that each person in an organization should take orders from and report to only one person.

VIDEO VIEWING QUESTIONS

1. How can delegation actually increase a manager's work load?

2. Northwest's CEO John Dasburg speaks of "operating" businesses and "service" businesses. Which label does he apply to Northwest? How does his conclusion relate to the process of delegation?

3. Evaluate the statement made by Northwest executive Barry Kotar (about the airline's senior managers): "We're not in the position of making the decisions as to how this company is going to be run."

4. Summarize the viewpoints expressed by UCLA's Barbara Lawrence, USC's John Galbraith and Peter Robertson, and Harvard's John Kotter about the informal organization. What do they see as the informal organization's relationship to managers?

5. Compare and contrast delegation of decision-making authority at Northwest Airlines and Cable News Network. Discuss some of the differences between the ways in which the two firms treat the idea of authority in their daily operations.

SELF-TEST

1. The power gained from authority is called

   a. expert power.
   b. referent power.
   c. legitimate power.
   d. formal power.

2. Expert power derives from

   a. the respect generated by a person's character.
   b. demonstrated superior skills and knowledge.
   c. an individual's position in the organization.
   d. top management.

3. Of the five elements listed below, which is **not** necessarily involved in the process of delegation?

 a. Creation of accountability
 b. Assignment of tasks
 c. Acceptance of responsibility
 d. Delegation of authority
 e. Determination of compensation

4. In the process of delegation,

 a. a manager transfers responsibility for accomplishing the delegated task to the subordinate.
 b. a manager retains his or her basic decision making authority.
 c. the subordinate becomes accountable to the manager for performance of the assignment.

5. A philosophy of decentralized decision making generally

 a. is found at mature companies like GM.
 b. requires the addition of inspectors to insure adequate control.
 c. leads to a company with fewer levels of management and wider spans of control.
 d. leads to narrow spans of control.

6. In dealing with their firm's informal organization, managers should

 a. essentially ignore it because it has little effect on the form's primary objectives.
 b. seek to eliminate it because at any time it may become counterproductive.
 c. designate a trusted subordinate to act as a liaison between management and leaders of the informal organization.
 d. endeavor to identify and make special efforts to work with the leaders within the informal organization.

7. Which of the following is **not** an advantage to management of the informal organization?

 a. Can lend stability in the operating environment.
 b. Can help to make the overall management system effective.
 c. Can fill in gaps in a manager's knowledge.
 d. Can be relied upon to facilitate needed change.

8. Informal leaders

   a. usually also hold positions of power in the formal organization.
   b. derive their power from seniority.
   c. tend to be the people with the highest status in the informal group.
   d. normally will lead in all of the informal organizations within a company.

Certain functions within companies are commonly categorized as either line or staff activities. For each of functions listed below, specify the appropriate classification – "L" for a line classification, "S" for staff.

9. Finance

10. Human Resources

11. Public Relations

12. Production

13. Marketing

14. Legal Counsel

15. Sales

16. Advertising

EXPANDED ANALYSIS

1. Practicing managers, commentators, and academics speak of the many strengths of informal organizations. By definition, however, such phenomena lie outside management's formal functions of planning, organizing, staffing, directing, and controlling. Are there some general strategies managers should consider to obtain the maximum possible benefits from the informal organization for their firm? How might such strategies differ in different types of organizations? Consider and contrast possible strategies for the chief of the New York City Police Department and U.S. Postmaster General.

9 Heart of the Matter: Organizational Climate

L E A R N I N G   O B J E C T I V E S

Upon completing this lesson, you should be familiar with the facts, ideas, and processes contained in this lesson, and be able to:

■ Define corporate culture and its relationship to the climate that exists within an organization.

■ Explain why the concept of organizational climate is important to managers.

■ Identify those factors that influence organizational climate and enhance work group effectiveness.

■ Describe, in general terms, the concept of Total Quality Management (TQM) and the goals it seeks to achieve.

■ Describe the relationship between effective organizations and group processes.

■ Given specific dysfunctional situations, describe strategies that can be used to improve the effectiveness of an organization.

O V E R V I E W

Organizational Culture

Only occasionally do most of us stop to analyze the background processes that influence our daily lives. Mostly we tend to take the complex, pervasive systems around us – from municipal government to supermarkets – for granted, and go about our business. Although it may seem to be such a background process, **organizational culture** can provide imaginative managers with a dynamic resource to improve corporate performance.

The idea of culture affects every organization. In the business world, culture shapes how we work, set priorities, and accomplish goals. Organizational (corporate) culture generates the **organizational climate** – the quality of the work environment experienced each day by a firm's employees. Because people tend to do their best among motivated and supportive colleagues in challenging but congenial settings, a company's climate profoundly influences how successful the organization will be.

A company's culture helps to define what is important to the group and its people as they share a common identity. Each organization's beliefs and values create a unique climate. A coherent climate (one that is consistent with the firm's objectives) provides a means for people to endorse and commit themselves to the firm's mission. The more deeply a culture's values permeate the organization, the stronger the culture. Among the factors that shape culture are organizational processes, employees and other tangible assets, formal organizational arrangements, the dominant coalition, the social system, technology, and the external environment.

Culture doesn't simply happen, but is created by efforts of both managers and employees. Some facets of a culture emerge unplanned over time, but others are the result of carefully conceived management. When 68-year-old Marvin Runyon became Postmaster General in July 1992, he called his new assignment as head of the 730,000-strong U.S. Postal Service "next to being President, the most challenging management job in the country." Interviewed by Steve Lohr in the November 15, 1992, *New York Times*, Runyon said his goal is to fashion a more efficient postal system, one that will behave like a business catering to customers instead of like a government monopoly. "The Postal Service hasn't faced the fact that we need satisfied customers to succeed."

During his long career (he rose from an assembly line job at Ford to oversee 29 of its factories, then headed Nissan U.S.A. and later was chairman of the Tennessee Valley Authority electric utility) Marvin Runyon has often used corporate culture as a management tool, especially to motivate people. At Nissan, he wore the same uniform as the factory workers and ate in the company cafeteria. When he took over T.V.A., he ordered the lights that burned all night at the utility's Knoxville headquarters shut off because they symbolized waste. At the Postal Service, to stress a new business-like atmosphere, Runyon immediately announced that every department would pay its own postage, including the inhouse newspaper. "We've got to behave like a private business to compete," he said. Runyon's views underline another mark of effective culture – adaptability to the external environment.

Factors Shaping Culture

A company's managers – the dominant coalition – influence culture by deciding how employees gather information, communicate, make decisions, manage workflow, and produce goods and services. Managers' leadership styles set the tone for how employees are treated and how they feel about themselves and their work. CEO Yvon Chouinard's determination to implement his personal attitudes and philosophy at Patagonia illustrates the impact management can have on a company's climate. Similarly, the quantity and quality of an organization's people, facilities, and related resources shape culture and performance. A firm's formal and informal social systems, the technology and equipment used by employees, and outside elements such as competitors and regulatory agencies further influence its culture.

Culture Signposts

Signs of an organization's culture are often unimposing when considered one at a time – statements of principle, stories, slogans, heroes, ceremonies, symbols, and the physical environment. Such elements usually assume their true effect when assessed in the aggregate – IBM's decades of unassailable, striped-suit authority, for example, or Walt Disney's squeaky-clean, family-centered innocence. Sometimes, however, a single element – say a notable building – can take on almost magical qualities for a company's culture. Frank Lloyd Wright's landmark corporate headquarters for the Johnson's Wax Company in Racine, Wisconsin, in 1937, was said to inspire awe among employees. And from its opening in 1962, Eero Saarinen's TWA Flight Center at New York's Kennedy Airport evoked an almost reverential pride among the staff who bid eagerly for the privilege of a duty assignment in its elegantly seductive spaces.

Employees share in defining organizational culture, in part, by the intensity with which they embrace the culture. Following a Fed Ex truck to Los Angeles International Airport in Friday evening rush hour traffic offers proof of what determined drivers will do to meet the company's cherished schedules. The earnest professionalism that marks President's

Circle Award Dinners for high-performing Avon representatives partly explains that company's nearly $4 billion in 1992 sales. The commitment to customer satisfaction, employee empowerment, and quality that drives Patagonia's clearly enthusiastic managers seems to be a logical extension of the company's management-driven culture.

Quality and Organizational Climate

Patagonia, a California manufacturer of outdoor clothing, has carefully fostered a climate to help employees realize their potential while pursuing quality. CEO Yvon Chouinard encourages people to take risks and to speak up. Patagonia's operating philosophy is a strong belief in the inherent value of people, an attitude that influences virtually everything the company does. Patagonia's culture embodies a number of strongly held beliefs, among them the importance of doing things right, of making quality not a goal, but a requirement.

The idea of quality as a primary corporate objective has become a rallying cry of American business only relatively recently. But as it replaced the objectives of low cost and high volume that prevailed in the late 1940s, the notion of quality in recent decades has been called by some experts the most effective idea in modern business. A review of what those experts mean by quality can explain why the idea has become a key element of the corporate cultures of so many companies in diverse industries.

Definitions of Quality

No simple definition of quality captures all its relevant parts. The American Society for Quality Control defines quality as: "the totality of features and characteristics of a product or service (or process or project) that bear on its ability to satisfy stated or implied goals (or requirements of the producers or users of the outcomes). The dimensions of quality include performance, features, reliability, conformance, durability, serviceability, aesthetics, and perceived quality."

J. M. Juran says "quality is fitness for use," and links two major concepts to quality: "product performance [which generates] product satisfaction" and "freedom from deficiencies (which produce) product dissatisfaction." Famed management consultant W. Edwards Deming writes that quality can be defined only in terms of the supplier, producer, user or customer.

Philip Crosby defines quality as "conformance to requirements." Conformance, says Crosby, demands that products and services be measured against known customer requirements and continuously updated to ensure that they will meet the customer's needs; continual measurements determine conformance to those requirements, and the nonconformance detected is the absence of quality. "Quality problems become nonconformance problems and quality becomes definable [and controllable]."

Crosby also notes that, "Quality improvement is built on getting everyone to do it right the first time (DIRFT). But the key to DIRFT is getting requirements clearly understood and then not putting things in people's way."

The Creation of Total Quality Management (TQM)

Contemporary ideas about quality in American business are often implemented in a system known as **total quality management** (TQM). The origins of TQM were laid nearly half a century ago in the work of W. Edwards Deming in post-World War II Japan. Deming asserted that once the talents, skills, and energy of motivated and empowered employees are unleashed, a company can operate at peak levels of quality.

The movement was formalized by Robert Costello, then Under Secretary of Defense for Acquisitions. Costello, building on the pioneering work of Deming and other theorists, devised TQM for the Department of Defense. The department's TQM Master Plan, issued in August of 1988, defined TQM as:

> A strategy for continuously improving performance at every level, and in all areas of responsibility. It combines fundamental management techniques, existing improvement efforts, and specialized technical tools under a disciplined structure focused on continuously improving all processes. Improved performance is directed at satisfying such broad goals as cost, quality, schedule, and mission need and suitability. Increasing user satisfaction is the overriding objective.

Other contributors to modern thinking about quality include: G.S. Radford, whose *The Control of Quality in Manufacturing* (1922) advocated inspection as the cornerstone of industrial quality control; Bell Laboratories' Walter A. Shewhart, whose *Economic Control of Quality of Manufactured Product* (1931) recommended scientific methods and quantitative measures for quality control; Armand V. Feigenbaum, GE manager of quality control in the 1950s, who advocated total quality control (TQC); and Thomas J. Peters, a tireless lecturer and consultant whose many recent books continue to chronicle and generate useful ideas about management and quality.

Quality as an Element of Culture

Such a philosophy can create an organizational climate which encourages the participation of every employee in the functioning of the company. This greatly enhances morale, which ultimately leads to improvement in productivity and overall work quality.

UCLA management professor and author William G. Ouchi emphasizes quality as process:

> *Quality means a commitment at every level that you will measure what you do, understand the process of what you do, and focus not on developing a better product, but on developing a better process. You can only improve the product by improving the quality of the process.*

With the work of Deming providing a philosophical base, the issue of quality has become a central focus of modern management practice and organizational culture. TQM is based on the notion that, ultimately, corporate success rests on quality. Total quality management is a revolution, argue some observers, and "companies that are not using it now are few and far between."

"Think of it as energy," says professor George Labovitz, "energy that starts at the top of an organization and is driven down through every level and across every division or department of an organization. And as that energy rolls down through an organization it identifies the critical processes that lead to the customer. And those processes inevitably cut across the organization. It identifies those processes, it analyzes those processes and it gets them under control in statistical terms, reduces variation so they work the way they're supposed to every time. And once they work the way they're supposed to every time, they're improved. The things that make a management approach like total quality different from anything in the past is ultimately that it's value driven. And the values in total quality are: an absolute, fanatical obsession with customer satisfaction."

Its effect can be seen in companies of every variety and size. A typical example is San Diego-based Hybritech, whose CEO Don Grimm says: "I knew that I needed something to draw the organization together and work as one unit. I didn't know it was TQM at the time, but I knew I needed something like it." In such circumstances, the relationship between corporate culture and quality emerges clearly. Says Grimm: "One of the benefits that I see from all our quality training is that we're all speaking and thinking the same language and looking towards the same goal."

Changing the Corporate Culture: Teams and TQM

Because TQM requires everyone's support, supervisors, team leaders, and workers must be empowered by being given a say in planning and executing plans. Teams created to implement TQM include: **quality** circles, teams of employees (usually workers and their supervisors or team leaders) most closely connected to a quality problem who go to work defining and solving it; **quality improvement teams**, usually representing all the functional areas of a company to identify and solve common problems; **process improvement teams** made up of members who are involved with a process who meet to analyze how they can improve the process; and **project improvement teams** usually including people involved in the same project. Project improvement teams usually include those who are or will be customers or consumers for the project's output, and may be insiders as well as outsiders.

ASSIGNMENTS

- Read the Overview, familiarize yourself with the Learning Objectives, and peruse the Key Terms below. Then turn to Plunkett & Attner, *Introduction to Management*, and read pages 62–91 in Chapter 3, "Management's Commitments to Quality and Productivity" and pages 276–291 in Chapter 10, "Organizational Culture and Change."

- Next, scan the Video Viewing Questions and watch the video program for Lesson 9, "Heart of the Matter: Organizational Climate."

- After watching the video, answer the viewing questions and assess your learning with the Self-Test.

- Familiarize yourself with the Review Questions, Discussion Questions for Critical Thinking, and Skill-Building Exercises on pages 89–90 and 312 of Plunkett & Attner.

- Strengthen your understanding of the lesson's ideas and issues by undertaking the Expanded Analysis.

KEY TERMS

benchmark A standard by which a product, service, or process can be measured or judged; the level to match or exceed in design, manufacture, performance, and service.

continuous-improvement process (kaizen) The ongoing search for incremental betterment, especially as developed and practiced in the Japanese corporate setting.

organizational culture A system of shared beliefs, values, and norms unique to a particular organization, and which defines what is important to the organization, how people should behave, how they should interact with each other, and what they should be striving for.

organizational climate The feel or personality of an organization, largely evidenced through the corporate (organizational) culture.

process improvement team A group of people assigned to cooperatively assess a process and make it better.

quality The aggregate features and characteristics of a product, service, or process that bear on its ability to satisfy goals or requirements of producers and users of the outcomes.

quality audit A systematic assessment of how well customer and consumer requirements are being met by an organization, product, service, or process; may include recommendations and actual implementation of corrections to discrepancies.

quality circle A small group of employees who meet, as part of their jobs, to improve their unit's processes, products, and services.

quality control (QC) A system of production methods which economically produces quality goods or services meeting the requirements of customers; uses statistical measures and methods and is often called *statistical quality control* (SQC).

quality control audit A systematic check on an organization's and its systems' quality control efforts; two questions are asked and answered: "How are we doing?" and "What are the problems?"

quality improvement team A team of people from all functional areas of a company who meet regularly to assess progress toward goals, identify and work to solve common problems, and cooperate to plan for the future.

statistical process control (SPC) The application to processes of statistical tools and methods to measure and predict variations; establishes boundaries to determine if a process is in control (predictable) or out of control (unpredictable).

statistical quality control The use of statistical tools and methods to determine the quality of a product, service, or process.

subcultures Smaller units within the organization that bond around their own shared values, norms, and beliefs.

total quality management (TQM) A strategy for continuously and comprehensively improving performance at every level, and in all units throughout an organization.

VIDEO VIEWING QUESTIONS

1. From the comments made by managers and staff at Patagonia, how would you characterize the company's culture? What are its most distinctive elements?

2. How does cross-training appear to influence Patagonia's corporate culture?

3. Professor Labovitz compares quality to energy flowing from the top of an organization. How do energy and quality appear to relate to corporate culture at Patagonia? At Hybritech?

4. W. Edwards Deming and William Ouchi talk about quality as process. How does quality as process relate to a company's culture?

5. What similarities do you see between the cultures at Patagonia and Hybritech? What differences? Compare the evident influence on the cultures at each company of their respective CEOs – Yvon Chouinard and Don Grimm.

6. Compare the apparent significance of management's formal effort to achieve quality at Patagonia and Hybritech.

SELF-TEST

1. Organizational climate

   a. is a complex phenomenon beyond the control of managers.
   b. operates in a company independent of outside influence.
   c. is basically a social condition unrelated to technology.
   d. depends largely upon how employees feel about the organization.

2. A company's dominant coalition consists of

   a. its owners and directors.
   b. its hourly employees.
   c. its managers at all levels.
   d. its major customers.

3. Corporate culture may be **least** influenced by

   a. the company's formal mission statement.
   b. the physical environment of the organization.
   c. the presence or absence of a labor union.
   d. government regulations of the firm's industry.

4. Total Quality Management (TQM)

   a. depends primarily upon formal company policies.
   b. is a recent development adapted from Japanese corporate practice.
   c. relies largely upon sophisticated inspection systems.
   d. requires adaptation of the organization's culture.

5. When a company decides to implement TQM, it should

   a. achieve results swiftly once the policy is put in place.
   b. rely largely upon the commitment of department managers.
   c. employ periodic inspection to monitor results.
   d. expect to achieve success in increments and only over time.

6. Of factors determining effectiveness of organizational culture, the most critical today may be

   a. the relationship of the firm's culture to it mission.
   b. the degree of employee identification with the company's values.
   c. adaptability to the external environment.
   d. strong corporate leadership.

7. According to W. Edwards Deming, the key to quality

   a. lies in surveying customer needs.
   b. depends primarily upon thorough employee training.
   c. requires breaking a production process into individual steps to be analyzed one at a time.
   d. is precise management control over process.

8. Joseph Juran developed seven rules for adapting a firm's culture to TQM. The statement inconsistent with Juran's thinking is

   a. Provide participation.
   b. Make the change to TQM a dramatic company event.
   c. Work with the recognized leadership.
   d. Treat people with dignity.

9. A company's culture can best be defined as

   a. the direct result of its success in the market place.
   b. the sum total of its behaviors, beliefs, and values.
   c. the overall morale throughout the organization.
   d. the attitude of its senior managers.

10. The team category **least** likely to be established at a company implementing TQM is

    a. a quality improvement team.
    b. a process improvement team.
    c. a product improvement team.
    d. a project improvement team.

E X P A N D E D   A N A L Y S I S

1. From recent print or broadcast news or commentary, choose a company or institution whose organizational culture appears to play a significant role in present success or difficulty. What evidence of culture can you identify? What, if anything, would you advise the organization's leaders to do about that culture? (Consider IBM, General Motors, Chrysler, Microsoft, the Federal Bureau of Investigation, the U.S. Navy, Sears, the U.S. Postal Service, the Los Angeles Police Department, the United Auto Workers, the National Rifle Association.)

2. What company with which you have had first-hand experience do you think displays the strongest commitment to quality? What evidence leads you to choose the firm?

10 Shifting Gears: Managing Organizational Change

L E A R N I N G   O B J E C T I V E S

Upon completing this lesson, you should be familiar with the facts, ideas, and processes contained in this lesson, and be able to:

- Describe how external as well as internal forces can precipitate change within an organization.

- Describe the phases of change management.

- Recognize that resistance to change is natural.

- Discuss ways to initiate change that may minimize or reduce employee resistance.

- Describe the role and the limitations of the manager in the change process both for the organization and the individuals it employs.

- Recognize why change efforts fail.

- Explain how organizations learn from their own experiences.

O V E R V I E W

The Nature of Change

Few elements in the manager's universe today exceed the force of accelerating change. Everywhere and ceaselessly, change generates change. At the Boeing plant and in the nearby logging town. In Massachusetts General Hospital and the office of a small town doctor in upstate Maine. On the campuses of the City University of New York and St. John's College in Annapolis. Inside Wal-Mart's Bentonville headquarters and behind the cash register of a neighborhood convenience store in South Central Los Angeles. Under "responsibilities," the job description of managers everywhere should include a clause that says, "Embrace Change."

For the manager, **change** is any alteration in the context of the work environment . . . in the way things are perceived or in how they are organized, processed, created, or maintained. Often, external events beyond a person's or a company's control initiate the change. Sometimes change is planned, as when a company like Apple Computer decides to change its market strategy and cut its prices deeply in order to increase market share.

Whether external and uncontrolled or internal and exquisitely micromanaged, changes invariably trigger more change. Broad, deep reductions in the military establishment, for instance, generate powerful temblors of alteration that shake families, communities, industries, and entire nations, immediately and far into the future. Change is endless, difficult, implacable.

Change can originate both outside and within a firm's internal environments, sometimes simultaneously. External sources of change range from cyclic economic variables and government action, to technological advances and shifts in social values, to the actions of competing firms and the natural consequences of hurricanes and earthquakes. If their companies are to thrive, managers often have little choice but to accommodate and respond to change by changing certain aspects of the company and its operations.

Internal sources of change are no less diverse. They range from staff turnover and policy modifications to the installation of a voice mail telephone system. Employees as well as managers must cope with incessant change. It affects strategy, structure, process, and people at every level.

A company's strategy or mission may require change, perhaps the divesting of unrelated businesses, alterations to the company's structural design, or modified work processes. Such changes, of course, affect the corporate culture. Attitudes, behaviors, skills, and employee performance can be modified with retraining, staffing changes, and increasing performance expectations of new employees.

Management and Change

To cope effectively with change, managers often follow the well-entrenched patterns of management fundamentals based on their level within the organization. Senior managers focus on the broad outlines of desired change – strategy, structure, and process. Middle managers tend to concentrate on structural, process-oriented, or people-centered changes, areas that overlap somewhat with first-line managers. First-line supervisors institute and implement with their employees, the process-oriented and people-centered changes developed higher in the hierarchy.

Managing Change

Some managers adopt a philosophy of **planned change**. They systematically forecast possible alterations in the external and internal environments, then shape strong responses in advance. When such managers implement planned change, they become **change agents**. They clearly enjoy more control of their company's destiny than managers who wait passively until change batters them into potential failure.

Because organizations commonly progress through identifiable stages of evolution, from birth to maturity, managers can diagnose and predict their company's need for internal organizational change. They can chart the progress of their firm through five developmental phases suggested by consultant Larry Greiner: creativity, direction, delegation, coordination, and collaboration. At the heart of Greiner's model is a key point about change: the solution to one set of problems eventually creates another set of problems that require solving, affirming once again that the need for change is constant.

Concrete action to promote change begins with the creation of a favorable climate that includes mutual trust within the firm, some mechanism for organizational learning, and reasonable adaptability. Research studies confirm that an environment of mutual trust between managers and employees is the most important factor in creating effective organizations. When people can rely on their colleagues' character, ability, and truthfulness, they can function together while optimistically pursuing improvement.

Organizational learning also plays a crucial part in facilitating constructive change. This capacity to integrate the new ideas into established systems promotes flexibility throughout an organization and enables change to take place.

Organizational learning occurs in two modes. In single-looped **learning**, only one way of making adjustments exists: the company's established way. Such firms do not change their attitude, only their responses. **Double-looped learning,** by contrast, acknowledges that more than one alternative exists and proceeds on the premise that there may be multiple solutions to a problem. Managers who can envision more than one way to reach a goal free their colleagues to share ideas and the assumptions underlying the ideas. Double-looped learning facilitates change in both attitude and behavior.

Implementing (and Not Implementing) Change

To implement change, managers must overcome the resistance of those from whom change is required. People resist change because it threatens their sense of security, because they fear loss of money or power, because old habits are tough to alter, because they perceive a situation selectively, and even because of genuine weaknesses in the proposed change.

Competent managers can turn most such objections around with the truthful and good-faith use of five techniques:

- by inviting people to participate in the change process;
- by communicating openly with the people affected by planned change;
- by providing ample advance notice of imminent change;
- by displaying sensitivity to each employee's specific concerns and responding appropriately; and
- by explaining that income and job security are not affected by the change.

Even when initiated for excellent cause, change sometimes fails. Managers can fail to achieve change because of inadequate analysis. They can bungle selection or application of the change process. They can apply too little time and money to change efforts. They may not generate sufficient acceptance and commitment from other managers and employees. They may time their efforts poorly. Or the firm's culture may simply not be ready for the proposed change.

Methods of Affecting Change

A portion of managers' efforts in implementing change will focus on influencing subordinates to increase their skills and knowledge and to change their attitudes and behavior. In addition to the many conventional avenues of communication and persuasion discussed throughout this course, managers may wish to know some specific techniques that have been used to change behavior on an individual level. These include Kurt Lewin's **three-step approach** to attitude change, in which managers follow a process of unfreezing the desired behavior, changing to the new behavior, and refreezing the desired behavior. Another technique is to strengthen the forces that lead a person to change, and weaken or remove those that lead to resistance.

Other managers will prefer to maintain an environment conducive to healthy change by cultivating the principles of organizational development, or OD. **Organizational development** is a comprehensive strategy that uses various tools, devices, and methods for introducing change, and involves all activities and levels of management in dealing with ongoing problems that arise from external and internal sources.

ASSIGNMENTS

- Read the Overview, familiarize yourself with the Learning Objectives, and peruse the Key Terms below. Then turn to Plunkett & Attner, *Introduction to Management*, and read Chapter 10, "Organizational Culture and Change," pages 291–313.

- Next, scan the Video Viewing Questions and watch the video program for Lesson 10, "Shifting Gears: Managing Organizational Change."

- After watching the video, answer the viewing questions and assess your learning with the Self-Test.

- Familiarize yourself with the Review Questions, Discussion Questions for Critical Thinking, and Skill-Building Exercises on page 312 of Plunkett & Attner.

- Strengthen your understanding of the lesson's ideas and issues by undertaking the Expanded Analysis.

KEY TERMS

change Any alteration in the present work environment. The shift may be in the way things are perceived or in how things are organized, processed, created, or maintained.

change agent The person who implements change.

force field analysis A technique to implement change by determining which forces drive change and which forces resist change.

management by reaction A philosophy toward change where no energy is spent to anticipate change; rather, when change occurs a reaction takes place.

organizational learning The ability to integrate new ideas into established systems to produce better ways of doing things.

planned change A philosophy that involves trying to anticipate what changes will occur in both the external and internal environments and then developing a response that will maximize the organization's success.

subcultures Smaller units within the organization that bond around their own shared values, norms, and beliefs.

three-step approach A technique to implement change that is characterized by three phases: unfreezing, change, and refreezing.

V I D E O   V I E W I N G   Q U E S T I O N S

1. Summarize the "stages of change" experienced by the Apple Computer company from its founding to the present.

2. Identify some of the strategic and tactical actions that Apple undertook as they sought to change.

3. Why do employees resist change? What are the three phases of employee response to change as described by Les McCraw of Fluor Daniel?

4. Describe the principal methods used at Hybritech to bring about needed change. How does TQM relate to change?

5. Explain how peer pressure and training related to change at Hybritech.

6. What role did communications play in the major changes undertaken at the Fluor Daniel Corporation?

S E L F - T E S T

1. Of the following statements, which reflects the most productive management strategy?

   a. Because there is little management can do about change in the external environment, management should wait until changed conditions stabilize before reacting to them.

b. Playing a leadership role in responding to change is needlessly risky; it is better to let other companies pioneer change and learn from their mistakes.

c. Managers should constantly monitor the external environment for early indications of possible changes in the environment, then position the company to protect itself or take advantage of the new circumstances as quickly as possible.

d. Managers should insulate the company from change as thoroughly as possible in order to minimize the costs of constant adaptation.

2. Corporate change is sometimes classified by its focus. Which of the following is **not** a common category of change focus?

   a. Strategic change
   b. Financial change
   c. Process-oriented change
   d. People-centered change

3. Process-oriented and people-centered change are generally instituted by

   a. first-line and mid-level managers
   b. top level managers
   c. first-line managers only
   d. top- and mid-level managers

4. According to Larry Greiner, the phase of corporate development characterized by team problem solving, risk taking, and innovation is

   a. the coordination phase.
   b. the collaboration phase.
   c. the delegation phase.
   d. the creativity phase.

5. According to the Greiner model, a company moves from one growth phase to the next when

   a. it has resolved the conflicts inherent in one phase and is therefore capable of productive growth again.
   b. internal conflicts reach crisis, thereby stimulating major change.
   c. external factors make growth essential for survival.
   d. it has developed an organizational climate that inhibits conflict.

6. Resistance to change is

    a. practically universal and must be planned for in any systematic approach to change.
    b. usually overcome soon after change has been introduced.
    c. seldom a difficulty in a well-managed firm.
    d. not a significant issue when compared to the long-term benefits of change.

7. The most effective way to deal with widespread resistance to change is to

    a. make a coordinated effort to introduce as little change as possible into the firm.
    b. postpone proposed changes until resistance dies down.
    c. ignore the resistance on the grounds that it is necessary and people will eventually come around.
    d. enlist as many people as possible in the change process.

8. Which of the following elements is **least** likely to cause a company's change efforts to fail?

    a. Improper analysis
    b. Lack of funding
    c. Conflicting corporate culture
    d. Action of competing firms

9. The process of thoroughly analyzing a company's problems and then systematically designing long-term solutions to them is called

    a. organizational learning.
    b. planned change.
    c. organizational development.
    d. the three-step approach.

10. Which of the following actions is **least** consistent with the principles of organizational development?

    a. Periodic review of policies and procedures by outside consultants
    b. Occasional inhouse management seminars to explore mutual problems
    c. Continuing training programs at all levels
    d. Across-the-board salary reductions for all employees during an extended period of declining sales.

EXPANDED ANALYSIS

1. In characterizing contemporary management trends, the University of Southern California's Professor Warren Bennis says that the three words which define traditional bureaucratic structures – control, order, and predict (COP) – "are no longer possible," and that "the watchwords of organizations **will** be: align, create, and empower" (ACE). What does Professor Bennis mean?

2. Identify what you believe will be the most significant change factor for U.S. management in the next ten years. Does your factor pose primarily an opportunity or a threat? Suggest strategies that (a) managers of private companies and (b) the federal or state governments might adopt either to address the problem or to capitalize on the opportunities represented by your change factor.

11

Help Wanted: Recruitment and Selection of Employees

Upon completing this lesson, you should be familiar with the facts, ideas, and processes contained in this lesson, and be able to:

- Explain why staffing is an essential management function.

- Discuss the relationship between organizational structure and human resource planning and staffing.

- Describe the primary factors to be considered in human resource planning and management.

- Suggest effective strategies for recruiting both within and outside the organization.

- Describe in general terms the employee selection process.

- Identify major laws and regulations applicable to recruitment, selection, and other employment practices.

- Analyze and assess, from a personal perspective, the effectiveness of various compensation and benefits programs presented in the video and text.

O V E R V I E W

The Right Person in the Right Job

No effective manager disputes the assertion that people are any organization's most valuable resource. Competent and committed employees at every level, from CEO to bottle washer, determine whether a company will succeed. Every aspect of management involves people in countless important ways, but in the functional area of human resources management, people and people issues are the manager's primary concerns.

The importance of recruiting and hiring the best people for a company simply cannot be overstated. Some critics of contemporary American business performance believe that industry has focused on other aspects of management and paid too little attention to human resources issues. The one thing that can make a difference in the world market, they assert, is people. And it's up to human resources managers to find and hire those crucial people, and to put the right person in the right job.

Modern management practice recognizes the importance and complexity of human resources. While smaller companies must rely on their generalist managers to accomplish personnel tasks, it is difficult to imagine a large firm that would attempt to do business without a dedicated department headed by **human resource managers** to assist others with their staffing tasks. Human resources staffers are experts in sound staffing theory and practice. Specialists concentrate on compensation, training, and recruiting. And increasingly, human resources managers are included at the highest levels of corporate planning so that important personnel-related questions can be integrated into strategy from the outset.

The Staffing Process

Staffing activities normally occur in a logical sequence. Some aspects of this process are non-recurring for each employee, some continuous. The eight generally accepted steps are: planning, recruiting, selection, orientation, training and development, performance appraisal, compensation, and the ongoing employment decisions of promotions, transfer, demotion, and separation.

In planning, senior managers integrate human resource requirements into their overall plans for the organization. Job analysis, inventory, and forecasting techniques are used to align personnel needs with strategic plans. In conducting a job analysis, human resource specialists use two coordinated documents: the **job description** which summarizes the details of each actual job, and the **job specification** which identifies the qualifications a person needs to perform the job successfully. Inventories catalogue the firm's present personnel and forecasting permits managers to relate strategic plans of the company to long-term people needs.

Recruiting and Selecting

When they have prepared their forecasts, inventories, and job descriptions and specifications, managers begin the actual **recruiting**. They find and invite qualified candidates to apply for vacant jobs. Recruiting strategies are many and diverse, and include: newspaper and periodical advertising; notices to suitable trade unions, private or state-operated employment services; requests to current employees to recommend qualified friends and relatives; participation in job fairs; contact with local schools and colleges. Internship and apprenticeship programs can generate especially qualified and committed people. Industry trade shows and conferences are often good recruiting sources, and in some industries, "raiding" competitors is common, if controversial.

When recruitment has identified suitable candidates for a vacant job, the **selection** process – deciding which candidate is best qualified – can begin. Among selection tools are applications forms, interviews, testing, reference checks, and physical exams.

The Staffing Environment

A company's external environment, especially its customers, affects staffing plans and strategies. Among the most powerful influences on today's American business operations is the huge body of statutes built up in this century to advance the nation's social and political agenda. From early concerns with child labor and monopolies, to trade unions, civil rights, and securities trading, the volumes of federal statutes and case law have grown to fill good size libraries. A fair percentage of the regulations apply to staffing, and deal with three areas: **equal employment opportunity**, **affirmative action**, and **sexual harassment.**

At the center of the regulatory construct lies the large body of federal laws which prohibit discrimination on the basis of race, color, religion, sex, age, national origin, or handicap. Particularly at large companies, managers at every level in an organization must carefully avoid making employment decisions that can put the firm and its managers at legal risk. One way to avoid problems with equal opportunity laws is to use only those criteria that are job-related in making decisions about recruitment, hiring, promotion, training and development, compensation, and separation.

The Social and Cultural Environment

America's expanding labor force continues to become more culturally diverse. Two-thirds of the nation's workers are either women or people of color, and that figure is likely to grow. Not long ago, companies tended to treat everyone alike, and to make people fit the company's dominant culture. Today, such an approach is unlikely to build a stable, committed group of employees. Differences in languages, personal goals, and ethnic backgrounds require a thoughtful response, and corporate America seems to be learning, at least in markets with notable cultural turbulence. The morning newspaper tells the story. In the *Los Angeles Times*, on June 1, 1993, under the headline "Creating a Bias-Free Corporate Structure," George White writes: "While some companies develop their own diversity managers – often using human resources staff – most companies turn to outside consultants with special credentials in such areas as personnel development, cross-cultural communications, and equal employment practices."

Compensation

The purpose of **compensation** is to attract, help develop, and retain talented performers. It includes all varieties of financial payments to employees: salaries and wages, benefits, bonuses, gain-sharing, profit-sharing, and awards of goods or services. The trend today is to link increased compensation to proven increases in performance and added value to the firm, a practice sometimes labeled "pay at risk." People who believe themselves fairly paid feel that they are being treated with recognition and respect. Compensation should also create an adequate sense of security, so that employees may devote their best efforts to their work, knowing that their financial needs are met. Companies assess each job and devise compensation packages consistent with the firm's other jobs in a process known as **job evaluation.**

Compensation other than wages, salaries, and bonuses falls under the classification of employee benefits. Some – Social Security, workers' compensation, and unemployment insurance – are legally required. Others – paid holidays and vacations, profit sharing, health and life insurance, and retirement programs – the employer offers "voluntarily." Many companies offer innovative benefits: child day care, flexible scheduling, and parental leaves.

A S S I G N M E N T S

- Read the Overview, familiarize yourself with the Learning Objectives, and peruse the Key Terms below. Then turn to Plunkett & Attner, *Introduction to Management*, and read Chapter 11, "Staffing," pages 314–337 and 347–355.

- Next, scan the Video Viewing Questions and watch the video program for Lesson 11, "Help Wanted: Recruitment and Selection of Employees."

- After watching the video, answer the viewing questions and assess your learning with the Self-Test.

- Familiarize yourself with the Review Questions, Discussion Questions for Critical Thinking, and Skill-Building Exercises on page 354 of Plunkett & Attner.

- Strengthen your understanding of the lesson's ideas and issues by undertaking the Expanded Analysis.

K E Y   T E R M S

affirmative action A requirement placed upon organizations that have discriminated against protected individuals or groups to make an extra effort to improve the employment situations of those people through specific actions with goals and time tables.

assessment center Outside groups or agencies that specialize in screening candidates for managerial positions.

benefits Legally required or voluntary programs provided to employees in addition to their salaries or wages.

collective bargaining Negotiation between the representatives of organized workers and their employer or employers to determine wages, hours, rules, and working conditions.

compensation All forms of financial payments to employees, including such things as salaries, wages, and benefits.

discrimination Using illegal criteria while making employment decisions resulting in an adverse impact on one or more members of protected groups.

disparate impact The result of using employment criteria which have a significantly greater negative result on one or more protected groups than they do on others.

equal employment opportunity Legislation designed to protect individuals and groups from discrimination.

human resource manager A manager specializing in the execution of one or more personnel or human resources functions.

job analysis Studying a job to determine both its duties and the human qualities needed to perform it; results in the preparation or updating of a job description and job specifications.

job evaluation The process of studying a job in order to determine its worth and importance to the organization and what compensation should be assigned to it.

perks From perquisite, a payment or benefit received in addition to a regular wage or salary; commonly associated with executives and top management.

personnel manager Another name for a human resource manager.

recruiting An organizations efforts to locate and encourage people to apply for each position that needs to be filled.

selection The process through which applicants are evaluated and those most closely matching the requirements of the job and offering the best "fit" into the organization's culture are hired.

sexual harassment Unwelcome sexual advances, requests for sexual favors and other verbal or physical conduct of a sexual nature which negatively affects an employee.

staffing Efforts designed to attract, hold, develop, reward, and retain the people needed to accomplish an organization's goals and the efforts designed to assist all employees in gaining job satisfaction.

test Any criterion or paper-and-pencil exercise or performance measure used as a basis for any employment decision.

transfer Moving an employee to a job with similar levels of status, compensation, and responsibilities.

V I D E O   V I E W I N G   Q U E S T I O N S

1. Identify three historic reasons for the emergence of the modern human resources/personnel function in management.

2. Why should human resources personnel participate in strategic planning?

3. Describe some of the effects of labor regulations on private corporation. How may such regulations influence a firm's costs?

4. How does the process of job definition relate to recruitment and employee selection?

5. Describe the Four Seasons Hotel hiring process. Would so elaborate a process be appropriate for a company that is not in the service business? Why or why not?

6. What is the significance of the term "pay at risk" to corporation? To employees?

S E L F - T E S T

1. The task of matching the right people with the right positions is best described as

   a. selection.
   b. recruitment.
   c. staffing.
   d. human resource planning.

2. Which of the following is **not** generally considered as an integral component of staffing?

   a. Organizational planning and goal setting
   b. Induction and orientation of new employees
   c. Employee training and development
   d. Employee separation, including retirement and separations

3. In order to plan human resources effectively, a manager needs all of the following **except**

   a. a large staff of qualified personnel from which to obtain a number of new candidates.
   b. knowledge of broad organizational goals, including plans for expansion or reduction.
   c. knowledge of employees' present qualifications.
   d. information about upcoming retirements, resignations, promotions, and terminations.

4. Unknown to the people who administer the bank's personnel tests, as part of its employee screening process for the last five years Porcine Bank has used a vocabulary test that is biased in favor of native speakers of English. Hal Wiggly, the bank president who insists on the test, observes that American-born Caucasians almost invariably perform somewhat better on the test than foreign-born applicants or people of color – none of whom have been hired by the bank since the test was introduced. Use of the test as described

   a. is an example of nondiscriminatory testing.
   b. is an example of performance appraisal testing.
   c. is an example of overt discrimination.
   d. would produce a disparate impact.

5. A minority applicant who was not hired as a result of her vocabulary test score could claim adverse impact if she

   a. met all other requirements for the job.
   b. could show that the test was not job-related.
   c. knew that the bank had never hired a minority applicant.
   d. could show that the test was not used by other local financial institutions in their hiring process.

6. Which of the following best describes the difference between a job description and a job specification?

   a. A job description is used internally, while a job specification is used for external recruiting.
   b. A job description is a general statement applying to all jobs on a given organizational level.
   c. A job description covers the scope, function, and responsibilities of a job while the specification focuses on the required education, skills, and experience.
   d. The labels are essentially synonymous; there is no significant difference between the two documents.

7. Which of the following questions is an interviewer legally allowed to ask a job candidate?

   a. What is your age?
   b. What is your maiden name?
   c. Have you ever been arrested?
   d. Do you have military experience?

8. Identify the federal legislation that establishes requirments for affirmative action plans.

    a. Title VII 1964 Civil Rights Act
    b. Executive Orders 11246 and 11375 (1965)
    c. Revised Guidelines on Employment Selection (1976, 1978, and 1979)
    d. Equal Employment Opportunity Guidelines of 1981 – National Origin

9. Which of the following is **not** among the groups protected from discrimination in employment decisions by federal law?

    a. homosexuals
    b. women
    c. the handicapped
    d. American Indians

10. What is the most valuable piece of information a reviewer is likely to learn from perusing a candidate's job application?

    a. The candidate's height and weight
    b. The candidate's birthplace
    c. The candidate's social security number
    d. The candidate's ability to follow directions

EXPANDED ANALYSIS

1. The cover story of the March 29, 1993, issue of *Time Magazine*, was titled "The Temping of America." The central argument of the story, written by Janice Castro, appeared on page 43:

    [T]he U.S. is increasingly becoming a nation of part-timers and freelancers, of temps and independent contractors. This `disposable' work force is the most important trend in business today, and it is fundamentally changing the relationship between Americans and their jobs. For companies large and small, the phenomenon provides a way to remain globally competitive while avoiding the vagaries of market cycles and the growing burdens imposed by employment rules, anti-discrimination laws, health-care costs and pension plans. But for workers, it can mean an end to the security and sense of significance that came from being a loyal employee.

    Senior editor Lance Morrow concluded:

    America has entered the age of the contingent or temporary worker, of the consultant and subcontractor, of the just-in-time work force —

fluid, flexible, disposable. This is the future. Its message is this: You are on your own. For good (sometimes) and ill (often), the workers of the future will have to constantly sell their skills, invent new relationships with employers who must, themselves, change and adapt constantly in order to survive in a ruthless global market.

What do you think of this view of U.S. business? Assuming its basic accuracy, what, if anything, should be done about the situation, and by whom?

12 High Performance: Staff Development and Maintenance

Upon completing this lesson, you should be familiar with the facts, ideas, and processes contained in this lesson, and be able to:

- Relate effective orientation programs and employee success.

- Discuss the importance of employee training and development, and related benefits for employees and the organization.

- Examine the impact of increasing cultural diversity in the workforce on the training and development process.

- Compare and evaluate subjective and objective methods used to assess and appraise employee performance.

- Discuss the glass ceiling and how it affects women and minorities.

- Suggest job coaching techniques to overcome performance deficiencies.

- Discuss effective approaches to employee termination.

- Examine the role of the manager in influencing an employee's organizational and professional future.

O V E R V I E W

Finding qualified candidates to fill vacant positions is a company's first step in developing committed, competent, and productive employees. But employee selection only begins an ongoing process of staff development that must be thoughtfully designed and vigorously implemented for the duration of each employee's career with the company. Staff development should start the moment a new employee walks in the door.

Orientation, simple or elaborate, welcomes a new employee to a firm's environment. It begins a socialization process that nourishes employees' relationships, attitudes, and commitment to the company. While the hiring process may have provided some familiarization, the object of orientation is to create a sense of genuine welcome, to get the new person on line quickly, and to establish realistic expectations that will help provide motivation for the long haul.

An effective orientation is thoroughly planned and skillfully executed. Work rules, policies, and procedures are explained, paperwork completed. The employee is introduced to workstation, supervisor, and co-workers. Questions are answered promptly and with candor. The goal is to ensure that first impressions and early experiences are realistic and positive.

Training and Development

Both training and development teach attitudes, knowledge, and skills and are ongoing and critical in business environments. **Training** concentrates on present and near-term needs, development on the future. Both require three elements in order to succeed: (1) needs assessments to determine content and objectives; (2) training and development people who know their business; and (3) the willing participation of everyone involved.

The five major aims of training are to increase knowledge and skills, to increase motivation to succeed, to promote chances for advancement, to improve morale and a sense of competence and pride in performance, and to increase quality and productivity. Increasingly culturally diverse workforces will continue to require more training than in the past, particularly in language and basic skills. If employees are to cope successfully with job demands and prepare for greater opportunities, many firms need to conduct remedial training as well.

Training Techniques

Modern companies have a wide array of training strategies they can utilize. Options include training on the job site, at a corporate training center, a college classroom, or various workshops, seminars, and professional gatherings. Among the most common in-house training approaches are: on-the-job training (OJT); machine-based training with computers, simulators, or other machines; vestibule training that simulates the work environment and uses the actual equipment and tools in a laboratory setting; and job rotation.

Sound training is realistic and teaches necessary material in ways that apply directly to the work setting once training ends. Constant feedback from trainees is required in order to accurately determine their progress and mastery of material.

The Purposes of Development

Development attempts to prepare a person for new and greater challenges that will be encountered in another, more demanding job and to enhance career progression. Workers need development to prepare for a management job; supervisors need development to prepare to move into middle management. All development is really self-development, and cannot occur without the employee's personal commitment. People can be pressured into training and must often undergo training just to keep their jobs; but development, when offered, can be rejected. It should also be noted that employees cannot depend on their employers for development. Small companies can't afford it, and many large employers will not pay for development when it is not directly related to an employee's current job or career track.

Development techniques include sending people to professional workshops or seminars; job rotation; sponsoring memberships in professional associations; paying for an employee's formal education courses; and granting a person a sabbatical (leave of absence) to pursue further education, engage in community service, or pursue other activities that can enhance the person's abilities to perform his or her job. Company-sponsored programs should be seen as a reward and as a clear statement about one's worth to the company.

Development efforts should never end; indeed, they can be made part of a daily routine. Regular reading of professional journals and business publications and constant interaction with those on the cutting edge of technology can do a lot to keep people current. Volunteering for tough assignments that will make a person stretch his or her abilities is another example of a "developmental experience."

One final approach to development should be mentioned: finding someone to act as a mentor. **Mentors** are professionals who are one or two steps above a person in his or her profession. They can come from a person's present environment or from another organization. They are persons who are willing to share experiences and give competent advice on how to handle such things as opportunities for advancement, company politics, and the best way to proceed in self-development.

Performance Appraisal

Some assessment of job performance takes place at least informally every day in most organizations. When the results for a given time period are summarized and shared with those being appraised, **performance appraisal** becomes a formal, structured system designed (within legal limits) to measure the actual job performance of an employee by comparing it to designated standards. These standards are introduced and taught to employees in the selection and training processes.

The Purposes of Performance Appraisal

Most organizations use appraisals to accomplish the following major objectives:

- To provide feedback on the success of previous training and to disclose the need for any additional training.

- To develop individuals' plans for improving their performance and to assist them in making such plans.

- To determine whether such rewards as pay increases, promotions, transfers, or commendations for excellence are due, and whether warning or termination is required.

- To identify areas for additional growth and the methods that can be utilized to achieve that growth.

- To develop and enhance the relationships between the person being evaluated and the supervisor doing the evaluation.

- To give the person being evaluated a clear understanding of where he or she stands in the supervisor's eyes and in relation to the performances of specific duties and achievement of specific goals.

Company policy establishes the frequency and form of the appraisal. Whatever form appraisals take, managers should provide daily feedback to employees on performance so the formal performance review contains no surprises.

Types of Appraisal Systems

Performance appraisal systems include (1) criteria for measuring employee performances; (2) ratings that summarize how well the employee is doing; and (3) methods – the specific forms, people, and procedures – used to determine the ratings. All three elements are tailored specifically to the firm's employees, jobs, organization structure, and subsystems.

Performance appraisals may be subjective, reflecting very personal points of view. Or they may be objective, representing a deliberate effort to remove personal biases, with chosen rating factors that are clearly defined and shared well in advance of the actual rating. Three appraisal methods are often found today: management by objectives (MBO), behaviorally anchored rating scales (BARS), and computer monitoring, all of which must be carefully utilized to ensure that implementation remains within legal constraints.

With **management by objectives**, manager and subordinate agree on specific performance goals for the subordinate over a fixed period. Employees are evaluated at the end of that period on the goals achieved. **Behaviorally anchored rating scales** (BARS) identify specific behaviors an employee must exhibit in order to be judged to have performed successfully. **Computer monitoring** tracks an employee's performance as it is taking place.

Implementing Employment Decisions

Employment decisions include determination of personnel changes through promotions, transfers, demotions, and separations (voluntary or involuntary). These changes are influenced by appraisals and by how an organization recruits, hires, orients, and trains. **Promotions** reward devoted and outstanding effort, and serve as incentives by offering personal growth and challenge. **Transfers** are lateral moves that require new skills and are often used by companies to train and develop employees. **Demotions** occur when an employee accepts a position of lower rank in the hierarchy. This approach may be used to retain employees who lose their positions through no fault of their own. Finally, **separations** take place when people resign or retire, are laid off or terminated.

A S S I G N M E N T S

- Read the Overview, familiarize yourself with the Learning Objectives, and peruse the Key Terms below. Then turn to Plunkett & Attner, *Introduction to Management*, and read Chapter 11, "Staffing," pages 337–347.

- Next, scan the Video Viewing Questions and watch the video program for Lesson 12, "High Performance: Staff Development and Maintenance."

- After watching the video, answer the viewing questions and assess your learning with the Self-Test.

- Familiarize yourself with the Review Questions, Discussion Questions for Critical Thinking, and Skill-Building Exercises on page 354 of Plunkett & Attner.

- Strengthen your understanding of the lesson's ideas and issues by undertaking the Expanded Analysis.

K E Y　T E R M S

demotion　A reduction in an employee's status, pay, and responsibilities.

development　Efforts to give employees the knowledge, skills, and attitudes needed for a move to a job with greater authority and responsibility.

orientation　Welcoming new employees into the organization, and introducing the to their duties, co-workers, and work environments.

performance appraisal　A formal, structured system that compares employee performance to established quantity and quality standards.

promotion　Changes in a job that result in increased status, compensation, and responsibilities for the employee.

separation　The voluntary or involuntary departure of employees from a company.

test　Any criterion or paper-and-pencil exercise or performance measure used as a basis for any employment decision.

training　Giving employees the knowledge, skills, and attitudes needed to perform their jobs.

transfer　Moving an employee to a job with similar levels of status, compensation, and responsibilities.

VIDEO VIEWING QUESTIONS

1. Identify the general objectives of orientation programs as described by the human resources managers from Four Seasons, Patagonia, Arthur Anderson, and Ford. Include the advise of consultant Michael Deblieux.

2. What relationship do you discern between "orientation" and "training" as discussed by both Peter Pesce of Arthur Andersen and Nancy Badore of Ford?

3. How does Ford Quality Director Gurminder Bedi relate training to new product introduction?

4. From Apple Computer Employee Services Manager Kathleen McEnroe's references, what sort of an enterprise do you suppose "Apple University" to be?

5. USC's Edward Lawler suggests that one single factor determines the effectiveness of a performance appraisal session. What is that factor? Do you agree with Lawler? Why or why not?

6. What does Northwest Airlines' Barry Kotar mean when he says, "We really want to get to the point where everyone judges everyone else's performance?"

7. Arthur Andersen's Peter Pesce describes his company's performance evaluation system. Identify features of that system that seem unusual in comparison with others in this lesson.

8. Describe the relationship between the orientation and termination processes at the Four Seasons Hotels.

SELF-TEST

1. Perhaps the most significant characteristic of a sound, well-structured orientation program is that it

   a. can be completed during the employee's first day on the job.
   b. prepares an employee to proceed independently without having to depend on others for information.
   c. sets the stage for a long-range, productive relationship between the employee and the company.
   d. quickly pinpoints an employee's major strengths and weaknesses.

2. The immediate goal of employee orientation is to

   a. prepare employees for advancement.
   b. ensure that an employee is, in fact, qualified for the job.
   c. establish a basis for subsequent performance evaluations.
   d. bring an employee into the firm's mainstream.

3. At what point in an employee's tenure with a company does training typically occur?

   a. Training commonly occurs when a need for it is discovered during performance evaluation.
   b. Training is an ongoing process that should continue throughout an employee's association with an organization.
   c. Training usually occurs within an employee's first six months to one year with the company.
   d. Essential training should be a prerequisite of employment, so that an employee is prepared to work productively immediately upon completion of orientation.

4. Which of the following is **not** an example of an employee development program?

   a. An employee is placed in a simulated work environment to learn needed skills without the pressure of meeting production quotas.
   b. A company offers an executive one year's unpaid leave in order to pursue a master's degree.
   c. A company offers tuition reimbursement to all staff who participate in a nine-week management seminar offered at the local university.
   d. An assistant magazine editor participates in a job rotation program, performing one editorial job for a few weeks, then moving on to another.

5. Performance appraisal has several critical objectives. Which of the following is **not** one of them?

   a. Documenting performance information to facilitate decisions on promotions.
   b. Identifying opportunities for professional growth and development.
   c. Developing individual plans for improvement based on each employee's identified strengths and weaknesses.
   d. Effective disciplining of an employee who has not met company expectations.

6. Regardless of the rating scale used in performance assessment, it is important that the rating criteria (work quality, attitude, and the like)

   a. not be revealed to the employee far in advance of the performance evaluation.
   b. be broad enough to apply to virtually any job within the employee's general professional field.
   c. be explicitly defined so that both employee and evaluator know precisely what is being evaluated.
   d. avoid rating any tasks which are "team" efforts, where the employee is not completely responsible for the outcome.

7. Which of the following is **not** an objective of training?

   a. To increase job-related knowledge and skills.
   b. To increase quality and productivity.
   c. To improve morale and pride in performance.
   d. To expand employee enjoyment of leisure time pursuits.

8. Manufacturing and processing companies in many U.S. cities find it difficult to find native speakers of English to apply for entry-level jobs at wages that will let the companies offer competitive prices. Simultaneously, corresponding local labor pools include growing numbers of otherwise qualified applicants who do not read or write English proficiently. Of the following alternative policies for such firms, which is most likely to be effective for both firms and their communities?

   a. Raise starting wages to attract more English speakers.
   b. Relocate to a city where language is not a problem.
   c. Arrange with a local adult school to provide convenient English language training classes and redesign some jobs to be less language-dependent.
   d. Subcontract as much work as possible to low-wage companies elsewhere.

9. Suppose a company decided for some reason not to use any performance appraisal system. Which of the following would be the most likely outcome of such a decision?

   a. More relaxed and more frequent communication between managers and their subordinates
   b. Increased motivation among employees at all levels
   c. Decreased opportunity for employee advancement
   d. Greater insight among managers regarding company problems

10. Which of the following is **not** an example of separation?

    a. A company must temporarily lay off workers due to decreased production.

    b. A department manager is granted a six-month leave to teach a course at the local university.

    c. A corporate head resigns after 30 years with the same firm.

    d. A new employee is terminated within the first year for insubordination.

EXPANDED ANALYSIS

1. Robert Rosenblatt, in the *Los Angeles Times* on June 1, 1993, in a piece entitled "Analysts Fear Minorities' Education Won't Keep Pace," writes:

The new workers won't fit the new jobs. That's the fear of economists, government experts, and community officials as they peer into the future, looking at the diverse work force of the 21st century. Many ethnic minorities . . . will make up a bigger portion of the labor pool, but if current trends hold, many of them will lack the education the new jobs demand.

What action can and/or should the business community, individual firms, and government and other public agencies undertake to address this problem?

13 Keeping in Touch: Interpersonal and Organizational Communication

---

L E A R N I N G   O B J E C T I V E S

Upon completing this lesson, you should be familiar with the facts, ideas, and processes contained in this lesson, and be able to:

- Describe communication as both a mechanical process and a human behavior.

- Summarize the steps in the interpersonal communication process.

- Discuss the significance of nonverbal communication in facilitating or countering the message.

- Describe the importance of communications in enhancing an organization's ability to achieve its objectives.

- Compare the effectiveness of various media in communicating among functional units and levels of the organization.

- Identify communication barriers, spot symptoms of problem situations, and devise remedies to overcome them.

- List and describe techniques to improve organizational communications.

O V E R V I E W

Few managers will disagree with Kathy Hagler, founder of the Technology Exchange Center, when she asserts that "The most essential ingredient in an organization's culture is the quality of the communication between the organization's members." Ms. Hagler's link of communication to culture offers a good starting point for this lesson, for communication is no abstract phenomenon; it is a virtual life force for management.

Communication: The Vital Link

Isolated for a moment from a management context, **communication** may be seen in linear terms as a process that requires three elements: (1) active persons to start and complete transmission (senders and receivers), (2) something substantive and recognizable to send and receive (the information or message), and (3) a medium for physical transfer.

In a management setting, communication is essential. The five management functions, after all, begin as ideas. But as USC's Warren Bennis reminds us, "An idea unless acted upon or understood is not really an idea." To be understood, an idea must be communicated. Without communication, therefore, the manager cannot plan, organize, direct, staff, or control.

The influence of communication extends far beyond functional mechanics. The nature and quality of a firm's communication are powerful shapers of corporate success. At the same time that communication allows organizations to accomplish objectives and do business, it also creates the pathways among people which allow them to convey their attitudes, beliefs, values, ambitions, and emotions.

Because process without content is meaningless, competent managers know that effective communication in the workplace centers around well-defined objectives that support the company's mission. They strive to achieve a common understanding – agreement as to the meaning and intent of a message – among parties to their communications. And they are concerned with feedback and continuing dialogue.

Mediums of Communication: General, Formal, Informal

For all of today's impressive technology, the primary means of communication are still words and images. Interpersonal communication involves face-to-face conversations in real time and allows instant feedback. Conversation is especially valuable when the message is personal and when give and take is vital. When the luxury of face-to-face dialogue is impractical, spoken messages can be delivered by any of today's diverse electronic means, from the simple telephone to transoceanic satellite uplink.

Despite the advantages of spoken communication, in many circumstances the power and effect of the written word remain unsurpassed. Transmittal options are virtually limitless; thoughtful selection of the best medium for each communication need is important. Written documents allow careful construction and confidentiality, may be contemplated at leisure, and provide a record for the sender and receiver.

Under the heading of **nonverbal communications** fall two broad subcategories. The first is body language – gestures, facial expressions, posture, and the like. The second is the vast array of channels for conveying visual information: photographs, film, charts, tables, graphs, and video. These powerful and persuasive tools are rich supplements to verbal communication. They do not substitute for language, however. Articulate, economical, and descriptive speech and writing are likely to be management's strongest communicative resource for the foreseeable future.

Barriers to Interpersonal Communication

Because words often mean different things (or sometimes nothing at all) to different people, carelessly chosen words (including jargon at the wrong time) can quickly derail communication. Therefore, it is advisable to strive for straightforward language and avoid unusual, specialized, or vague words and constructions. Conversely, familiarity may lull people into hearing what they expect to hear instead of the actual message. By ignoring information that conflicts with what we know, we close our minds and inhibit growth and change. Divergent perceptions among people of differing values compromise understanding, as do contradictory nonverbal signals and anger (opponents are notoriously bad communicators). Poor timing and noise also sabotage understanding.

Organizational Communication

The primary difference between interpersonal and organizational communication is the structural context provided by the organization, which establishes a pattern of formal communication channels to carry information vertically and horizontally. An organization chart conveniently displays these channels, maintained and made accessible to employees for interchange throughout the organization and with the outside world.

Their formal structures notwithstanding, today's organizations increasingly depend on communication mechanisms and organizational realities that are of recent vintage. Computer networks, fax machines, satellite communications, teleconferencing, and the like enable the interchange of information among newly empowered employees, often organized in integrated teams. Today more communication flows from bottom to top and across the organization than from the top down in companies exhibiting unprecedented institutional flexibility. With layers of middle management having been eliminated to reduce costs and bring decisions closer to the front line, communication is faster and more direct than in the past.

Downward communication occurs from managers to subordinates, and upward communication allows feedback, requests for assistance, reports, and complaints. A large proportion of both downward and upward communication follows established channels to accommodate the organization's day-to-day operating needs. Horizontal communication connects people of similar rank and status – co-workers, peers, and team members – with inside and outside customers or suppliers.

Formal and Informal Communication

The designation of **formal communication networks** applies to electronic links between people and their equipment and between people and data banks where vital information is stored. From the integrated electronic networks with which the world's banks transfer and reconcile hundreds of billions of dollars every day to Apple Computer's E-mail system, variations on such networks profoundly shape the way the world does business. Whether it's Fluor Daniel's engineering sites in the Middle East, Arthur Andersens' clients in Japan, or Northwest's dispatchers in Minneapolis coordinating flights along their global routes, today's enterprise absolutely depends upon swift and reliable operation of sophisticated communications networks.

Despite their wide variety and undeniable influence, formal communication processes do not function in isolation. They are invariably complemented by informal communication channels. Known as the grapevine, this network of informal channels buzzes and crackles with rumors, gossip, information truthful and false, and even official communications on occasion. Messages can originate with anyone in the organization or outside of it. The messages are transmitted in many ways – face-to-face, by telephone, by E-mail, or by fax. Managers must recognize the operation of the grapevine in order to utilize it to their own and the company's advantage.

Barriers to Organizational Communication

Communication blockages arise all to easily, from obvious difficulties such as poorly designed facilities that needlessly separate potentially communicative individuals and work units from one another. Managers at one GM plant tell an illustrative story. Plant remodeling required that the division's manufacturing engineers be temporarily shoe-horned into offices alongside the product design staff. Instead of complaining, the engineers were soon conversing with one another and solving old problems with unheard of speed. Division costs shrank and, at their request, the two staffs were moved into a common space permanently.

Common communication barriers include:

- information overload, where non-essential data clogs the system and hampers individuals;
- excessive management levels that corrupt information as it flows from source to destination;
- inappropriate delay, often caused when information must pass through too many hands;
- lack of respect among communicators, a difficulty that can arise from secretiveness;
- excessively wide or narrow spans of control;
- poorly managed change;
- misperceived or misused company rank or position that can inhibit candid sharing of information;
- divergent managerial priorities; and even
- electronic noise that degrades the speed and audibility of messages.

The responsibility to strengthen and improve communication is both individual and organizational. Senders should define the purpose behind their message, construct each message with the receiver in mind, select the best medium, time each transmission thoughtfully, and seek feedback. Receivers must listen actively, be sensitive to the sender, recommend an appropriate medium for messages, and initiate feedback efforts.

A S S I G N M E N T S

- Read the Overview, familiarize yourself with the Learning Objectives, and peruse the Key Terms below. Then turn to Plunkett & Attner, *Introduction to Management*, and read Chapter 12, "Communication, Interpersonal and Organizational," pages 356–383.

- Next, scan the Video Viewing Questions and watch the video program for Lesson 13, "Keeping in Touch: Interpersonal and Organizational Communication."

- After watching the video, answer the viewing questions and assess your learning with the Self-Test.

- Familiarize yourself with the Review Questions, Discussion Questions for Critical Thinking, and Skill-Building Exercises on page 386 of Plunkett & Attner.

- Strengthen your understanding of the lesson's ideas and issues by undertaking the Expanded Analysis.

KEY TERMS

communication The transmission of information and understanding from one person or group to another.

diction The choice and use of words in speech and writing.

feedback Ways in which senders and receivers seek to ensure that mutual understanding has taken place in a communication.

formal communication channel Management-designated pipelines used for official communication efforts that run horizontally, up, and down.

formal communication network An electronic link between people and their equipment and between people and data banks where vital information is stored.

grapevine The informal networks or channels that exist outside the formal channels and are used by people to transmit casual, personal, and social interchanges at work.

informal communication channels A path of communications used for messages that are essential to performing one's tasks.

information Processed data that is useful to the receiver.

interpersonal communication Face-to-face or voice-to-voice (telephone) conversations that take place in real time and allow for instant feedback.

jargon The specialized technical language of a trade, profession, or other group.

medium The way in which a sender transmits a message.

message The information that the sender wants to transmit.

noise Anything in the physical environment of a communication that interferes with the sending and receiving of messages.

nonverbal communication Images, actions, and behaviors used to transmit messages.

perceptions   Ways in which people observe and bases for their judgments about the stimuli that they experience.

receiver   The person or group for whom the communication effort is intended.

semantics   The study of meaning in language forms.

sender   The person or group that initiates the communication process.

stereotype   Predetermined sets of beliefs about people and groups which cause us to rect in positive or negative ways towards them.

understanding   The situation that exists when all the parties – senders and receivers – to a communication are of one mind as to its meaning and intent.

V I D E O   V I E W I N G   Q U E S T I O N S

1. What is communication? What is information?

2. Describe Solectron's use of surveys and face-to-face interchanges between managers and employees.

3. Differentiate between formal and informal communication processes.

4. In a corporate structure, what is lateral communication? How does it differ from vertical communication?

5. Describe the application of video teleconferencing at Arthur Andersen.

6. What are some of the values of Management by Walking Around (MBWA)?

7. Describe Apple Computer's use of electronic mail (E-Mail) systems. Why might such a system might be particularly effective at Apple?

S E L F - T E S T

1. The primary purpose of feedback is to

    a. provide a critique of the message.
    b. demonstrate that one is being an active listener.
    c. summarize the main points of a message.
    d. request clarification of indicate understanding.

Following is a list of possible purposes for communicating. Match each purpose with the level at which it is most likely to occur.

   a. Communication with superiors
   b. Communication with peers
   c. Communication with subordinates

2. To keep them informed of your progress

3. To seek clarification of orders and instructions

4. To appraise performance

5. To coordinate your activities with theirs

6. To clarify instructions you have provided

7. Which of the following is **not** a communication responsibility of the sender?

   a. Be sure the communication is necessary.
   b. Initiate feedback from the receiver.
   c. Know the receiver.
   d. Select the proper medium for communicating.

8. Impersonal communications are totally inappropriate in certain contexts, largely because

   a. so many people are offended by them.
   b. they tend to be long and complex.
   c. they are frequently ignored or lost in the shuffle.
   d. they convey a false sense of urgency.

9. Which of the following is **not** a typical organizational barrier to communication?

   a. Over-reliance on an open communication network
   b. Differences in rank between those communicating
   c. Numerous management levels within the organization
   d. A large number of employees

10. Which of the following objectives is probably **not** suitable for formal horizontal communication?

   a. Define, investigate, and solve problems
   b. Gather, process, and distribute information
   c. Create, examine, and improve methods
   d. Promulgate new corporate strategy

E X P A N D E D   A N A L Y S I S

1. Dr. Stephen Covey says:

   Trust and communication are inseparable ideas, they really are. Most people have separated them. They think you can train people in the field of communication apart from the human context of what the trust relationship is in the relationships: not so. When trust is high, communication is effortless, it's instantaneous.

   How would you define trust in this context? How do you think such trust might relate to communication? Accepting Dr. Covey's statement at face value, what can (and should) managers do to establish trust?

2. In addition to the corporate communication requirements of any multi-national firm, operation of a large airline like Northwest clearly generates a variety of special communication needs. Identify as many as you can, and suggest suitable solutions.

14 All Systems Go: Motivating for Excellence

Upon completing this lesson, you should be familiar with the facts, ideas, and processes contained in this lesson, and be able to:

■ Recognize factors that influence human behavior.

■ Define **motivation**.

■ Distinguish between content and process approaches to motivation.

■ Indicate the impact that the cultural and social diversity of today's workforce has on the selection of motivational approaches.

■ Describe how managers can create environments in which people can motivate themselves.

■ Contrast the content theories of Maslow, Herzberg, McClelland, and Alderfer and indicate their significance for managers.

■ Summarize the relationships between each of the following process theories and motivation:
  a. expectancy theory
  b. reinforcement theory
  c. equity theory
  d. goal-setting theory

OVERVIEW

The Challenge of Motivation

When a method actor asks, "What is my motivation?" he is asking, "What is my reason for doing something?" When managers discuss **motivation,** they are generally talking about creating an environment that will provide employees with reasons for doing certain things. Organizations depend on accomplishing activities that are necessary to achieve their goals – indeed, activity analysis and the formulation of job descriptions are primary steps in organizing – and for every job that needs to be done, people need to be motivated.

For many years, managers thought the only way to motivate employees was through pay. For example, Frederick Winslow Taylor (1856–1915), known as the Father of Scientific Management, assumed that workers were essentially lazy and motivated mainly by the best pay for the simplest work. He devised systems that could divide work into simple, repetitive tasks that could be performed with little thought and no creativity. While these systems facilitated mass production, they put a low ceiling over the level of skills workers could achieve and how much pride or motivation they could feel in their work.

A shift in approach began in the 1920s with experiments conducted by Elton Mayo at Western Electric's Hawthorne facility near Chicago. Mayo and his associates set out to test how workers' output could be affected by changing light levels. Surprisingly, they found that whether they raised or lowered the light level – or just pretended to change it – the worker's output increased. Mayo hypothesized and further experiments confirmed that workers were responding to the attention being paid to them. The Hawthorne experiments opened the door to thinking of workers as complex beings, not just as cogs in the industrial machine. Increasingly, managers looked to the emerging field of psychology for ways to understand the human nature of employees and how to motivate them.

Motivational theories have fallen mainly into two categories: content and process. **Content theories** focus on the needs that motivate people. **Process theories** focus on the behaviors that people choose to meet their needs.

Content Theories:
Motivation Theories that Focus on Needs

The fundamental idea underlying content theories of motivation is that unsatisfied needs can motivate or be used to motivate people to action. The managerial goal, of course, is to synchronize the actions that employees take to satisfy their needs with the activities that the organization needs to achieve its goals.

A basic motivation model portrays needs and the satisfaction of needs as a loop. A person feels a need (for example, hunger) that triggers a want (for food) that leads to behavior (cooking a hamburger) that results in action (eating) that satisfies the need. When the hunger returns, the cycle is repeated.

In applying this model to complex business situations, a number of factors can be integrated. Suppose that an employee feels a need for respect that triggers a want for recognition from her boss which in turn leads her to choose the behavior of volunteering for a project on which she takes effective action, for which she earns the boss's respect. At every point in this cycle, especially in choosing her course of action, the employee is likely to consider numerous factors. Her past experiences may give her clues about what has and hasn't worked in similar situations. Environmental influences such as organizational values and management expectations may suggest a course of action. The company may have set up special incentives, such as awards or bonuses, that motivate her toward one course of action over another. Since no two people think alike, this employee's behavior will be influenced by her perceptions of herself and the situation. Finally, her personal skills will strongly influence her choice of behavior.

One theory that managers have often used to analyze basic human needs (that can become the basis for motivation) has been psychologist Abraham Maslow's hierarchy of needs (1943). Maslow compared needs to the levels in a pyramid. The bottom level consists of basic physical needs, such as food and shelter. Only when these are met can a person direct substantial energy to the next higher level, safety needs such as for security and protection from harm. Next come social needs (companionship and belonging), then esteem needs (recognition and self-respect), and finally, at the pinnacle, self-realization needs (independence and creativity).

For managers, one value of Maslow's hierarchy is that it can often help a manager to identify the need level that a particular worker is attempting to satisfy and to provide appropriate outlets. For example, a manager who is aware that an employee is struggling to adjust to a new work group – a social need – may encourage that worker to become involved in recreational activities. A manager dealing with an employee who is eager to get ahead – a self-realization need – may provide guidance in charting a career path or recommend the employee for special training.

Psychologist Frederick Herzberg (1975) developed a needs theory that distinguished between factors that are part of the environment surrounding a job and factors that are intrinsic to the job. The former, which he called **hygiene factors**, include salary, job security, working conditions, status, company policies, and quality of technical supervision and interpersonal relations. According to Herzberg, hygiene factors bear only on dissatisfaction, which it is their goal to minimize. Job satisfaction depends on factors intrinsic to the work, which Herzberg called **motivation factors**. These include achievement, recognition, responsibility, advancement, and the chance for growth.

The implication for managers of Herzberg's two-factor needs theory is that managers must pay attention to both realms, hygiene and motivation. Hygiene factors, while supportive, will not by themselves motivate workers or lead to satisfaction. That must come through motivation factors in the work itself. Herzberg's emphasis on motivation intrinsic to work helped to pave the way for movements such as empowerment, participative management, and intrapreneurship (see Lesson 15).

A third needs theory, developed by David McClelland (1971), identified three types of needs – achievement, power and affiliation – and recognized that individuals can be differentiated into distinct personality types depending on which need predominates. McClelland focused mainly on high achievers, people who perform tasks because of a compelling need for personal achievement, not necessarily for rewards. High achievers are often loners who tend to work independently and take personal responsibility for solving problems.

One implication of McClelland's theory is that it can be extremely valuable for managers to identify high achievers and provide ways for them to satisfy their drive to do excellent work. It's particularly important, for instance, to provide high achievers with immediate, concrete feedback. McClelland's identification of power-motivated and affiliative personality types also offers useful clues to managers, particularly in understanding how different employees may be too prone either to engage in or avoid conflict.

Clayton Alderfer (1972) compressed Maslow's five levels of needs into three: existence needs relate to a person's physical well-being (and correspond to Maslow's physical and safety needs), relatedness needs focus on satisfactory relationships with others (and corresponds to Maslow's social needs), and growth needs call for the realization of potential and the achievement of competence (and correspond to Maslow's needs for esteem and self-realization).

Alderfer's **ERG theory**, named after the initials of the three needs, differs from Maslow in one vital respect. Maslow held that unsatisfied needs are the key to motivation. Alderfer agreed with regard to lower-level needs but believed that it is crucial for managers to provide opportunities for employees to maintain satisfaction in meeting their higher level needs, principally for growth. Growth tends to be self-perpetuating, and workers who become frustrated in attempts at growth may redirect their energies to lower level needs.

In many ways the several needs theories are like variations on a theme. They repeat many of the same elements, but each highlights particular points that can help managers to motivate employees.

Process Theories: Motivation Theories that Focus on Behaviors

Motivation is the result of the interaction between a person's internalized needs and external influences that determine behavior. While content theories of motivation focus on internalized needs, process theories focus on external influences, which are often more readily accessible to managers.

The **expectancy theory** developed by Victor Vroom (1964) states that before choosing a behavior, an individual will evaluate various possibilities on the basis of anticipated work and reward. Motivation – the triggering mechanism of action – is a function of how badly we want something and how likely we think we are to get it.

Several key variables influence expectancy. First, the individual assesses whether his effort will achieve performance. Does he have the skills to accomplish the task, or will he spin his wheels? Next, he assesses whether achieving performance is likely to lead to the desired reward or outcome. Will his boss recognize his achievement, or perhaps feel threatened? Finally, the individual assesses how attractive the reward is. If he suffers airsickness he's not likely to work hard to win a trip to Hawaii, but he may work hard for a cash prize.

Expectancy theory bears a number of implications for managers. They should provide training or guidance to strengthen employees' perceptions that they can successfully perform tasks. They should clearly communicate desired behaviors and outcomes and quickly reward acceptable performance. They should find out what rewards are perceived as desirable by employees and provide them. And they should recognize that people differ, and should set up tasks and rewards to suit the talents and desires of individuals.

Another process theory of motivation, reinforcement theory, is based on the behaviorist psychology of B.F. Skinner (1969). Skinner held, in essence, that behavior is learned, and that the most effective means to influence people's behavior is not through exploring their needs or other deep matters of human nature, but rather by responding in an appropriate fashion to their actions. How a person behaves in a given situation will be strongly influenced by the rewards or penalties experienced in similar situations in the past. Behaviors can be shaped in different directions. For example, punishing a behavior will tend to decrease it and ignoring it will tend to extinguish it. But the approach which most often leads to long-range growth in individuals and produces lasting and positive behavioral changes is positive reinforcement of desired behaviors.

Reinforcement theory has several implications for managers. It emphasizes how crucial it is to make clear to employees what behaviors are desired and to reward them promptly. It points out the power of praise and recognition and the relative ineffectiveness of punishment and criticism. And it makes clear that managers who take desirable behavior for granted aren't just leaving well enough alone but are tending to extinguish that behavior and confuse employees about what is desired. As management consultant Michael Deblieux points out: "We tend to focus on the bottom end of the organization, the problem employees, and the super stars. We forget that ninety percent of the work is being done by folks who are just doing the job we asked them to do, and we ignore them. And I don't think we need to throw big parties. I don't think we need to slap them on the back all the time. But I do think we need to look at being creative and finding ways to say to those ninety percent, 'You're doing what I want you to do.' And to me, that's where the motivation comes from."

Another process theory of motivation, the **equity theory**, states that people's behavior is closely connected to their perception of the fairness of treatment they receive. People base their feelings of equity on several comparisons. Most employees have a perception of a proper ratio between the effort they are expected to invest in the job and what they expect to receive after investing that effort. They also compare what they receive with what workers in similar jobs receive and what workers in other jobs in the company receive. If an experienced worker is receiving what she considers a fair salary but learns that a new worker has been hired at a higher salary, her sense of equity is likely to feel violated. Similarly, if workers are being asked to take a cut in pay at the same time as the company awards huge bonuses to top executives, worker motivation is likely to plummet. A major issue of equity that is becoming widely recognized is the disparity between the levels of pay that men and women receive for performing comparable tasks.

The implication of equity theory for managers is that they must make conscious efforts to establish and retain equity in the work environment. The motivating effect of pay will depend not simply on the amount but on the employee's perception of fairness. Often fairness will be reinforced by organization-wide policies and procedures.

A final process theory holds that people's behavior is strongly influenced by goals. Like expectancy theory, **goal-setting theory** emphasizes the value of the projections and conscious choices that people make. Goals provide targets for motivation and help employees to assess in advance what needs to be done and how much effort will need to be expended. Guidelines for managers using goal-setting include: (1) make goals specific, (2) provide feedback on performance, and (3) involve employees in setting goals.

Philosophies of Management

Since motivation systems are deeply connected with the psychology of workers, it can be extremely valuable for managers to become aware of the basic assumptions they make about human nature. These assumptions, or **philosophies of management**, are likely to exert a strong influence over the climate of the workplace and over the success or failure of attempts to create motivational systems.

Douglas McGregor (1960), a professor of industrial management, observed that managers tend to operate from one of two radically different sets of assumptions about workers. He called these Theory X and Theory Y. **Theory X** takes the negative position that workers (subordinates) dislike work, need to be closely supervised and threatened with punishments, and possess little creativity or problem-solving ability. In many ways Theory X reflects attitudes about motivation similar to those of Frederick Taylor.

Theory Y, by contrast, takes the stance that people are naturally inclined to seek meaningful work and responsibility, to become committed to organizational objectives, and to creatively solve problems. John Dasburg, President and CEO of Northwest Airlines, expresses an almost pure Theory Y philosophy in regard to training workers to provide good service to customers: "Employee motivation is less lecturing and teaching than it is bringing out in the individual that's providing the service their own best instincts and their own natural desires to do a good job, to be proud of what they do, and to help and serve other people."

Another point of management philosophy, formulated by Chris Argyris (1957), notes the frequent conflicts that experienced employee encounter with the rules and structures of organizations. In Argyris's **maturity theory**, experienced employees tend to become more active rather than passive, independent rather than dependent, self-aware rather than unaware, and self-controlled rather than needing control by others. Ideally, an organization should be able to capitalize on the increasing maturity of employees and give them greater freedom and responsibility. In reality, formal chains of command and narrow job-descriptions often force passivity and dependence. In recent years, recognition of these problems has fueled the growth of the movement toward employee empowerment and caused many companies to make jobs and work structures more flexible (see Lesson 15).

A final point of management philosophy addresses the importance of expectations. Good managers – like good parents and teachers – are adept at the art of setting expectations that are high but within the reach of employees. These expectations, like goals, provide targets for motivation and affirm employees' sense of self-esteem. When a manager's high but realistic expectations for employees are communicated clearly and reinforced consistently, they usually create a self-fulfilling prophecy that employees will live up to.

ASSIGNMENTS

- Read the Overview, familiarize yourself with the Learning Objectives, and peruse the Key Terms below. Then turn to Plunkett & Attner, *Introduction to Management*, and read Chapter 13, "Human Motivation," pages 388–416.

- Next, scan the Video Viewing Questions and watch the video program for Lesson 14, "All Systems Go: Motivating for Excellence."

- After watching the video, answer the viewing questions and assess your learning with the Self-Test.

- Familiarize yourself with the Review Questions, Discussion Questions for Critical Thinking, and Skill-Building Exercises on page 426 of Plunkett & Attner.

- Strengthen your understanding of the lesson's ideas and issues by undertaking the Expanded Analysis.

KEY TERMS

cultural diversity A value a manager needs to incorporate in the motivational environment. It involves the changing composition of the work group. Minorities – African Americans, Hispanics, and Asians – are collectively becoming the majority in the workplace.

empowerment A method to increase motivation. It occurs when an individual is given autonomy, authority, and trust, and is encouraged to make the decisions necessary to get the job done.

equity theory A motivation theory stating that people are influenced in their behavior choices (motivation) through the comparison of relative input-outcome ratios. People compare the ratios of their input (efforts) with outcome (rewards) to others' ratios to see if equity exists.

ERG theory A motivation theory stating that people have three categories of needs: existence needs, relatedness needs, and growth needs.

expectancy theory A motivation theory stating that a person's behavior is influenced by the value of the rewards, the relationship of the rewards to the performance necessary, and the effort required for performance.

goal-setting theory A motivation theory stating that a person's behavior is influenced by the goals that are set. The goals, whether set by management or mutually, tell the employee what needs to be done and how much effort will need to be expended.

hygiene factors Herzberg's list of causes most closely identified with unhappiness on the job. These extrinsic factors, if provided in the right qualities by management, can result in no job dissatisfaction.

motivation The set of processes that determine choices. It is the interaction of a person's internalized needs and external influences (equity, expectancy, previous conditioning, and goal setting) that determines behavior designed to achieve a goal.

motivation factors Herzberg's list of conditions that can lead to an individual's job satisfaction. They are intrinsic to the job and offer satisfactions for psychological needs.

needs Physical or psychological conditions in humans that act as stimuli for behavior until satisfactions for them have been provided or achieved.

philosophy of management A manager's attitude about work and the people who perform work. It influences the motivation approaches a manager will select.

reinforcement theory A motivation theory stating that the behavior choices of a person are influenced by the supervisor's reactions to them and the rewards or penalties experienced in a similar situation.

VIDEO VIEWING QUESTIONS

1. How did Frederick Winslow Taylor's assumptions about workers discourage thinking about motivation?

2. What are parallels among the Hawthorne Effect, Maslow's concept of social needs, and Skinner's concept of positive reinforcement?

3. How does the reward system at the Four Seasons Hotel echo ideas such as Vroom's expectancy theory of motivation?

4. Why are rewards that are intrinsic to the work sometimes more effective than extrinsic rewards such as pay and bonuses?

5. How does the commitment strategy of motivation differ from the control strategy, and why is it becoming more important in today's marketplace?

6. How does Northwest Airlines encourage employees to be self-motivating?

S E L F - T E S T

1. In analyzing what motivates workers on the job, most researchers would probably agree that

   a. human motivation remains largely a mystery.
   b. human motivation is generally well understood
   c. the need to study human motivation is no longer critical, as it was in the nineteenth century.
   d. we are beginning to understand human motivation, but the need to know more has never been greater.

2. A need can best be defined as

   a. an unsolved problem.
   b. a deficiency experienced by a person at a particular time.
   c. a desire for something different.
   d. a stimulus triggering a particular reaction.

3. An unsatisfied need may be met in various ways. In selecting a behavior or action that will fulfill an unsatisfied need, a person will be influenced by all of the following **except**

   a. the extent to which personal needs parallel the needs of others.
   b. the values and expectation inherent in the environment.
   c. past experience, good and bad, in similar situations.
   d. perceptions of the probably effort required, and the reward likely to be gained from that effort.

4. According to psychologist Abraham Maslow, human needs occur on a five-level hierarchy. This hierarchy is based in part on the premise that

   a. both satisfied and unsatisfied needs can influence human behavior.
   b. if a person's needs are not met on one level, he or she advances to the next level to seek satisfaction.
   c. a person's needs are arranged in distinct priority from very basic to highly complex.
   d. once a need has been effectively satisfied, it will generally remain satisfied from that point on.

5. According to David McClellan's need achievement theory, the person identified as a high achiever will be marked by a

   a. compelling desire for high status and power.
   b. tendency to set goals that others often regard as unattainable.
   c. need to be constantly in control of his or her situation.
   d. marked absence of the need for personal feedback.

6. It is sometimes suggested that effective managers should make a concerted effort to identify and work with persons who are high achievers. The main reason for this is that

   a. left to themselves, high achievers tend to lose their motivation to excel.
   b. the achiever's strong desire for responsibility makes it easy for the manager to delegate tasks.
   c. high achievers have a very difficult time setting goals for themselves.
   d. without close supervision, many high achievers defy authority and attempt to assume control.

7. In using motivation factors to increase job satisfaction, perhaps the most important thing for managers to recognize is that

   a. many workers cannot be motivated, regardless of the factors present in the environment.
   b. no amount of recognition or personal satisfaction will make up for mediocre salary and poor benefits.
   c. desire for personal development is the one universal motivator.
   d. what motivates one person may have little appeal to the next.

8. Motivation factors are sometimes said to be the primary cause of job satisfaction. Which of the following is **not** an example of a motivation factor?

   a. Job title or position
   b. Opportunity for advancement based on performance
   c. Recognition from one's superior for outstanding effort.
   d. The chance to acquire new responsibility.

9. According to the reinforcement theory of management, an effective manager will

   a. explain openly what unrewarded employees are doing wrong.
   b. let individuals learn from experience how and why they will be rewarded.
   c. allow some time to elapse between behavior and reinforcement.
   d. reward some individuals more than others, according to individual needs.

10. In order to motivate employees, an effective manager must do all of the following **except**

   a. establish a strong personal philosophy based on the premise that people are eager to achieve and to do their work well.
   b. create a supportive environment in which contributions are openly appreciated and positive risk taking is encourage.
   c. make a strong commitment to continuously increasing the responsibility and accountability levels of each employee.
   d. insure that all employees understand completely the expectations of the manager and of the corporation.

E X P A N D E D   A N A L Y S I S

1. Victor Vroom's expectancy theory suggests that people choose their behavior based upon a comparison of work and reward. B.F. Skinner's reinforcement theory says that a person's behavior is influenced by rewards or penalties experienced in prior, similar circumstances. Equity theory says that people's behavior relates to their perceptions of how fairly they are treated. Goal-setting theory suggests that people's behavior is influenced by the goals that are set for them. How do you think such theories might influence the management decisions of the owner of a five-person accounting firm? Of the senior management team at a medium-size clothing manufacturer with 50 employees? At a very large, multi-national firm like the Arthur Andersen group?

15 Pulling Together: Building Morale and Commitment

L E A R N I N G   O B J E C T I V E S

Upon completing this lesson, you should be familiar with the facts, ideas, and processes contained in this lesson, and be able to:

- Recognize indices of employee morale and factors that influence it.

- Define **quality work life** and its relationship to employee satisfaction.

- Compare strategies that might be used for effective job re-design.

- Discuss the concept of **empowerment** and its role in employee commitment, motivation, and productivity.

- Examine the use of teams in the work environment and the effect it has had on building commitment and morale.

- Suggest ways in which a manager and an organization can foster **intrapreneurship** within a corporate structure.

O V E R V I E W

Morale and Motivation

Strategies to motivate employees often seem mechanistic and manipulative unless viewed in the broader context of how managers can shape the work environment to make the work more meaningful to workers and to raise morale. Many key management ideas related to morale are just as integrally related to motivation.

The most ringing indictment of business's treatment of workers came from 19th-century German philosopher Karl Marx. In Marx's view, business is dominated by "capitalists" who only care about making money for themselves. They exploit workers, expose them to brutal working conditions, and strip their work of personal meaning. The widely influential Scientific Management Theory of Frederick Winslow Taylor – which broke work down into simple, repetitive tasks and minimized workers' decision making and creative input – also contributed to the demoralization and demotivation of workers.

While the ideas of Marx and Engels are dated – and the communist governments that adopted them as ideology have proven anything but humane – a fundamental conflict between the financial interests of companies and the treatment of workers as people often remains. In the words of author William Lareau: " 'Human resources,' is a word we use in this country, but do we really think they are a resource? Most companies think employees are like meat robots, they're just a lot of trouble, and it would be better if we just had a machine."

Gradually, though, managers are coming to recognize that high morale can make an essential contribution to productivity. Unmotivated performance and rates of defects that were acceptable during the era of mass production can't stand the test of increasing competition. Japanese corporations in particular have turned teamwork and other systems that simultaneously raise morale, quality, and productivity, into a competitive advantage. Organizations everywhere are seeking ways to create positive, supportive work environments and to make work more involving for employees.

Treating People as Individuals

If the most demoralizing management policy would be to treat people like machines and disregard their human needs, the management policy which would lead to the highest morale would be one which shows regard not only for human needs in general but for the needs of workers as individuals. All of us are different, and the more that management can adapt or give us leeway to adapt our jobs to meet our personal needs and bring out our personal talents and interests, the more highly motivated we are likely to feel. There is broad evidence that most people want to become deeply involved in their work and committed to their companies, if given the opportunity.

Treating employees as individuals is becoming increasingly important as the work force becomes more diverse. Mass influxes of immigrants from all corners of the globe, the growing presence of women in the workplace, and other forces challenge today's managers to learn about and become sensitive to the cultures and special needs of different people. Managers who accept this challenge become able not only to treat their employees as special but also to find ways to motivate them. Diversity can also provide an asset for managers to draw on, as different employees with different points of view contribute different ideas.

Empowering Employees

In the traditional bureaucratic view, managers didn't need to understand employees on a personal level. They could treat all of their subordinates the same, which basically meant telling them what to do. Today, with the rapidly changing pressures of the marketplace, bureaucracies are faltering, or at least being forced to change. Effective managers are not only learning to treat employees as individuals but reconsidering whether their role should be to tell people what to do.

Employee **empowerment** means various things, and they all can contribute to higher morale. It means unshackling employees from rules and policies that may slow them down and keep them from doing their jobs effectively. It means giving employees more decision-making power, letting them shape their own jobs. And it means seeking ideas from everyone who does the work, not just from managers.

One concept closely related to empowerment is **participative management**. George Labovitz describes how it can contribute to the flow of ideas in an organization:

> *Participative management involves people at every part of the process, when the idea is a gleam in your eye to the final implementation of your new system. Historically, senior executives or managers would sit down in little conference rooms and come up with a new idea and then go tell the employees what we just told you to do. Participative managers recognize that you waste a lot of time that way.*

Another closely related concept is employee involvement. Edward Lawler describes how it reaches down to the roots of a company:

> *High involvement management is a way of thinking about the role of management and the creation of organizations that emphasizes mov-*

ing four elements of an organization to the lowest possible level. And those four elements are: power to make decisions, information about how the business is doing; knowledge and skills about the operations of the business; and finally, rewards for the business's success.

Companies that implement these sorts of ideas frequently make their employees' work more meaningful not just by recognizing them as people but by clarifying how their particular jobs fit into the larger system of work. Edward Baker describes how this concept has been applied at Ford Motor Company:

To manage the enterprise as a system means to enable people to understand the purpose of the enterprise and where they fit in and how they can contribute. What I think is important is the ability of people to cooperate and understand each other, for people to under-stand who their suppliers and customers are within the organization, when they can cooperate, how they can help each other improve.

Systems thinking is often accompanied by teamwork. Teams can bring together ideas from different people and departments. They can help individuals to develop a broader view of the enterprise. And they can improve morale by replacing the isolation and competition rampant in many workplaces with cooperation, camaraderie, and a supportive work environment.

Many innovative forms of teams are revolutionizing organizational structures, the way work is approached, the role of managers, and the involvement of workers. Effective teams tend to share certain charac-teristics: commitment to shared goals; participation by all members; trust; consensus decision making; focus on problems, not symptoms; flexibility and innovation.

One revolutionary impact of teams has been to help break down departmental barriers. Although there are vertical teams that align with the formal chain of command, most innovative teams – unless they are contained within one work unit – are horizontal and bridge departments. **Cross-functional teams** harness the knowledge of people from various functional areas to solve operational problems on either a temporary or on-going basis.

The decision to create teams, like every management decision, gen-erates benefits and costs. On the benefit side, a team environment provides camaraderie and sharing often absent from traditional work structures, which can produce synergy, more creativity and energy than the same number of individuals working alone could produce. People teach each other skills and knowledge, learn more than one job, and become more valuable to themselves and the company. A cohesive team is flexible and can adjust to changes in work demands and work flow and respond constructively to emergencies. And because team members feel increased ownership in their work, they feel greater commitment to the company.

On the cost side, lower- and middle-level managers may have a hard time relinquishing control to the team and may resist. Both technical cross-training and training in group dynamics cost time and money. Time spent in team development is time not spent in production, and teams don't reach peak performance overnight. Some less committed team members may slough off and take a free ride, and some skilled, productive workers may have a hard time fitting in and decide to quit.

Team implementation may produce conflicts caused by adjusting to change or the demand on individuals to work more closely together. Generally, once the transition stage is past, teamwork results in a more open atmosphere and less disgruntled workers. Companies that implement teamwork frequently experience a radical drop in employee grievances. As Robert Galvin describes the effect of teamwork at Motorola:

> *Our effectiveness as an institution is multiplied when we learn to team, when we learn to work together with common process and common objectives, with a line of sight to what we're working on, to work toward an end solution of an issue. And the net effect is that we have people who are immensely more satisfied in their job and who contribute ever so much more on their job. They've discovered they have creativity and they have skills they never knew before.*

Re-Designing Jobs

Another concept that's closely related to empowerment and high morale is ownership. If capitalism, in Marx's view, deprives workers by putting all ownership into the hands of the money people, empowerment and related movements correct this condition by giving a portion of ownership back to the workers. Sometimes this ownership is financial, through profit-sharing, share-holding, or similar devices. More often it's psychological—the commitment a worker can feel to a company that treats him or her like a whole person, and the investment that a worker can put into a job that he or she helps to shape. In order to promote the latter feeling, many companies have undertaken programs of job re-design.

Contemporary job **re-design** is in many ways the opposite of that devised by Frederick Taylor. Taylor broke jobs down into the simplest, repetitive components, which could often be performed with minimal thought. The result was often bored, resentful workers. Contemporary job re-design takes advantage of automation technologies which enable many of the most boring, repetitive tasks to be performed by machines. It then takes the human work and divides it in ways that will be interesting and motivating to workers.

Edward Lawler summarizes research related to job re-design:

For people to be motivated by the task or tasks that they are asked to do, those tasks have to have certain characteristics. Basically, those can be summarized as a whole and meaningful piece of work, a relatively challenging piece of work, a piece of work over which the people doing it have some control over how it's done, and finally, a work in which people get feedback about how well they've performed.

One form of job re-design, called **job enlargement**, consists simply of increasing the scope or variety of tasks incorporated into a job. It can reduce boredom and increase feelings of accomplishment. Another form of job re-design occurs through **job rotation**, which is often implemented along with teamwork. Workers change jobs, usually in a cycle over a period of time. Again, variety reduces boredom. Also, workers gain a broader view of the company and become more valuable, since they can substitute for one another in times of need.

A third and more profound form of job re-design is **job enrichment**. Workers are encouraged to take on new and more difficult tasks, to handle complete units of work, to become expert in specialized tasks, and to take responsibility and exercise authority. Job enrichment can provide workers psychological satisfaction and tap into motivation factors such as achievement and advancement that can be inherent in the process of work itself.

Providing an Effective Reward System

Just as rewards are an integral part of motivation, they are also important to morale in an organization. To summarize and expand on ideas treated earlier and in Lesson 14, an effective reward system should satisfy the basic needs of all employees (pay, benefits, vacations, etc.); it should be equitable within the organization and in comparison to other organizations; it should to some degree be tailored to individuals, be flexible, and allow some choice of rewards. Perhaps most importantly, it should recognize that rewards are not just carrots to be dangled in front of employees. In many cases the most satisfying rewards come from the work itself and from empowering people to take ownership of the work.

As Roger McDivitt describes his experience working at Patagonia:

This place has been very good about leaving people to figure out the best course for their work, and I would say that that is, more than anything, the most attractive feature of working here. The company stands for a lot of things that I also think are important and that make it enjoyable. But none of those in and of themselves would be enough. For me, in my situation, it's more or less being left alone to figure out how to get the job done.

Promoting Intrapreneurship

Perhaps the purest expression of creativity, high motivation, and high morale in work is entrepreneurship, the pioneering of new ideas, products, and services. The term **intrapreneurship** has come to be applied to entrepreneurship within the boundaries of a formal organization.

While few managers would argue against intrapreneurship – and many would recognize that it has become a survival necessity in today's competitive marketplace – it's a difficult seed to nurture in many corporate environments. It can be stifled by rigid rules and procedures and by reluctance to take risks. Companies that seek to develop intrapreneurship are discovering that it is essential to give employees flexibility, promote informal communication, reward innovation, and, perhaps most critically, encourage risk-taking.

Steven Cerri tells a story about Thomas Watson, the founding President of IBM, that captures the spirit of intrapreneurialism:

> *A young product manager developed a product, spent a hundred thousand dollars – at the beginning of IBM that was a very large sum of money – and the product failed. And so Watson called him into his office. And the gentleman came in and proceeded to say, 'Well, I assume you want my resignation, Mr. Watson.' And Mr. Watson said, 'Heck no, why would I do that after I spent a hundred thousand dollars training you?' That is an entrepreneurial environment. That is an environment where risk is approved*

Creating Flexibility

Flexibility is vital to nurturing not only the intrapreneurship of innovative employees but the morale of all employees. It's a basic aspect of treating employees as individuals. And it's becoming more and more essential, especially to families in which both parents work.

But flexibility often comes hard to organizations. It forces them to break old habits and often raises the conflict between corporate profits and employee's human needs. William Lareau describes a typical conflict:

> *Daycare centers are one in a hundred now, one in a thousand. Why is that? It's because people running American business do not value family concerns over and above making a dollar. Because they don't value their people. If they valued their people, they wouldn't ask how much it costs. They'd say, 'We'd like to do that.' And they'd find that it did pay and reduced turnover and increased commitment to the company.*

Within the range of justifiable costs, in the interest of higher morale, and often over considerable resistance, many companies are giving employees more flexibility in how they situate their jobs within their lives. One innovative approach is **flextime**, which allows employees to decide, within a certain range, when to begin and end each workday, which eliminates many conflicts between work and personal needs. Another approach is a **compressed work week**, which allows employees to fulfill their work obligation in less than the traditional five-day work week – for example, four 10-hour days or three 12-hour days – thus freeing extra days for other commitments. A third approach is **job-sharing**, which permits two part-time workers to divide one full-time job.

A S S I G N M E N T S

- Read the Overview, familiarize yourself with the Learning Objectives, and peruse the Key Terms below. Then turn to Plunkett & Attner, *Introduction to Management*, and read Chapter 13, "Human Motivation," pages 416–424, and Chapter 15, "Team Management and Conflict," pages 462–480.

- Next, scan the Video Viewing Questions and watch the video program for Lesson 15, "Pulling Together: Building Morale and Commitment."

- After watching the video, answer the viewing questions and assess your learning with the Self-Test.

- Familiarize yourself with the Review Questions, Discussion Questions for Critical Thinking, and Skill-Building Exercises on page 426 and 492 of Plunkett & Attner.

- Strengthen your understanding of the lesson's ideas and issues by undertaking the Expanded Analysis.

K E Y   T E R M S

compressed work week A technique to provide facility in work by permitting employees to fulfill their work obligation in less than the traditional five-day work week.

cross-functional team Designed to bring together the knowledge of various functional areas to work on solutions to operations problems; has a continuous life.

<u>cultural diversity</u> A value managers need to incorporate in the motivational environment. It involves the changing composition of the work group. Minorities – African Americans, Hispanics, and Asians – are collectively becoming the majority in the workplace.

<u>empowerment</u> A method to increase motivation. It occurs when an individual is given autonomy, authority, and trust, and is encouraged to make the decisions necessary to get the job done.

<u>flextime</u> A technique to provide flexibility in work that allows employees to decide, within a certain range, when to begin and end each work day.

<u>intrapreneurship</u> A concept in large corporations which provides for entrepreneurship. It provides a process whereby an individual sees a need and promotes it within the organization.

<u>job enlargement</u> Increases in the variety or the number of tasks a job includes, not the quality or the challenge of those tasks.

<u>job enrichment</u> Designing a job to provide more responsibility, control, feedback, and authority for decision making.

<u>job re-design</u> The application of motivational theories to the structure of work for increasing output and satisfaction.

<u>job rotation</u> Sending people to different jobs on a rotating or temporary basis.

<u>job sharing or twinning</u> A technique to provide flexibility in work by permitting two part-time workers to divide one full-time job.

<u>morale</u> The attitude or feeling workers have about the organization and their total work life.

<u>motivation</u> The set of processes that determine choices. It is the interaction of a person's internalized needs and external influences (equity, expectancy, previous conditioning, and goal setting) that determines behavior designed to achieve a goal.

<u>participative management</u> A leadership approach in which a manager shares decision-making authority with subordinates.

<u>philosophy of management</u> A manager's attitude about work and the people who perform work. It influences the motivation approaches a manager will select.

<u>quality of work life (QWL)</u> A term used to describe management efforts focused on enhancing the dignity of workers, improving the physical and emotional well-being of people, and improving the satisfaction of individual needs in the workplace.

reinforcement theory A motivation theory stating that the behavior choices of a person are influenced by the supervisor's reactions to them and the rewards or penalties experienced in a similar situation.

team A group of two or more people who interact regularly and coordinate their work to accomplish a common objective.

work team A team composed of multi-skilled workers. A work team does all the tasks previously done by individual members in a functional department or departments.

VIDEO VIEWING QUESTIONS

1. In the view of Marx and Engels, why is capitalism destructive of worker morale?

2. How is Patagonia's emphasis on quality conducive to morale?

3. How do the ideas of W. Edwards Deming implemented at Ford Motor Company affect employee morale?

4. How do empowerment and the high involvement of work teams benefit companies such as Ford or Solectron?

5. What corporate values or working environments tend to support high morale?

SELF-TEST

1. In attempting to create a positive, supportive work environment, the manager should

   a. treat all employees uniformly in order to insure a sense of fairness throughout the department.
   b. attempt to group people of similar ethnic backgrounds in the same work location to insure cultural harmony.
   c. work with people's individual differences, consistent with fairness.
   d. make every effort to ensure that only people who get along well with others are hired initially.

2. The statement most appropriate for sound employee compensation practice is:

a. Compensation should be devised solely on an individual employee's performance.
b. Confidentiality of payroll records and information ensures that differences in pay rates are not a problem among employees.
c. Equitability is essential in setting pay scales, in part because employees generally learn about one another's compensation, and differences perceived as unfair can easily alienate employees.
d. Pay rates should be based only on the company's assessments of its corporate requirements, not on any outside factors.

3. Which of the following statements best reflects the ideas underlying employee empowerment?

a. Each employee should have control over a part of his or her job assignment.
b. For most employees, compensation is the key motivator: so long as wages are believed throughout the employee group to be equitable (or superior), other steps that management may take are merely "icing."
c. Employees should be encouraged to participate fully in the organization as long as they follow company rules and stay within the boundary of their assigned role.
d. Pushing decision-making power as far down the organizational hierarchy as possible enhances employee involvement in a firm's success.

4. Which statement **least** accurately reflects the principles of job re-design?

a. The primary function of job re-design is to simplify job supervision.
b. Job re-design usually tailors a job to the person who must perform it.
c. Two approaches to job re-design include modifying the variety of task and the level of employee discretion to alter a job.
d. Worker experience is a significant factor in job re-design.

5. The process of increasing the quantity of tasks, rather than the nature of the job is called

a. job enrichment.
b. job enhancement.
c. job re-design.
d. job enlargement.

6. Job enrichment includes all but one of the following elements. Which item does **not** belong?

   a. Employees are introduced to a variety of new and more difficult tasks.
   b. Quality of tasks rather than the nature of the job is changed.
   c. Employee handles specialized tasks that enable him or her to become an expert.
   d. Employee receives directly periodic and specialized reports on his or her performance.

7. The essential goal of job re-design in general and job enrichment in particular may be characterized as

   a. to counter the influence of labor unions.
   b. to lower the number of overall employees, thus controlling costs and improving overall efficiency.
   c. to heighten morale and improve productivity.
   d. to strengthen the performance of human resources managers.

8. Intrapreneurship is

   a. a common managerial response to the problem of bored executives.
   b. usually an inexpensive and easily implemented strategy to improve morale among middle managers.
   c. such a strong idea that, once introduced, it quickly and easily takes hold.
   d. fragile and must be carefully nurtured by managers if it is to accomplish much.

9. An adaptation of car manufacturing that has a team of workers assembling the entire car instead of the car proceeding down an assembly line can best be characterized as

   a. job enlargement.
   b. job rotation.
   c. job enrichment.
   d. a combination of all three of the above.

10. The extent to which a team functions effectively and retains the commitment of its members is influenced by all the factors listed below **except**

    a. its size – the larger the better.
    b. clear, shared goals.
    c. frequent interaction.
    d. identifiable successes.

E X P A N D E D   A N A L Y S I S

1. People costs are frequently a company's greatest expense. In order to remain competitive, many of America's largest companies continue to cut costs by laying off large numbers of employees. In 1983, American Airlines tried another approach to reducing labor costs by introducing a two-tier wage system. From 1983, people newly hired were paid a rate 37 percent below those hired earlier. Describe some of the merits and difficulties such a system poses for management. Specifically address the question of morale and commitment.

16 At the Helm: Styles of Leadership

LEARNING OBJECTIVES

Upon completing this lesson, you should be familiar with the facts, ideas, and processes contained in this lesson, and be able to:

- Define the term **leadership**, and list at least five traits that are generally linked with organizational leadership.

- Compare the skills and attributes necessary for successful leadership and successful management.

- Relate the importance of leadership to the success of an organization.

- Examine alternative styles of leadership and indicate when and in what situations these styles are most effective.

- Describe how the leadership needs of an organization tend to change as the organization matures.

OVERVIEW

Leadership Defined

Leadership can be defined as the process of influencing individuals and groups to set and achieve goals. But beyond this dry definition, there lie realms of mystique and mythology. Something in the human imagination seeks to transform leaders into heroic, larger-than-life figures, symbols of the group experience. We think of the civil war as Grant versus Lee or Lincoln versus Davis, or the Second World War as Churchill, Roosevelt, and that dark figure, Stalin, resisting and overcoming the aggression of Hitler, Mussolini, and Hirohito. On the one hand, the glorification of leaders seems to reflect a desire to simplify imponderably complex events into stories of individuals. But on the other hand, leaders clearly can exert a tremendous influence in bringing vision to situations and galvanizing groups of people.

Early theories about leadership concentrated on the character of individual leaders. Gary Yukl, in the book *Leadership in Organizations* (1981), extended this mode of thinking to describe 13 traits, 9 skills, and 19 behaviors that are common to leaders. Just to pick a few of each, traits include adaptable, ambitious, decisive, and dependable; skills include intelligence, persuasiveness and organizational ability; and behaviors include performance emphasis, consideration, and inspiration.

While each such item is thought-provoking and offers insight into certain situations, there are several limitations to analyzing leadership solely in relation to leaders. The first is that no two leaders are alike. In a survey at the end of World War II, U.S. soldiers were asked to describe their commanders. They came up with a list of fourteen traits, but none of the leaders possessed all of the traits and many lacked several.

The disparities become even greater in comparing leaders in radically different situations – how much does Stalin have in common with Gandhi or either of them with Mrs. Fields? – and suggest that the traits, skills, and behaviors of leadership depend on the situation. This view is confirmed by studies of the life-cycles of organizations. The leadership characteristics that are critical at start-up differ widely from those that are needed during expansion, or periods of gradual change, or crises.

Management Versus Leadership

In traditional corporations, with their tall hierarchies, centralized authority, and strict chains of command, it has been common to equate management with leadership, but managerial skills do not guarantee the presence of leadership ability.

John Kotter has outlined a number of contrasts between management and leadership. **Management** attends to functions such as planning, budgeting, organizing, staffing, controlling, and problem solving. **Leadership** focuses on establishing a vision and direction, and aligning, motivating and inspiring people. Management produces a degree of predictability and order. Leadership produces change.

The nature of leadership is often called **transformation**. Kotter describes it as "a process of identifying, in any particular situation, where we need to go, what's the vision of what we're trying to achieve, and what's the strategy for getting there, of getting the relevant parties that need to be on board and believing in that objective, on board and believing it not only in their heads but in their hearts."

In comparing managers and leaders in terms of the types of power (see Lesson 8), managers possess legitimate power, formal authority deriving from their organizational positions. Leaders are likely to possess expert power – deriving from their special skills and abilities – and referent or charismatic power – deriving from the kind of persons they are or appear to be.

There are no inherent conflicts between being a leader and being a manager, and there are many demonstrations that the ability to lead can be gained through managerial experience. As the rate of change and importance of dealing with change have multiplied in many fields, more and more companies have begun to seek ways to help managers develop leadership ability.

Leadership Styles

Differences in leadership styles can be analyzed on several different scales. One is in terms of positive versus negative motivation. Positive leadership styles involve the use of praise, recognition, or monetary rewards or increasing security or granting additional responsibilities. Negative leadership styles use sanctions such as fines, suspensions, and termination. Current thinking runs strongly against negative leadership styles – but countless managers haven't gotten the message.

Richard Branson, founder and CEO of the Virgin and Voyager Group of Companies, describes his extremely positive leadership style: "A leader should praise, praise, and praise, and I think that brings out the best in people. We all like to be told how wonderful we are, and that spurs us on to try to go to even better things."

Another comparison of different leadership styles focuses on three different types of decision-making: autocratic, participative, and free-rein. Managers who use an autocratic style do not share decision-making authority with subordinates. While this style, which used to be the norm, runs against the flow of recent thinking, there are situations, such as crises, when leaders need to make fast, solo decisions. There are also settings, such as brain surgery, which are structured around the idea of someone with great expert power being the central decision-maker.

Managers who use a participative style share decision-making with subordinates. This sharing can vary in degree, depending on how early and how fully the manager involves others in the decision making process. A participative style brings different minds to bear on a problem and facilitates implementation, since employees who help make a decision are more likely to carry it out willingly.

Barbara Nyden Rodstein, founder and CEO of Harden Industries, describes her participative leadership style: "We try to encourage one another through communication, the interplay of personality to personality and idea to idea. If you're just present while it's being discussed, you're encouraged to participate. Once I get that participation, I know I've got the commitment."

The free-rein leadership style takes place when managers empower individuals or groups to make their own decisions and function on their own. This style is most appropriate among experienced professionals. Even when managers use a free-rein style, they are still likely to set limits, remain available for consultation, and hold participants accountable through reviews and performance evaluations.

Leadership styles can also differ according to whether they are task- or employee-oriented. While task and employee orientations might seem to fall on opposite sides of the divide that Kotter outlined between management and leadership, both are integral to leadership. Studies at Ohio State University in the 1970s compared leadership behavior in terms of consideration (concern for subordinates' ideas and feelings) and initiating structure (concern for goal achievement) and found that, of the four possible high-low combinations, the most effective leaders combined a high level of consideration with a high level of initiating structure.

Another, less formal comparison of leadership styles is between male and female. UCLA professor Judy Rosener characterizes the traditional masculine image of a leader: "If you ask people to free associate what words come to mind when they hear the word leader, what they say is, 'Command, strong, linear thinker, competitive, and so forth,' and it's interesting that those are the very same attributes that are associated with the word male."

A female leadership style, by contrast, conjures up a flexible, cooperative leader who is less power-obsessed and seeks to bring out the best in other people. Interestingly, a female leadership style generally aligns with positive, transformational, participative and employee-oriented styles, and seems increasingly appropriate in today's organizations. As Rosener observes:

We don't have hierarchies. Information is communicated in a fast way. We can't wait for it to go up and down the line. So the attribute that women bring to the workforce – which are a comfort with ambiguity, a sharing of information, a sharing of power, because they've been outside the traditional structures of organization – turn out to be very effective in terms of motivating and leading organizations.

In comparing masculine and feminine leadership styles, it's important to keep in mind that women can use male styles and men can use female. Barbara Nyden Rodstein displays a female style when she says, "There's a lot of push-pull here. It isn't just me pulling." But so does Richard Branson when he says, "What I try to do is give people a lot of freedom, freedom to make mistakes as well as to make successes of themselves," as does Horst Schulze of the Four Seasons Hotels in saying, "Teaching is probably the most important thing that a leader can give. Teaching is truly giving."

Theories of Situational Leadership

Given that no one leadership style applies in all situations, a number of theorists have attempted to define which styles work best in which situations.

Fred E. Fiedler considered three situational variables – leader-member relationships, task structure, and leader position power – and charted them against each other to suggest whether an employee- or task-oriented style is likely to work best in a given situation. If **leader-member relationships** show a high level of respect, trust, and confidence, the leader should be able to inspire and influence subordinates. If the relationship is poor, the manager may have to resort to negotiating or to promising favors to get performance. When **task structure** is routine, a task oriented leadership style will work better, but when tasks are unstructured, complex, and varied, an employee oriented leadership style that gives people latitude for creative expression will work better. And a leader with much **position power** (clout in the organization) can usually play a stronger hand than one without, or if he or she so chooses.

Robert J. House and Terrence R. Mitchell developed a path-goal theory of leadership based on Victor Vroom's expectancy theory of motivation (see Lesson 14). In their view, leaders can influence employees by setting up goals or rewards and providing paths to achieve them. Leaders are called upon to train employees, define and clarify tasks, devise rewards that employees perceive as desirable, and act to support employees' efforts. In doing so, leaders must take into account two situational variables: the personal characteristics of employees (abilities, self-confidence, and individual desires and perceptions), and the work environment (organizational culture, management philosophy, rules and policies). In essence, leaders must know what their people want from work and what stands between them and successful performance.

Paul Hersey and Kenneth H. Blanchard developed the life-cycle theory of leadership, which relates leadership behavior to subordinates' maturity levels. Generally, new and inexperienced employees will need to learn how to do the job and will benefit from task oriented, autocratic leadership. As people learn and mature in their jobs and relationships on-the-job, they will become increasingly able to direct themselves and participate in decision making, and the appropriate managerial style will shift from autocratic to participative to free-rein.

Leadership Throughout an Organization

In the heroic configuration, leaders were people who stood above everybody else. They were the only people expected to think and act independently, at least on big issues. Everyone else might swing swords and yell, but they did so on cue. Now even line employees are being called upon to exercise leadership, and companies are discovering that **leadership – the process of influencing individuals and groups to set and achieve goals** – doesn't have to come from the top down. It can come from anyone in an organization, as long as he or she feels qualified and empowered to pick up the mantle.

How Managers Can Become Better Leaders

For people in positions of managerial authority and responsibility, two ideas about leadership seem paramount. The first is that – while continuing to draw on their personal strengths and without becoming chameleons – they should learn to adapt their leadership style to different situations and people. The second is that, if they are caught in the old mold of an autocratic, negative, task oriented, male leadership style, they will increasingly be challenged to stretch in the direction of transformational, positive, participative, employee oriented, female styles of leadership.

John Dasburg, CEO of Northwest Airlines, describes his course of personal growth:

> *I was not a natural leader and I was not a natural delegator. I was one of those people who did the assignments myself, and I was one of those people who viewed, early-on in my career, that the involvement of others was a complexity that I would prefer to avoid. It became apparent to me as my responsibilities increased, that it was ever more important that I learn to delegate and ever more important that I learn to rely on others. It was somewhere during that process a decade or so ago that I realized that the most important thing I can*

do is coach and counsel, develop the pride in the people who I'm relying on, so that they will then go out and see that we accomplish our mission.

ASSIGNMENTS

- Read the Overview, familiarize yourself with the Learning Objectives, and peruse the Key Terms below. Then turn to Plunkett & Attner, *Introduction to Management*, and read Chapter 14, "Leadership," pages 428–459.

- Next, scan the Video Viewing Questions and watch the video program for Lesson 16, "At the Helm: Styles of Leadership."

- After watching the video, answer the viewing questions and assess your learning with the Self-Test.

- Familiarize yourself with the Review Questions, Discussion Questions for Critical Thinking, and Skill-Building Exercises on page 460 of Plunkett & Attner.

- Strengthen your understanding of the lesson's ideas and issues by undertaking the Expanded Analysis.

KEY TERMS

autocratic style A leadership approach in which a manager does not share decision authority with subordinates.

contingency model A leadership theory holding that a manager should focus on either tasks or employees, depending upon interaction of three variables – leader-member relationships, task structure, and leader position power.

expert power Influence possessed by a manager due to abilities, skills, knowledge, or experience.

free-rein style Sharing decision authority with subordinates, empowering them to function without direct involvement from managers to whom they report.

influence The ability to inspire others, to sway them to subject their wills to a leader's.

leadership Influencing individuals and groups to set and achieve goals.

legitimate power Authority possessed by managers and derived from the positions they occupy in the formal organization.

life-cycle theory A view of management asserting that the leader's behavior toward a subordinate relates to the subordinates' maturity level; the focus on tasks and relationships will vary as the subordinate matures in the job and the organization.

managerial grid Blake and Mouton's two-dimensional model for visualizing the mix of managers' focus on tasks and on people.

participative style The sharing of management decision authority with subordinates.

path-goal theory A view of management asserting that subordinates' behaviors and motivations are influenced by the behaviors managers exhibit toward them; suggests leadership style depends on leader influence and support of subordinate perceptions, goals, rewards, and goal paths.

referent power Influence that comes to people because of the kinds of persons they are – their traits, personalities, and attractiveness to others.

sanctions Penalties such as threats, fines, suspensions, and termination used to influence people's behaviors.

VIDEO VIEWING QUESTIONS

1. In what ways do leaders empower others?

2. Could a person be a leader without having a strong vision?

3. What are some distinctions between leadership and management?

4. Why can leadership only be described in relation to specific situations?

5. Could Horst Schulze be described as a servant-leader?

6. Would you characterize Barbara Nyden Rodstein's leadership style as female? Horst Schulze's? Richard Branson's? Explain your answer in each case.

7. Does Richard Branson use an autocratic, participative, or free-rein leadership style?

8. What would you think if you woke on an airplane to find Richard Branson giving you a massage?

S E L F - T E S T

1. The term leadership is best defined as the process of

   a. putting management into action.
   b. influencing a group or individual toward the achievement of a goal.
   c. exercising power or control over others.
   d. helping others make effective decisions.

2. Truly effective leadership is generally found

   a. among persons with extensive managerial experience.
   b. at top management levels.
   c. from mid-management levels on up.
   d. among managers and non-managers throughout all levels in an organization.

Management and leadership are not synonymous terms. As you read the descriptions below, indicate whether each is more closely related to

   a. management
      or
   b. leadership

3. Planning and budgeting

4. Developing a vision for the future and the strategies necessary to achieve it

5. Communicating the vision and aligning staff to support it

6. Establishing and structuring and staffing the organization to accomplish plans

7. Monitoring results and solving problems that are identified

8. Motivating and inspiring staff

9. The autocratic leadership style is probably most appropriate when applied with

   a. extremely experienced and knowledgeable employees.
   b. new employees undergoing orientation.
   c. high achievers.
   d. employees with a strong need for challenge.

10. Hersey and Blanchard's life cycle theory of leadership is based on the premise that

    a. leaders tend to become increasingly autocratic with experience.
    b. most leaders go through a predictable cycle from autocratic to free rein leadership styles.
    c. it takes a lifetime of managerial experience to qualify for assuming a leadership role.
    d. managers need to change their leadership styles in response to the varying organizational maturity of employees.

11. A manager who employs a negative motivation approach to leadership usually does so mainly because

    a. such an approach is the quickest way to dramatically increase productivity.
    b. he or she has little faith in the notion that people can be motivated by desire to achieve.
    c. budgetary restrictions make positive motivation impractical.
    d. he or she has attempted a positive approach and found it unproductive.

12. A manager who exhibits high task orientation and low employee orientation is generally one who

    a. sets and meets goals with a minimum of stress.
    b. has strong autocratic leadership tendencies.
    c. has great faith that employees will perform well with a minimum of direction.
    d. really has little or no interest in her or his position.

EXPANDED ANALYSIS

1. In their book, *Leaders* (New York, Harper & Row, 1985, p. 33), Warren Bennis and Burt Nanus, say:

   Leaders articulate and define what has previously remained implicit or unsaid; then they invent images, metaphors, and models that provide a focus for new attention. By so doing, they consolidate or challenge prevailing wisdom. In short, an essential factor in leadership is the capacity to influence and organize meaning for the members of the organization.

   Does this description of what leaders do differ from your understanding of what managers do? If so, what are the differences?

17 Working it Out: Managing Organizational Conflict

Upon completing this lesson, you should be familiar with the facts, ideas, and processes contained in this lesson, and be able to:

- Assess some of the problems that occur when individuals operate in a group environment.

- Describe the sources and symptoms of organizational conflict.

- Identify the types of conflict commonly experienced in organizations.

- Describe the consequences of intergroup competition.

- Compare positive and negative aspects of conflict.

- Discuss the manager's role in conflict management.

- Suggest strategies to optimize the productivity of organizational conflict.

O V E R V I E W

Conflict can be defined as disagreement between two or more organizational members or groups. There are three basic philosophical views that managers hold toward conflict. The **traditional view** sees it as unnecessary and harmful to an organization and seeks to wipe it out. The **behavioral view** attributes it to human nature, concedes that it can sometimes produce positive results, but generally seeks to resolve and eliminate it as soon as it occurs. The **interactionist view** – which is the most current philosophy – holds that conflict is inevitable and can be good or bad. A manager with an interactionist view attempts to harness conflict to maximize its positive potential for organizational growth and to minimize its negative effects.

Louann Parker of Mercy Hospital describes the positive role of conflict: "Conflict is an imperative for an organization to grow. It challenges us to think differently. It challenges us to rethink ways that we've done things. It challenges us to come up with better ideas. It makes us stretch. If we just stayed real comfortable we would never go through that, we would never get better, and eventually we would be passed by."

Sources of Conflict

Sources of conflict include competition, differences in objectives, differences in values or perceptions, disagreements over role requirements, disagreements about work activities, disagreements about individual approaches, and breakdowns in communication.

Competition can take the form of individuals or groups trying to outperform each other (the Lakers and Celtics during the 1980s) or it can erupt over a struggle for limited resources. Most cases of positive conflict emerge from performance competition.

Breakdowns in communication are not only sources of conflict in themselves, they can aggravate virtually every other form of conflict. Many of the most stunning cases of conflict resolution occur when people start or resume talking with each other. Mountains are turned back into molehills.

Strategies for Managing Conflict

The first steps in managing a conflict situation are to analyze who is in conflict, the source of conflict, and the level of conflict. In answering these questions, it's important to try to view the situation through the eyes of all parties involved. Depending on the situation, a manager can choose from among seven strategies for addressing the conflict.

Avoidance may be the most appropriate response if the conflict is trivial and not likely to have significant consequences. Also, there are many situations in which the level of conflict does not justify a manager becoming involved.

Smoothing, or downplaying the conflict and calming the parties, may be appropriate if there are no major issues.

Compromise, in which each party gives up something to get something, may be effective when the parties are about equal in power, major values are not involved, a temporary solution to a deeper problem is desirable, or time pressures require a quick solution.

Collaboration, or mutual problem solving through open discussion, can often provide the most satisfying solution, especially when communication can help both parties to understand each other's needs.

Confrontation is like collaboration, but under less propitious circumstances, often with parties at each other's throats. Forcing both parties to verbalize their positions and disagreements may clear the air and point to a solution – or it may pour fuel on the fire.

Decisions by a third party – often the manager – may produce a judgment that both parties can accept.

Finally, **appeals to superordinate objectives**, shared needs or values, can sometimes enable parties to rise above their conflicts. Louann Parker of Mercy Hospital describes an appeal to a superordinate objective: "When we really have a lot of conflict what we do is stand back and say, 'If I were the patient or if that were my family member, what would I want? How would that change my answer?' A lot of times it does."

Conflict Stimulation

Peter Robinson paints the need for conflict from a manager's perspective:

> If groups are making decisions without any conflict, this is a bad sign. This is a symptom that they are not being very honest and open, that they're not sharing their ideas, that they're not being critical. So managers, if their group is running too smoothly, can take note of this and say, 'I need to generate more conflict in here.'

Robert Cooley of Mercy Hospital is more blunt:

> If you don't have conflict, you've got people that aren't thinking. If everybody did exactly what they were told, or exactly what everyone else thought was right, then you don't have employees that are thinking and are even able to be empowered.

Situations in which managers should consider stimulating conflict are usually ones in which performance is low or people are passive or afraid to do anything other than the norm.

The manager's challenge in any of these situations is, in essence, to shake things up. Strategies for shaking things up include: bring in an outsider, change the rules, change the organization, change managers, and encourage competition. Many of these strategies can be seen on about half of professional sports teams every year, as managers are fired and hired, players traded, and contracts dressed up with extravagant incentive clauses.

When shake-ups succeed they can increase group cohesion, task focus, and efficiency. When they fail, they can lead to open hostility, with competitors perceiving each other as enemies, cutting off communication, and sabotaging each other's efforts.

ASSIGNMENTS

- Read the Overview, familiarize yourself with the Learning Objectives, and peruse the Key Terms below. Then turn to Plunkett & Attner, *Introduction to Management*, and read Chapter 15, "Team Management and Conflict," pages 462–492.

- Next, scan the Video Viewing Questions and watch the video program for Lesson 17, "Working It Out: Managing Organizational Conflict."

- After watching the video, answer the viewing questions and assess your learning with the Self-Test.

- Familiarize yourself with the Review Questions, Discussion Questions for Critical Thinking, and Skill-Building Exercises on page 492 of Plunkett & Attner.

- Strengthen your understanding of the lesson's ideas and issues by undertaking the Expanded Analysis.

KEY TERMS

avoidance A conflict strategy in which the manager withdraws or ignores the conflict situation.

collaboration Conflict strategy in which the manager focuses on mutual problem solving by both parties. Parties seek to satisfy their interests by openly discussing the issues, understanding differences, and developing a full range of alternatives.

compromise A conflict strategy option in which each party is required to give something up and find a middle ground.

conflict A disagreement between two or more organizational members or teams.

confrontation A conflict strategy that forces parties to verbalize their positions and area of disagreement.

dysfunctional conflict Conflict that limits the organization's ability to achieve its objectives.

functional conflict Conflict that supports organizational objectives.

smoothing A conflict strategy in which the manager diplomatically acknowledges that conflict exists, but downplays its importance.

superordinate objective A conflict strategy in which the parties adopt an objective that overshadows their own interests.

work team Comprises multi-skilled workers; does all the tasks previously done by individual members in a functional department or departments.

VIDEO VIEWING QUESTIONS

1. Why is conflict inevitable in some circumstances?

2. How can communication serve to resolve or reduce conflict?

3. What is the connection between pressure and conflict at CNN?

4. Why do periods of organizational change tend to increase conflict?

5. Why and how has Mercy Hospital moved toward a policy of bringing conflict into the open?

SELF-TEST

1. Conflict is best described as

   a. a disagreement between two or more organizational members or teams.
   b. the internal psychological environment of an organization.
   c. the general readiness of an organization to expand or move forward.
   d. the capability of the organization to respond to change.

2. Which of the following statements about conflict in the work environment is **not** true?

   a. Conflict in any work environment is inevitable.
   b. The presence of conflict in an organization signifies failure on the part of management to control resources and personnel.
   c. Conflict is inherently neither positive nor negative.
   d. A manager's attitudes towards conflict can actually influence the extent to which conflict exists within an organization.

3. Which of the following is **not** usually a major source of conflict within an organization?

   a. A manager's preference for an open, informal communication system
   b. A difference between individual and organizational goals
   c. Lack of structure within the organization
   d. Differences in personal style or ways of approaching the work

4. Sometimes a manager feels that avoidance is the most effective approach to dealing with conflict. Avoidance is the best solution

   a. because it is the easiest to implement.
   b. if the resulting hurt feelings do not create other problems.
   c. when a speedy solution is necessary.
   d. when the conflict is trivial.

5. Before she or he is equipped to handle conflict effectively, a manager must determine all of the following **except**

   a. the underlying source of the conflict.
   b. whether the conflict exists between individuals, groups, or individuals and groups.
   c. how significant or serious the conflict really is.
   d. how many other people already know about the conflict.

6. Which of the following remarks best represents the interactionist view of conflict?

   a. "A certain amount of conflict is inevitable – but if you catch it in time, it seldom has any long-range negative effects."
   b. "Conflict can be healthy if it's managed right – how else are you going to spur people to their best efforts?"
   c. "Some people say you can't do anything about conflict – that attitude shows a real deficiency in interpersonal management skills."
   d. "Conflict is the worst enemy a healthy organization faces – our job as managers is to wipe it out."

7. Under which of the following conditions might an effective manager choose to increase the level of conflict?

   a. When a serious communications problem surfaces between two departments, groups, or individuals
   b. When members of an organization seem well satisfied with present performance levels
   c. When a verbal confrontation session seems to produce more stress and hostility than predicted
   d. There are no conditions under which an effective manager should deliberately increase the level of conflict

8. Which of the following actions on the part of the manager is **least** likely to increase conflict within an organization?

   a. Changing the rules to allow a person or group to function in a way that would ordinarily not be permitted.
   b. Giving a work group a new manager who offers a relatively dominant style of leadership
   c. Restructuring work groups, thus giving individuals an opportunity to interact with new people and gain new perspectives
   d. Bringing groups or individuals together to openly discuss issues and problems

9. Strategically, which of the following would a behaviorist probably consider the best time for a manager to interfere in order to be truly effective at resolving conflict in an organization?

   a. As soon as it occurs.
   b. As soon as the conflict becomes serious enough to affect the stability of the organizational climate.
   c. As soon as the conflict threatens to precipitate a true crisis.
   d. Only when it becomes obvious that there is no chance the conflict will resolve itself.

10. As part of the so-called confrontation strategy, employees are encouraged to confront

   a. each other.
   b. management.
   c. competitors
   d. their problems.

E X P A N D E D   A N A L Y S I S

1. In management contexts, the term conflict is too often used loosely to embrace any disagreement or contrasting views of facts or circumstances, any competition or divergence. In general usage, the word may be too severe for most management situations. The 1992 *American Heritage Dictionary* defines conflict as: "a state of disharmony between incompatible or antithetical persons, ideas, or interests." In many management circumstances, the word tension, may be more appropriate. ADH defines tension as: "A balanced relation between strongly opposing elements." Think of an example of true incompatibility in a work situation and suggest a suitable course of action for the responsible manager.

18 Keeping Track: Management and Control

Upon completing this lesson, you should be familiar with the facts, ideas, and processes contained in this lesson, and be able to:

- Explain why management needs the control function.
- Describe the link between planning and controlling.
- Indicate the importance of establishing control system standards.
- List and describe typical control methods.
- Discuss the factors a manager must consider in designing and evaluating a control system.
- Describe the characteristics of an effective control.
- Recognize barriers that may inhibit successful operation of a control system.
- Discuss effects of controls on organizational behavior.
- Recognize that Total Quality Control (TQM) is only as effective as the corporate culture allows it to be.

O V E R V I E W

Controlling: Purpose and Process

In its most basic form, controlling is the management function in which managers set and communicate performance standards for people, processes, and devices. In the management process, controlling is the companion bookend to planning. Planning reaches forward into all the other functions, and controlling reaches back and brings the management cycle full circle. Controlling is, as Lester Bittel noted, "the steering mechanism that links all the preceding functions of organizing, staffing, and directing to the goals of planning." If an organization's trip from plan to goal can be compared to a voyage to a distant island, controlling is the navigator.

To consider the connection between controlling and each of the other functions, suppose that Proctor & Gamble is going to introduce a new soap.

In planning, P&G calls for a 15 percent profit, 10 percent share of the soap market, and other goals. These become the foundation for controls. From the inception, P&G designs and establishes controls to provide feedback about profits, costs, sales, market penetration, and so forth.

In organizing, P&G modifies its organizational structure by adding a product team to launch the new soap. Senior managers create controls to monitor production and determine whether the allocation of resources and authority has been appropriate to the job.

In staffing, P&G hires workers at all levels to accomplish its plan. Managers create controls to evaluate the effectiveness of the recruiting, hiring, compensation, and training of the new product team and those who assist them in manufacturing and support positions.

In directing, P & G coordinates employees in many different units to accomplish the goals set by the plan, within the means set by the budget. Managers establish controls to ensure smooth work flow and progress toward goals, to enforce standards, to evaluate workers and be evaluated themselves, and to monitor rewards and corrective actions.

And throughout the entire process, controlling meets the vital need of monitoring resources, which are the lifeblood of any organization.

Controls in an Organization

The four primary types of controls are: personnel, financial, informational, and operational. Taken together, they represent a formidable arsenal.

- **Personnel controls** include human resource inventories, job descriptions, job specifications, performance appraisals, and statistics about absenteeism, safety, and so forth.

- **Financial controls** focus on income, expenditures, cash flow, asset mix, and the acquisition and investment of funds.

- **Information controls** give managers the information they need to make timely and intelligent decisions. Management information systems that electronically collect, process, disseminate, and store information have become a major control tool.

- **Operational controls** monitor anything that is of value but not covered by the others. In general, they monitor the use of physical resources, and their provinces include policies, procedures, inventories, and products and services.

The Control Process

The control process utilizes four steps: (1) establishing performance standards, (2) measuring performance, (3) comparing measured performance to established standards, and (4) taking corrective action.

Standards are the cornerstone of control. A **standard** is any guideline established as the basis for measurement. Whether quantitative or qualitative, standards must be precise, explicit statements of expected results. Standards and controls usually address time, cost, quality, productivity, or behavior.

- **Time standards determine priorities, schedules, and sequences of** events. They might, for instance, ensure that goods are reordered before stock runs out or that customers receive deliveries on time.

- **Cost standards** keep organizations on track with their budgets and monitor cost-effectiveness.

- **Quality standards** make sure that the features and characteristics of a product or service satisfy customers' needs. Top managers should involve everyone, including suppliers and customers, in the quest for quality.

- **Productivity standards monitor ratios between output and input. They can be quantitative (units produced per machine-**hour) or qualitative (customer feedback about a customer-**service** representative).

- **Behavioral standards** seek to create compatibility between individual and organizational goals. For instance, a division manager evaluated by short-term profits might ignore long-term investment that would benefit the company.

In the second step of the control process, managers must **measure** actual performance to determine variation from standard. The mechanisms for this purpose can be extremely sensitive, particularly in high-tech environments. Computers are becoming increasingly important as tools for measuring performance. Many retail stores, for example, use computerized scanning equipment that simultaneously accesses prices and tallies sales then tracks inventory by department, vendor, and branch store.

The third step in the control process is to **compare actual** performance to the standards set for that performance. If deviations from the standards exist, the evaluator must decide, first, if they are significant enough to require corrective action. If so, then a search for the cause of deviation begins. Perhaps suppliers shipped faulty materials. Perhaps a worker made an error. Perhaps a machine broke.

Problems may also be inherent in the standards and measuring processes themselves. If a control is too loose, a product (or service) may meet specifications but not in fact be satisfactory. If a control is too tight, it may cause the rejection of satisfactory products, bog down the process in red tape, or cause resentment among the people being controlled.

In the productivity- and quality-centered environment of today, workers and managers are often empowered to evaluate their own work. This not only reduces the potential for resentment but, in many cases, puts the authority to make decisions in the hands of the people who know the job best and can take remedial action most quickly. George Labovitz describes the goal: "Everybody eventually should get trained in this stuff: rip a process apart, gather data on that process, be able to analyze the data, come up with new ways of doing things."

Once the evaluator determines the cause or causes of deviation, he or she can take the fourth step in the control process: **corrective action**. The most effective course may be prescribed by policies or may be best left up to employees' judgment and initiative. It may require fixing something, training someone, or adjusting either the system or the control itself.

Types of Controls and Control Systems

Controls can be divided into three types depending on whether they occur before the process begins, during the process, or after it ceases.

Controls that focus on operations before they begin are called **feedforward controls**. Their goal is to prevent defects and deviations from standards. Safety systems, training programs, and budgets – to name a few – can all function as feedforward controls. Good maintenance feeds forward to prevent problems, as does close coordination with suppliers.

Controls that apply to processes as they are happening are called **concurrent controls**, or steering controls. Any sort of guiding mechanism – including a steering wheel – is a concurrent control. Automated systems can be equipped with extraordinarily sophisticated concurrent controls, but the most important element in many such systems is the skilled and experienced operator who recognizes when something isn't right. In the Toyota Production System, for example, all employees on the production line are empowered to pull a cord that stops the line any time they detect a problem.

Controls that focus on the results of operations are called **feedback controls**. Measurements and comparisons made after an operation has been concluded serve to guide future planning, goals, inputs, and process designs. Annual or quarterly budget and other reports are a staple of feedback control. Many companies are discovering a need for even more timely reports. Walter Wilson describes the approach at Solectron: "We do weekly profit-and-loss analysis. We can't wait a month. We can't wait a quarter. We do that every week. Coming out of that, then, we understand how we're doing relative to the objectives we've set and can make almost an instantaneous adjustment to keep us on track."

The Characteristics of Effective Controls

Perhaps because they represent such highly analytic and systematic modes of thinking, control systems are subject to gross errors of common sense. In weighing the effectiveness of controls it can be helpful to consider several features that might seem obvious.

- Controls should focus on points that are critical to an organization's success or survival. There's little point measuring trivia.

- Controls should be comprehensible, which in many cases means as simple as possible. They should produce clarity, not clutter and confusion.

- Controls should be integrated into operations and help people to work smoothly. They shouldn't impede operations and put people at cross-purposes.

- Controls should be timely and get people the information they need when they need it. In the words of Richard Brumbaugh of Santa Anita Racetrack: "It doesn't do us any good to find out twelve months later that something was done incorrectly."

- Controls shouldn't cost more than they save.

- And controls should be accurate. Wrong information is worse than no information.

Control Monitoring

Every attempt to create a control is, in a sense, a scientific experiment. It may be a resounding success or failure, or it may succeed on it's own ground but cause undesirable side effects. As scientific experiments, controls can be tested by two basic tools of inquiry. One is before-and-after comparisons, which amount to saying, "Let's look at the way things were and the way things are now (or the way they are now and the way they will become) in order to judge whether the control is achieving its desired effect." The second tool is the use of control groups. Change may occur during the course of an experiment but not be due to that experiment. Comparing the "after" situation with another group that hasn't been subject to the experiment can help to gauge what changes are due to the experiment.

The main negative side effect that controls are likely to cause is related to employee morale. Excessive or confusing controls can cause stress and resistance. Surveys of employees can provide positive and negative feedback that will help managers to evaluate whether a control is truly beneficial to the organization. On a preventive level (as a feed-forward control), managers can involve workers in designing and implementing controls. Workers who take an active role in improving performance are less likely to feel that demands are being imposed upon them.

Controls also need to be monitored as a simple function of time and change. Controls which worked brilliantly yesterday can become – through changes in an organization's mission, structure, decision making, human relations, or technology – excess baggage from the past.

People tend to get comfortable with the way things are. By simply relying on controls and systems that are in place, managers fail to make full use of the preventive nature of the controlling process. The instant that changes occur or are planned, managers should begin to determine if present controls will be adequate and applicable in the new situation. In sum, controls themselves need to be controlled!

A S S I G N M E N T S

- Read the Overview, familiarize yourself with the Learning Objectives, and peruse the Key Terms below. Then turn to Plunkett & Attner, *Introduction to Management*, and read Chapter 16, "Controlling: Purpose and Process," pages 494–515.

- Next, scan the Video Viewing Questions and watch the video program for Lesson 18, "Keeping Track: Management and Control."

- After watching the video, answer the viewing questions and assess your learning with the Self-Test.

- Familiarize yourself with the Review Questions, Discussion Questions for Critical Thinking, and Skill Building Exercises on page 516 of Plunkett & Attner.

- Strengthen your understanding of the lesson's ideas and issues by undertaking the Expanded Analysis.

KEY TERMS

concurrent controls Controls that apply to processes as they are happening; often called steering controls.

control process A four-step process involving (1) establishing standards, (2) measuring performance, (3) comparing measured performance to established standards, and (4) taking corrective action.

control system Feedforward, concurrent, and feedback controls operating in harmony to make certain that standards are enforced, goals are reached, and that resources are used effectively and efficiently.

controlling The process through which standards for performances of people and processes are set, communicated, and then applied to those processes.

critical control point An area of an organization's operations that directly affects the survival of the firm and the success of its "key" or most essential activities.

feedback controls Controls that focus on outputs of or results of operations; feedback controls are post-performance or after-action controls.

feedforward controls Controls concerned with preventing defects and deviations from standards; feedforward controls are sometimes called preliminary controls and focus on operations before they begin.

integrated controls Controls that are supported and enforced through the corporation's culture and climate; those that have the support and commitment of organization members.

standard Any established rule or basis of comparison in measuring or judging capacity, quantity, content, value, quality, or performance of outputs.

VIDEO VIEWING QUESTIONS

1. How do computerized control systems coordinate operations at Santa Anita Racetrack? At Solectron?

2. How does Harden Industries involve employees in designing and implementing control systems?

3. In what ways is the quest for continuous improvement a control concept?

4. What is a six sigma standard and what is its broader significance?

5. How does Solectron include customers and suppliers in its control system?

6. What is benchmarking, and how does Solectron use it?

7. How would you compare the degree of accuracy needed for controls at Solectron with those at Harden? At Santa Anita?

SELF-TEST

1. The term "control" can best be defined as

   a. the process through which standards for performance of people and processes are set, communicated, and applied.
   b. knowledge of one's own capabilities and limitations.
   c. the authority to ensure that one's subordinates will carry out their responsibilities in acceptable fashion.
   d. a centralized management approach, which assumes a strong power base.

2. Which of the following is **not** a fundamental step in the control process?

   a. Establishing standards for performance
   b. Refining the fundamental mission of the organization in light of current standards
   c. Measuring performance, and noting any deviations – positive and negative from expectations
   d. Taking whatever actions are necessary to correct deviations from established standards

3. Which of the following statements about performance standards is **not** correct?

    a. Standards can be either qualitative or quantitative in nature.
    b. Standards apply not just to people, but to equipment, goods, services, and processes as well.
    c. Experience, strategic and tactical plans, and feedback from employees are all important sources of input in establishing standards.
    d. Standards should rarely be changed unless a company dramatically revises its overall mission or objectives.

4. When an inspector on the production line at Evergreen Microchip discovers a problem and corrects it on the spot, this action can best be described as a

    a. prevention control.
    b. diagnostic control.
    c. concurrent control.
    d. feedback control.

5. The primary purpose of feedback controls is to

    a. compare real costs with budget projections.
    b. determine customer satisfaction.
    c. evaluate managerial effectiveness.
    d. obtain information that will help prevent future problems and errors.

6. In making any control system effective, a manager must do all of the following **except**

    a. establish overlapping controls, so that if one system fails, another will provide backup.
    b. continually update the system to accommodate changes.
    c. ensure that standards are attainable, yet realistically stringent.
    d. monitor the controls to be certain they do not cause more problems than they resolve.

7. Standards and controls generally deal with all of the following **except**

    a. metric measurements
    b. time standards
    c. costs
    d. quality and productivity

8. Measuring performance to determine variation from standards increasingly calls for

   a. visual inspection.
   b. third-party evaluation.
   c. the involvement of top-level managers.
   d. the use of computers.

9. Effective controls have all but one of the following characteristics. Identify the **incorrect** item.

   a. Limited to a few highly trained individuals
   b. Supported and enforced by the corporate culture
   c. Provide information in an accurate and timely manner
   d. Benefits of the system outweigh its costs

10. In the future, which of the following is a trend in relation to controls that is expected to continue?

    a. With growing decentralization and empowerment, the need for workers (individually and in teams) to plan, organize, direct, staff, and control their areas of influence will increase.
    b. Rapid advancement in technology will lessen the need for real-time, instant feedback in operation.
    c. Controlling for quality will become a secondary focus: productivity will be the key.
    d. Changes will slow down for most organizations, eliminating the need to re-evaluate plans and controls as frequently.

EXPANDED ANALYSIS

1. In his book, *Thriving on Chaos*, (New York: Alfred A. Knopf, 1987 [HarperPerennial, 1991]), Tom Peters talks about the three principal management controls over individuals – performance appraisals, the setting of objectives, and job descriptions. He says that these three personnel controls are "downright dangerous – as currently constituted." Why might Peters say that, and what kinds of changes might make these controls genuinely effective?

19 It All Adds Up: Financial Methods of Control

Upon completing this lesson, you should be familiar with the facts, ideas, and processes contained in this lesson, and be able to:

- Explain why business organizations use financial controls as the predominant means of control.

- Compare responsibility for financial control at various levels of management.

- Describe the budgeting process and principal types of budgets.

- Delineate non-budgetary types of financial controls, including financial statements and ratios.

- Compare controls used in production and operations, in human resource management, in marketing, in financial management.

O V E R V I E W

The Importance of Control Techniques

To function effectively, an organization must have controls. Without them, managers cannot monitor the organization's performance to know if resources are being properly utilized, the mission fulfilled, objectives realized. Controls affect every facet of operations, and are central to financial operations. An organization cannot survive without proper management of its financial resources; without cash to hire staff, maintain inventory, or produce a product. To provide for continuous management of financial resources, three primary classes of controls have been developed and refined: feedforward, concurrent, and feedback. With them, progress toward achievement of objectives can be measured by both quantitative and qualitative standards.

As with the other management functions, the necessary matrix for designing controls to monitor resources, processes, trends, and changes throughout the company emerge during the planning phase. A firm's strategic plan guides the overall control system; department (subsystem) plans play a similar role at their particular level. The companywide operating budget, for instance, is built up from forecasts and predictions developed in each line and staff department. Line departments whose operation depends upon efficient and reliable control techniques include finance, marketing, operations (production), and human resources. Suitable controls are also necessary in the company's staff departments – management information systems (MIS), legal services, computer services, and public relations.

Finance Controls, Corporate and Departmental

Finance managers commonly forecast and budget for one month and six months; and one, two, and five years. They need comprehensive information about the organization's ability to meet its monetary commitments. in cooperation with marketing personnel and others, these managers project income and expenditures, prepare appropriate financial statements, and apply formulas and ratios to analyze developed information.

Although they share a common base of theory and procedures, operating controls are tailored for each of the line and staff departments. Because their operations are so essential, and mistakes so costly, controls for the marketing-based tasks of advertising, sales, distribution, and research have benefited from the vigorous analysis many companies have instituted. Some of industry's most innovative control systems appear in this discipline: market research, test marketing, ratio analysis, sales quotas, and inventory levels. Production functions requiring controls include product design, procurement of raw materials and other resources, production layout and flow, supply inventories, work in process, and finished goods. For human resources activities, control techniques range from performance appraisals to human asset valuation and attitude surveys.

Financial Controls and Financial Statements

Two primary financial statements – the balance sheet and the income statement – provide a common measure of corporate financial operations and conditions. Both documents are used to prepare budgets and other kinds of plans and controls, and to monitor the organization's financial health.

The **balance sheet** lists a company's assets – what is owned and the nature of the ownership – at a fixed point in time. As its title suggests, the balance sheet's aggregate numbers result in an equation: the total assets equal (balance) the sum of stockholders' equity and liabilities. Periodic preparation of balance sheets allows comparisons from year to year so trends may be spotted.

With the **income statement**, managers can review expenses and revenue on an ongoing basis, for any discrete period of time. Its content also can be stated as an equation: income minus expenses equals profit or loss. Seven items are considered: net sales, cost of goods sold, gross profit, operating expenses, net income (or loss) before taxes, taxes, and net income – the bottom line. Like the balance sheet, the income statement yields information needed to track the firm's health – particularly trends in costs and income – and each provides a measure of feedback and concurrent control over financial and related activities.

Financial Ratios

A financial ratio involves selecting two relevant figures from financial statements and expressing their relationship as a ratio or percentage to measure both the company's progress toward goals and its financial health. By emphasizing relationships, ratios dramatically illustrate possible problems that may be not be readily apparent in partially analyzed data. A firm's balance sheet, for example, may show substantial assets; yet if the ratio of current assets to current liabilities is less than two to one, the company may not have enough cash to meet short-term debts. A firm's ratios can be compared year to year and to the ratios of competing companies to determine change and relative achievement. The four most common types of ratios are liquidity, profitability, debt, and activity ratios.

Liquidity ratios measure the ability of a firm to raise enough cash to meet short-term debts; the current ratio is obtained by dividing the current assets by the current liabilities. **Profitability ratios** indicate a company's profits from several perspectives – for example, from sales. **Debt ratios** assess capacity to meet debts. **Activity ratios** assess key internal areas such as inventory levels to reveal performance. Still other ratios can be used to monitor diverse important activities.

Financial Responsibility Centers

All management control relies upon the simple idea – responsibility accounting – that says each manager is responsible for a part of the company's total activity. A variety of responsibility centers routinely operate in most companies; each controlled with appropriate assessment tools. Center categories include:

- financial responsibility centers that contribute costs, revenues, investments, or profits;
- discretionary expense centers, usually administrative departments for which there is seldom a practical way to establish the relationship between inputs and outputs;
- profit centers, where the manager is responsible for the best combination of costs and revenues; and
- investment centers in which the manager is responsible for the assets employed, and in which trade-offs are made between current profits and investments to increase future profits.

Financial Audits

Because financial output depends upon quality data and interpretation, reliable control is needed to ensure that data is accurate and that control systems are working as designed. Most organizations achieve this through **audits** – formal investigations that determine if financial data, records, reports, and statements are correct and consistent with policies, rules, and procedures. Audits may be conducted by insiders or outsiders. At most companies, a manager's regular appraisal of subordinates functions as a kind of internal audit. In addition, internal audit teams are sometimes designated to review department performance.

Scheduled external audits are routine in many firms. A wide range of companies must, by law, be regularly audited according to rigorous standards. Banks, insurance companies, many public agencies, and other organizations whose satisfactory performance depends upon high credibility and reliability fall into this category. Such audits are performed by independent public accounting firms which provide expert accounting and management services. Many governmental bodies maintain separate audit branches, of which the huge U.S. General Accounting Office may be the best-known example.

Budgets

Even people who know virtually nothing else about management know something about budgets. This disarmingly useful device is almost universally accepted as the primary financial control used in the daily management of organizations everywhere. Budgets come in every size and degree of complexity.

As a planning mechanism, a budget includes estimates (projections) of revenues and expenses for a given period of time. It then provides the standard for measuring performance (controlling) as actual revenues and expenses are tracked against projections. To budget, managers must (1) set goals, (2) plan and schedule activities to reach the goals, (3) identify and price resources, (4) locate needed funds, (5) and adjust goals, plans, and resources to match actual fund availability. Four approaches to budgeting have emerged as trusted standards, usually in some combination: top-down, bottom-up, zero-based, and flexible budgeting.

Top-down budgeting has senior managers preparing budgets and distributing them to lower levels. Bottom-up budgeting utilizes the knowledge and line experience of the men and women closest to the planned activities to build the budget. **Zero-based budgeting** launches each budget from scratch with a clean sheet of paper instead of carrying over items from one year to the next. It requires each manager to justify every dollar requested each period. Any budgeting exercise can incorporate **flexible budgeting**, which sets "meet or beat" standards to which expenditures can be compared.

Two Main Budget Types

Operating budgets serve as financial plans and controls for each financial responsibility center's revenues, expenses, and profits. Both the company at large and each revenue center use: **revenue budgets**, which forecast total revenues from all sources; **expense budgets** for each cost center and the whole organization; and **profit budgets** that simply merge revenue and expense budgets to calculate derived profit – for the organization at large and for each profit center.

Financial budgets detail how each financial responsibility center will manage its cash, and capital expenditures. **Cash budgets** (often called cash flow budgets) project the amount of cash that will flow into and out of an organization and its subsystems during a fixed period. **Capital expenditures** budgets allow managers to project short- and long-term funding needed to acquire capital goods – expensive assets that will be paid for over more than one year.

A S S I G N M E N T S

- Read the Overview, familiarize yourself with the Learning Objectives, and peruse the Key Terms below. Then turn to Plunkett & Attner, *Introduction to Management*, and read Chapter 17, "Control Techniques," pages 518–549.

- Next, scan the Video Viewing Questions and watch the video program for Lesson 19, "It All Adds Up: Financial Methods of Control."

- After watching the video, answer the viewing questions and assess your learning with the Self-Test.

- Familiarize yourself with the Review Questions, Discussion Questions for Critical Thinking, and Skill Building Exercises on page 550 of Plunkett & Attner.

- Strengthen your understanding of the lesson's ideas and issues by undertaking the Expanded Analysis.

K E Y T E R M S

audit A formal investigation conducted to determine if records, statements, and reports – and the data on which they are based – are correct and conform to the organization's policies, rules, and procedures.

balance sheet The listing of a business's assets and both the owner's and outsiders' interests in them; the balance sheet formula is: assets equal liabilities plus owner's or stockholders' equity.

budget Periodic plan and control for the receipt and spending of income over a fixed period.

financial budget The details of how a financial responsibility center will manage its cash and capital expenditures.

financial ratio See ratio.

financial responsibility center An organizxational unit which contributes to an organization's costs, revenues, profits, or investments.

flexible budgeting Budgeting and living within one's budget in accordance with established "meet or beat" standards against which expenditures will be compared.

human asset accounting Treating employees as assets, not expenses, by recording the money spent on people – hiring, training, development, and salaries and wages paid – as increases to the value of those assets.

income statement A listing of the income/revenue and expenses of an organization over a fixed period and the deduction of expenses from income/revenue to determine a profit or loss.

just-in-time (JIT) inventory control The receipt of inventoris on an "as needed" basis; JIT often results in several deliveries per day and in zero or minimal stockage levels.

operating budget A financial plan and control for each finaancial responsibility center's revenues, expenses, and profits.

ratio The expression of the relationship between numbers; the selection of two critical figures from financial statements expressing their relationship in terms of numbers or percentages.

zero-based budgeting A budgeting system that starts from scratch for each period in all spending categories and requires justification for all expense amounts requested for the coming period's plans and goals.

VIDEO VIEWING QUESTIONS

1. Explain how a budget is both a plan and a control.

2. How do the budget, the financial plan, and the business plan relate to one another?

3. At Santa Anita, says Glennon King, there are three primary budgets: operating, cash flow, and capital expenditure. How is each used?

4. Describe "top down" and "bottom up" budgeting techniques and suggest how they are combined.

5. In talking about Santa Anita's marketing budget, Glennon King says, "We evaluate whether [a] promotion in fact was profitable, whether there was an incremental benefit as compared with the incremental cost." How do you think management might know which promotion is "incrementally beneficial" for budgeting purposes?

6. Compare and contrast the functions of the balance sheet and the income statement.

S E L F - T E S T

1. The primary tool that managers use for financial control is the

   a. budget
   b. audit
   c. balance sheet
   d. income statement

2. A budget is an example of a

   a. prevention control.
   b. feedforward control.
   c. feedback control.
   d. any and all of the above, depending upon circumstances.

3. Which of the following statements is **not** true of an effective organizational budget? An effective organizational budget is

   a. based on input from everyone affected by that budget.
   b. highly sensitive to change.
   c. based on thorough research.
   d. useful as a standard for measuring organizational performance.

4. Ideally, the concept of profit should be used as a measure of a manager's financial accountability only when

   a. the manager can influence profits directly through his or her actions or decisions.
   b. other measures of accountability fail to yield a complete picture of performance.
   c. it can be demonstrated that corporate assets outweigh liabilities.
   d. the manager is head of a corporate profit center.

Match each item on the left with one of the labels on the right:

   a. Current Asset
   b. Fixed Asset
   c. Current Liability
   d. Long-term liability

5. Equipment used by a company in manufacturing its products

6. A company trademark

7. A mortgage

8. Product inventory

9. Income taxes

10. A patent

11. Financial ratios can help accountants and managers assess a company's financial health. The main purpose of calculating ratios is to show

a. where a company is likely to be in five or more years.
b. how a company's current performance compares to past performance and to the performance of other companies.
c. where profits are being lost.
d. how close the company is coming to achieving a good balance between income and expenses.

EXPANDED ANALYSIS

1. Arthur Andersen's Gary Peterson says, "There are a lot of key factors in effective financial management, but to me, communication is the key and most important factor, especially as it relates to non-financial people." What does Mr. Peterson mean?

2. Sketch the designs of revenue and expense budgets for a college. Choose whatever type and size you wish for your school, and at any level of complexity you choose, but plan your document accordingly. Identify all likely sources of revenue, and include all the fixed and variable costs you can. Line items will be sufficient; if you come up with some truly creative funding sources, feel free to share them with your instructor.

20 Taking Stock: Production/Operations Management

L E A R N I N G   O B J E C T I V E S

Upon completing this lesson, you should be familiar with the facts, ideas, and processes contained in this lesson, and be able to:

■ Describe the relationship between planning and productivity and quality.

■ Summarize factors to be considered in

    a. locating facilities and designing their layout
    b. determining capacity
    c. developing processes and utilizing technology

■ Describe in general the types of operations controls that are used to verify quality and productivity at various stages in the creation of a product or service.

■ Discuss the significance of managing and controlling the purchase and acquisition of materials.

■ List and briefly describe control techniques used in scheduling.

■ Describe the function and purpose of major product control methods, and when each can be used effectively.

■ Compare principal inventory control methods and indicate how they can assist managers in meeting their objectives.

■ Recognize the ultimate importance of the human factor in creating quality products and services.

O V E R V I E W

The Nature of Operations Management

Operations management consists of the managerial activities and techniques used to convert resources, such as raw materials and labor, into products and services. It embraces design, implementation, and control processes, and in all areas it focuses on improving productivity and quality and, in effect, squeezing the bottom line for profits. While the concepts of operations management tend to conjure up manufacturing, they apply equally to service organizations.

Historically, design planning has not been acknowledged as part of operations management. Marvin Lieberman describes the old approach: "In the U.S. the standard process has been for the design people – let's say it's an automobile company – the design people first design the car, then the term is they `throw it over the wall' to the engineering people." The engineering people do the same to manufacturing. At each step of the way different departments have to go back and forth to correct problems and oversights, which causes costs, delays, re-dos, and compromises in quality. The process almost seems intended to do it wrong and laboriously make it right rather than make it right in the first place.

Japanese companies solved this problem by integrating representatives from later stages of operations into the design process. In Lieberman's description: "They have a design team which would involve design people and engineering people and manufacturing people, so a lot of these communication problems would be eliminated and a lot of the problems of having to rework the design or rework engineering that doesn't fit what the production people can do." This approach, called **design for manufacturability and assembly** (DFMA) improved speed, efficiency, quality, and competitiveness – all of which are key goals in operations management.

Not surprisingly, DFMA is being rapidly adopted in the U.S. and other countries. In many cases integration is being extended even further, with representatives of finance, marketing, customer service, and other departments – and even outside suppliers – being included on design teams. Operations strategy is becoming an increasingly important component of strategic planning.

Planning for Production

After design, the next step in operations management is to plan actual production. Elements of production planning include facility location, facilities layout, capacity, and process and technology.

Facility location involves two decisions: how many facilities should there be and where should they be located? Both decisions connect closely to the company's long-range objectives. Will these be served better by a large number of small facilities, a small number of large facilities, or some combination? And how can facilities be situated to make optimal use of resources, labor pools, costs, markets, and special advantages?

Facilities layout aims at efficiency for the particular operations to be performed. A process layout places all equipment that performs the same function together, which makes efficient use of equipment and people but requires moving product from step to step. A production layout, such as an assembly line, arranges machines and tasks in progressive steps and is most efficient for turning out large volumes of identical products. A cellular layout groups together all the equipment and people required for a sequence of operations on the same product. It requires less moving of product than a process layout, and it's conducive to teamwork. A fixed-position layout involves keeping the product – usually something large like a ship or airline – in one place and moving people and equipment to it.

Capacity planning involves trying to convert sales forecasts into production capabilities. Too little capacity results in failure to meet demand and loss of customers. Excess capacity results in people and facilities sitting idle. A company can increase capacity by building new facilities, refitting existing plants, creating additional shifts and hiring new staff, paying present staff overtime, or subcontracting work to outside firms. It can decrease capacity by laying off workers, reducing hours of operations, or closing facilities. For example, General Motors closed many facilities in the early 1990s when its diminished market share left it with massive over-capacity.

Process and technology are issues of how best to approach the job. Usually they involve questions of how to blend people and technology. On one hand, the trend is toward technology, with new, often computerized machines performing jobs that used to require people. On the other hand, new technologies create new jobs, and one of the recent revolutions in operations management – again spearheaded by the Japanese – has been the development of systems that increase the level of employee performance and involvement in their work.

In manufacturing, several rapidly emerging technologies stand out. **Robotics** replaces people with machines that can perform repetitive, dangerous, or extremely precise tasks. **Computer-aided design** (CAD) allows engineers to develop new products by using a computer monitor to display and manipulate three-dimensional drawings, thus slashing design time and eliminating much of the need to build prototypes for testing. **Computer-assisted manufacturing** (CAM) programs computers to guide and control manufacturing processes, which can reduce waste and costs and improve quality and safety. A **flexible manufacturing system** (FMS) is an automated production line that can be programmed to make rapid model changes and custom variations. And **computer- integrated manufacturing** (CIM) controls production machinery through a system of interconnected computers, and orchestrates people, information, and processes to produce quality products efficiently.

Computers have also revolutionized delivery of services. For example, they have enabled companies like Federal Express and UPS to track orders almost instantaneously. In retail, computerized point-of-sale terminals constantly update inventory records and hasten response to customers' needs.

The Management of Operations

Methods of coordinating overall production activities include aggregate planning, master scheduling, and structuring for operations.

Aggregate planning draws a "road map" for operating activities and resource needs for a period of up to a year. By examining demand and capacity, the operations management team sets materials requirements, production rates, labor needs, and inventory levels.

The **master schedule**, derived from the aggregate plan, specifies the quantity and type of each item to be produced and how, when, and where it should be created. It indicates materials requirements and the level of inventory that will be needed at different times.

Finally, the operations management team must decide how to **structure** departments, which involves questions such as whether and how to use teams, the nature of authority relationships, and the extent of decentralization. The desired result is an integrated, flexible organization structure that can respond to changes in the aggregate plan.

Controls for Quality and Productivity

To achieve high quality and productivity, managers use a number of operation controls over areas including design, materials, scheduling, products, and inventory.

Design controls focus on creating new products engineered for reliability, functionality, and serviceability. As discussed earlier, a team approach can enable managers to integrate quality and performance controls during the design stage.

Materials control is achieved through effective purchasing. Production depends on the availability of materials and supplies. Purchasing used to focus largely on quantity, but increasing attention is being paid to quality. In place of the old practice of pitting suppliers against each other in dog-eat-dog price competition, managers are developing long-term relationships with fewer suppliers and expecting suppliers, in return for steady business, to guarantee to meet quality specifications.

There are two basic **scheduling control** techniques. A Gantt chart tracks a project from beginning to end, comparing the time estimates for the steps involved with the actual time they require and adjusting the starting and ending times of steps if necessary. Gantt charts are linear and work best for scheduling and tracking sequential events. For projects that involve different operations that run simultaneously, network scheduling accommodates a more complex mesh of events (circles) with processes (lines and arrows). An adaptation of network scheduling called Program Evaluation Review Technique (PERT) assigns four different time estimates to each activity – optimistic, most likely, pessimistic, and expected – and provides managers with a graphic view of trouble spots when a project falls behind schedule.

At one time the entire concept of operations control focused on inspection of the physical product. With the advent of Total Quality Management, inspection was placed in a new perspective as only one part of controlling. Now **product control** utilizes a number of techniques to encompass controls from purchasing to end use. Acceptance sampling inspects a representative group of products prior to the beginning of any new phase of production and determines whether entire batches are accepted or rejected. When it's critical to detect all parts that do not meet standards – for example, with medicines – detailed inspections and tests are used instead of sampling. These also serve to pinpoint inadequate processes. Control sampling uses periodic tests to correct problems as they occur. And qualification testing extensively examines sample products for performance, reliability, and safety. New car models, for example, are driven hundreds of thousands of miles so engineers can test the overall car and its components.

Inventory control is critical to operations management because inventory can represent a massive investment. Most organizations carry three types of inventory – raw materials, work-in-process, and finished goods – and the investment in any material increases as work is performed on it. Ironically, managers once prided themselves on maintaining large inventories as a measure of wealth. Managers today recognize that a large inventory ties up money that could be used elsewhere and represents a tremendous waste.

Various techniques have been developed to keep inventory to the minimum necessary to sustain operations. Economic order quantity (EOQ) uses several formulae to calculate ordering and holding costs in relation to the rate of inventory use. **Materials requirement planning** (MRP) facilitates ordering large numbers of interrelated components, such as in airplane assembly, by forecasting customer orders, analyzing product design, and determining all the parts and supplies needed to manufacture the finished product. **Manufacturing resource planning**

(MRPII) is a comprehensive planning system that coordinates all of a firm's resources with its production and materials management. It creates a model of the overall business, allowing top managers to control production scheduling, cash flow, human resources, capacity, inventory, purchasing, and distribution.

Just-in-time inventory control – another Japanese innovation – arranges for deliveries from suppliers to arrive just as they are needed for production. Thomas Everhart, President of Caltech, sketches the consequences:

> *You have only the few parts that you need around to assemble, rather than a vast number of each of the parts. So it tightens up the production line. It speeds up the process. It cuts down the storage space. It means the factory can be smaller. And since the cost-per-unit of the factory is an important part of the cost of producing something, through the depreciation of the space and so on, it really does improve the productivity and the cost of making things.*

Just-in-time inventory control exemplifies a general rule of operations management, in which waste in any area is likely to lead to waste elsewhere, and efficiency in any area is likely to lead to efficiency elsewhere and tighter integration of operations as a whole. In the just-in-time philosophy, inventory is compared to the water in a river. When the inventory level is high, it covers up the problems of the company, which are like rocks at the bottom of the river. When a company lowers its inventory, it exposes these problems and makes it easier to remove them.

ASSIGNMENTS

- Read the Overview, familiarize yourself with the Learning Objectives, and peruse the Key Terms below. Then turn to Plunkett & Attner, *Introduction to Management*, and read Chapter 18, "Operations Management," pages 552–581.

- Next, scan the Video Viewing Questions and watch the video program for Lesson 20, "Taking Stock: Production/Operations Management."

- After watching the video, answer the viewing questions and assess your learning with the Self-Test.

- Familiarize yourself with the Review Questions, Discussion Questions for Critical Thinking, and Skill Building Exercises on page 582 Plunkett & Attner.

■ Strengthen your understanding of the lesson's ideas and issues by undertaking the Expanded Analysis.

KEY TERMS

acceptance sampling A product control technique in which inspection is made on a sample of items prior to the beginning of the next phase.

aggregate planning An element of operations management that involves the planning of production activities and the resources needed to achieve them.

CAD/CAM CAD (computer-aided design) and CAM (computer-assisted manufacturing) are computer technologies used in manufacturing environments.

capacity planning An element of operations planning which determines the organization's capability to produce the desired number of products or services to match demand.

computer-integrated manufacturing (CIM) A technology in which computers coordinate people, information, and processes to produce quality products efficiently.

continuous-improvement process (*kaizen*) The ongoing search for incremental betterment.

control sampling A product control technique designed to detect variations in production processes and workmanship.

design controls An area of operations control that focuses on engineering reliability, functionality, and serviceability into new products.

design for manufacturability and assembly (DFMA) Designing products for functionality while simultaneously considering how they will be manufactured and assembled.

detailed inspection and tests A product control technique in which thorough examinations or performance tests are made on every finished item.

economic order quantity (EOQ) An inventory technique that helps managers determine how much material to order by minimizing the total of ordering costs and holding costs based on the organization's usage rate.

facilities layout The element of operations planning concerned with the physical arrangement of equipment and work flow.

flexible manufacturing system (FMS) A technology in which an automated production line is coordinated by computers.

Gantt chart A scheduling and control technique that uses a graph to plan and control a process with sequential events.

just-in-time inventory system (JIT) A technique for inventory control designed to eliminate raw material and supply inventories by coordinating production and supply deliveries.

manufacturing resource planning (MRPII) A comprehensive planning system that controls the total resources of the firm.

master scheduling An element of operations management which specifies the quantity and type of each item to be produced and how, when, and where it should be produced.

materials requirement planning (MRP) A production planning and inventory system that uses forecasts of customer orders to schedule the exact amount of materials needed to support the end product.

operation management The managerial activities directed toward the processes used by an organization to convert resources like raw materials and labor into products and services.

outsourcing A purchasing strategy in which a company contracts with a supplier to perform functions in lieu of the company performing the functions themselves.

PERT Program Evaluation and Review Technique; A network scheduling technique that plans and charts the progress of a complex project in terms of the time it is expected to take, an estimated derived from probability analysis.

productivity The determination of how much input is needed to produce an amount of output, usually expressed as a ratio.

product control A component of operations control concerned with reducing both the probability and costs of poor quality and unrealistic products by exerting controls from purchasing to end use.

project improvement team A group of people engaged in executing a project whose purpose is to make the subject project better.

qualification testing A product control technique in which products are tested for performance on the basis of reliability and safety.

quality The totality of features and characteristics of a product, service, or process that bear on its ability to satisfy stated or implied goals or requirements of producers and users of the outcomes. For a compelling analysis of quality, see Robert Pirsig's *Zen and the Art of Motorcycle Maintenance* (New York: William Morrow, 1974).

quality improvement team A team composed of people from all functional areas of a company who meet regularly to assess progress toward goals, identify and work to solve common problems, and cooperate to plan for the future.

quality control (QC) A system of production methods which economically produces quality goods or services meeting the requirements of customers; uses statistical measures and methods and is often called statistical quality control (SQC).

robotics The use of programmed machines to handle production in place of people.

total quality management (TQM/TQC) A strategy for continuously and comprehensively improving performance at every level, and in all areas of responsibility throughout an organization.

VIDEO VIEWING QUESTIONS

1. How can separation among departments detract from overall efficiency?

2. How does "listening to customers" influence operations management at Rutherford Hill Winery?

3. What factors have influenced facility location and facilities layout at Rutherford Hill?

4. How does just-in-time inventory control contrast with a just-in-case mode of production?

5. How do computers and other technological developments contribute to integration of operations?

6. How does Convair integrate employee empowerment and continuous improvement (*kaizen*) into operations management?

S E L F - T E S T

1. The element **not** conventionally included in the flow of operations that produce goods and services is

   a. inputs.
   b. the transformation processes.
   c. advertising of outputs.
   d. the output of products and services.

2. Product and service design for manufacturability and assembly involves four concepts. Which of those listed below does **not** belong?

   a. Cost
   b. Marketability
   c. Quality
   d. Reliability

3. Four main types of facilities layouts are currently much used in manufacturing plant design. Which of those listed below does **not** belong?

   a. Fixed-position layout
   b. Cellular Layout
   c. Process layout
   d. Product layout
   e. Sequential layout

4. The manufacture of very large or hugely complex products, like Boeing 747s or Cray Supercomputers, are most likely to use which type of facilities layout?

   a. Cellular
   b. Fixed position
   c. Production
   d. Process

5. A small publisher of cookbooks moving a number of titles through acquisition, writing, editorial, design, printing, and distribution steps would be most likely to use which of these production control devices?

   a. A PERT chart
   b. Network scheduling
   c. A Gantt chart
   d. Manufacturing Resource Planning

6. Many companies today rely on computerized inventory control systems. Perhaps the main reason for this reliance is that

   a. the vast amounts of data needed in a modern inventory control system cannot be processed efficiently any other way.
   b. in the computer age, this approach is demanded by boards of directors.
   c. computers take the place of inventory control specialists
   d. such a system eliminates most conventional administrative costs associated with inventory control.

7. A good computerized inventory control system will do all of the following **except**

   a. identify every item in the inventory by its unique number.
   b. pinpoint all inventory shortages.
   c. identify all items for which current supply is below probable demand.
   d. project which items will become obsolete in a given time frame.

8. Prototypes of a car were built to test the ease of manufacture. In response to an observation that three different sizes of wrenches were required on various fasteners for a single part, engineers simplified the design by making all the fasteners the same. This is an example of

   a. design for manufacturability and assembly (DFMA).
   b. design for disassembly (DFD).
   c. qualification testing.
   d. operations management.

9. A purchasing strategy in which a company contracts with a supplier to perform functions in lieu of performing them themselves is called

   a. finished goods inventory.
   b. outsourcing.
   c. just in time inventory.
   d. acquisition control.

10. Operations management applies to

    a. service organizations only.
    b. organizations that produce goods only.
    c. organizations that produce goods and services.
    d. organizations that produce neither goods nor services.

EXPANDED ANALYSIS

1. While the principles of operations management clearly apply to manufacturing and many kinds of service companies, their usefulness in some settings may not be readily apparent. Do you think those principles might benefit the operation of a large university or a major sports franchise? Choose one of these two operations, or both if you would enjoy the challenge, and suggest suitable operations management applications for a university setting. Consider service design planning, facility location and layout planning, operations control, materials and inventory control, technology planning, and schedule control.

21

Point of Information: Information Systems Management

L E A R N I N G   O B J E C T I V E S

Upon completing this lesson, you should be familiar with the facts, ideas, and processes contained in this lesson, and be able to:

- Identify the categories of information that are important in managing a business, whatever the size.

- Give examples of technological systems currently enhancing productivity in the workplace.

- Compare Management Information Systems (MIS) and Decision Support Systems (DSS) and their utility as management tools.

- Suggest business situations in which Artificial Intelligence and Expert Systems might be valuable and cost effective.

- Discuss the social and organizational impact of information system technologies.

Information is an inherent and vital component of everything a manager does, or contemplates. Its universality places information and its competent use at the top of every manager's priority list. Not only managers, but every member of the organization, must have quality information in order to act intelligently and make sound decisions.

In order to create useful information, raw data must be selected, processed, and organized in some meaningful pattern. The term **useful** means that the information is understandable, reliable, relevant (concise), sufficient (complete), timely, and cost effective. Further, it must be conveyed to those who need it in an undistorted and immediately useable form. In addition to acquiring sufficient quantities of information, those responsible for gathering and processing data must take care that everything formally entered into the system is accurate, consistent with fact, actual, and verifiable. Conjectural or speculative material must be so identified.

The Information Needed by Managers

An immense volume and variety of information flows through every organization. The particular information managers need varies with their position, functional assignments, and management level. Both line and staff managers require operational information, for instance, and line managers often utilize staff-specific information. Production, marketing, and finance and accounting managers all have topical information needs. Top-level managers need information on strategic and wide-ranging external factors; middle managers need information on their particular divisions and operations; lower-level managers and autonomous teams need information and feedback about daily, weekly, and monthly activities.

Management Information Systems

Managers have always needed information. The accelerating technology of the modern era vastly expanded the scope and complexity of organizations and their need for information of every kind. Increasingly, managers found that their need for quality information was outstripping their organization's capacity to gather and process data efficiently. From that recognition arose the idea of consolidating information-related activities into a dedicated management information system.

In its contemporary form, a **management information system** (MIS) is a formal collection of processes through which managers obtain necessary and sufficient information to discharge their functions effectively and efficiently. The basic work of an MIS can be done manually, and often still is at small or fledgling firms. But today's information management at a growing proportion of companies of all sizes largely relies upon computers. A **computerized information system** (CIS) is an MIS built upon computer hardware and software to collect and process data and store and disseminate the resulting information. Such reliance generates this synopsis: An MIS (CIS) gathers and transmits data (input); combines and files data (conversion); and retrieves, formats, and displays information (output). MIS (CIS) managers monitor progress and ensure that the system performs as designed.

Developing an MIS

Putting a new MIS in place requires common sense and imagination. Ideally the process starts with an assessment of user needs, both to determine the best design and to promote acceptance by people who might otherwise resist the change. A successful MIS does not merely make old practices more efficient; it can also significantly alter basic management. Says UC Irvine's John King:

> The special thing that the MIS vision provides is the ability to take the information you already have for operational uses – for control, accounting, etc. – and apply it to management problems like planning for the future, strategic thinking about where you should be going next, marketing your products, new product development and design. That's the vision of management information systems. It's to move information to the foreground of planning for the future.

Most experts agree that installers of an MIS should involve its users in the system's design; establish clear lines of authority and direction for MIS personnel; establish clear procedures for system operation; clarify the roles of technical specialists; and build an MIS staff consistent with service requirements. Equally importantly, an MIS should (1) meet organizational objectives, (2) provide information flow, and (3) deliver the right quality and quantity of information.

CIS Tools for Managers

Computers are enormously useful to managers in every management function, but their greatest strength may be in the realm of information management. An example is a variant of CIS called the **decision support system (DSS). By joining the manager's experience, judgment, and** intuition to the computer's data access, display, and calculation strengths, the DSS allows managers to manipulate models and stored data to display likely outcomes.

Another variant of decision support programs is the **expert system** – software that stores the knowledge of an authority or group of authorities for application to suitable problems. Such programs are occasionally characterized under the label of **artificial intelligence** (AI) – the use of computers to model the behavioral aspects of human reasoning and learning. Consultant Steven Cerri amplifies: "The concept of artificial intelligence is that we can take certain decision-making processes that a human being would use and put them in an electronic medium, into a computer. The concept is that I can take rational as well as subjective processes that a human being would go through, and put them into a computer – that was the ideal." Practical applications in business remain limited.

Another decision support variation is the **group decision support system** (GDSS), which allows group members to exchange information and ideas interactively and functions as an analytical support system. **Executive information systems** (EIS) constitute still another variant, and emphasize forecasting, strategic planning, risk and cost-benefit analyses, and other senior management concerns.

Consultant Steven Cerri emphasizes that a CIS can be considerably more than the sum of its parts: "As computers began to evolve . . . executives began to realize that there is all kinds of information that exists within their database, within their computer systems, that can allow them to get a glimpse of issues and of trends and of concepts that they would never be able to access without this computer system having all this information." That potential for dynamic synergy should be a part of every manager's thinking.

A related phenomenon of information management in today's companies is the tendency of CIS implementation to generate opportunities for integration, networking, and sharing throughout the organization. To promote efficiency and effectiveness, functions and processes must be linked both by networks and often by physical proximity.

Emerging Information Technologies

The success of information systems depends upon imaginative conception, skilled application, and flexibility. The seemingly endless proliferation of new information technology and imaginative applications has infused the field of MIS with rising expectations. Today's systems, it is suggested by some observers, contain the nucleus for still greater change. Consider this observation from John King: "The objective . . . is to create an apparatus that takes data from lots of different sources and . . . [puts] those data together in a way that creates information for people to use to do something differently, to change their minds, to try something that they haven't tried before. This is . . . where the big payoffs are supposed to happen." But King adds an important cautionary note of realism:

> *You are dealing with the intersection of very complicated, very fast changing technology – computer technology – that's altering in its capacity, in its price performance, in its ability to do things literally on a daily basis, together with just the complex world of organizations. So when you put together rapidly changing technology with the inherent complexities of organizations, you've already got something that's hard to do. Building systems to deal with management problems using technology is a very big challenge.*

ASSIGNMENTS

- Read the Overview, familiarize yourself with the Learning Objectives, and peruse the Key Terms below. Then turn to Plunkett & Attner, *Introduction to Management*, and read Chapter 19, "Information Management Systems," pages 584–605.

- Next, scan the Video Viewing Questions and watch the video program for Lesson 21, "Point of Information: Information Systems Management."

- After watching the video, answer the viewing questions and assess your learning with the Self-Test.

- Familiarize yourself with the Review Questions, Discusson Questions for Critical Thinking, and Skill Building Exercises on page 606 of Plunkett & Attner.

- Strengthen your understanding of the lesson's ideas and issues by undertaking the Expanded Analysis.

KEY TERMS

artificial intelligence (AI) The ability of a machine to perform those activities that are normally thought to require intelligence; giving machines the capability to learn, sense, and think for themselves.

computerized information system (CIS) An MIS built upon computer hardware and software to collect and process data and store and disseminate the resulting information.

data Unprocessed facts and figures.

database A collection of (computerized) data arranged for ease and speed of retrieval; sometimes called data bank.

decision support system (DSS) A specialized variant of CIS, an analytic model that joins a manager's experience, judgment and intuition to the computer's data access, display, and calculation processes; allows managers to interact with linked programs and databases through the keyboard.

distributed data processing (DDP) Computer systems in which two or more using organizations can share information and tap into common databases to monitor and modify transactions; sometimes called electronic data interchange.

executive information system (EIS) A decision support system custom designed to facilitate executive decision making; may include forecasting; strategic planning and other elements.

expert system A specialized end-user decision support program that stores the knowledge of a group of authorities for access by non-experts faced with the need to make topic-related decisions.

group decision support system (GDSS) A variant decision support system that allows groups focusing on a problem to interact with one another and to exchange information, data, and ideas.

information Data that have been deliberately selected, processed, and organized to be useful to an individual manager.

management information system (MIS) A formal collection of processes that provides managers with suitable quality information to allow them to make decisions, solve problems, and carry out their functions and operations effectively and efficiently.

networking The electronic linking of two or more computers.

VIDEO VIEWING QUESTIONS

1. Describe Apple Computer's use of information systems in its marketing operations. In what other applications does Apple appear to be using CIS as a management tool?

2. Identify some of the applications for computer information technology at the "front line" of a service company's operations.

3. How does Solectron appear to use its CIS capabilities on the product manufacturing line?

4. UC Irvine's John King and Kenneth Kraemer identify two principal causes for the failure of information systems. What are they?

5. Kenneth Kraemer speaks of the "linkages" that make information management systems effective. Identify those linkages and how they work.

6. Consultant Stephen Cerri tells how Campbell Soup used its computer systems to "compensate" for the retirement of their chief of soup recipes. What kind of a system did they construct?

S E L F - T E S T

1. Which of the following pairs best characterizes useful information?

   a. Concise and reliable
   b. Timely and incomplete
   c. Relevant and somewhat outdated
   d. Exhaustive and excessive

2. The information most needed by top managers

   a. appears in quarterly figures on quality, productivity, and schedules.
   b. is contained in current reports on employee attrition, positions opening, and new hires.
   c. covers economic conditions, legal developments, and the activities of competitors.
   d. includes sales quotas and their achievement.

3. Management Information Systems may be expected to perform each of the following **except:**

   a. gather and transmit information
   b. retrieve, format, and display information
   c. refine decisions on corporate strategy
   d. combine and store data

4. The first step related to the installation of an MIS should probably be

   a. notification from top management that the system is going to be installed.
   b. selection of the software needed to run the system.
   c. choice of the hardware needed to run the system.
   d. a survey of potential users of the system.

5. An Expert System is a computer-based system

   a. designed to make complex managerial decisions.
   b. that allows application of previously accumulated technical knowledge and experience to suitable problems in a decision support system.
   c. that surveys databases for technical information.
   d. that cannot be utilized by inexperienced staff.

6. Wide area networks

   a. facilitate computer aided manufacture by linking plans and production machinery.
   b. are a world-wide network of computers linked by phone lines.
   c. allow companies to link their remote operations and to connect them to the operations of their customers, partners, and suppliers.
   d. is a decision support system.

7. Executive information systems

   a. should be operated separately from other other corporate information files for security reasons.
   b. are specialized decisions support systems that facilitate decision making by senior management.
   c. are too sophisticated and costly for any but the largest companies.

8. Which of the following statements is **not** consistent with initial installation and management of a computerized information system?

   a. Information specialists should become familiar with the intended users' analytic techniques before designing the system.
   b. For a small company, if an "off-the-shelf" program is not available to meet their needs, it may be most efficient to postpone the project until the firm is bigger.
   c. Substantial familiarization and training is necessary for everyone who will use the system.
   d. Management by exception is a concept well suited to a CIS because it allows system operators to focus on key indicators for management action.

9. In general, when selecting or designing and implementing a CIS,

   a. managers should anticipate an immediate improvement in the quality of decision making in all affected departments.
   b. managers should not worry about employee resistance to the new system, because as soon as staffers see how much more productive they can be, they'll accept the change.
   c. permit long-time employees to continue to use existing information handling procedures for as long as they wish if they are uncomfortable with the new technology.
   d. plan on regularly updating the system as new technology and experience require.

10. A computer application program is

   a. any program designed to let a computer system accomplish specific sets of tasks.
   b. the software that controls the operation of the computer itself.
   c. software used by the human resources department to process new hires.
   d. software designed to assist managers in selecting the best applications for a particular company.

E X P A N D E D   A N A L Y S I S

1. The computer's capacity to store and allow swift access to huge quantities and varieties of information has undoubtedly changed the way managers manage. One way is the dramatic increases in the speed and precision of certain operations. A second and more important effect may be the radical changes in the way whole industries conduct their affairs. Can you think of one such industry and briefly describe some of the differences computer information management has caused in its operation?

22 Above and Beyond: Managing for Productivity

Upon completing this lesson, you should be familiar with the facts, ideas, and processes contained in this lesson, and be able to:

- Define the concept of **productivity**: what it is, what it isn't, and how it is measured.

- Explain how productivity, quality, and profitability relate.

- Describe the ways in which each of the following affects an organization's productivity:

  a. government influences
  b. union/management relations
  c. quality of the workforce

- Examine the various ways management can influence and encourage productivity improvement.

O V E R V I E W

Productivity, Quality, and Profitability

Marvin Lieberman offers a clear definition and illustration of **productivity**:

> *Productivity is output per unit of input. If you were thinking of an automobile factory, for example, you might measure the number of cars produced as output. The inputs would be the workers – in other words, the amount of labor that's needed by this plant – the amount of capital or equipment that's used in the plant, and also the amount of materials that are used, parts that are bought from suppliers, energy that is required to run the plant. So, if you were able to increase the number of cars and keep the plant fixed and keep the number of people fixed, you have in effect raised the productivity of that plant. Or if the number of cars stays constant, and you're able to reduce the number of people, or the amount of materials or energy, then you've also raised the productivity of the plant. So, productivity is output divided by all of these inputs.*

The purpose of productivity measurement is to help managers examine critical aspects of production. It can be used to compare countries, industries, companies in an industry, or operations within a company. There is no one formula for measuring productivity. It is usually measured either in terms of a single-factor index, such as output per hour of labor or output per amount of capital invested, or a **combined-factor index**, such as Lieberman's, which integrates different inputs into one overall measure. Even broader measures attempt to take into account factors such as quality and sales, since a product or service that doesn't sell can hardly be described as productive.

Indeed, the connection between productivity and quality is profound and has only recently become widely recognized. Through most of the twentieth century America thrived through simple mass production. In the absence of competitors, the amount of goods the country turned out generated enormous domestic and international sales and prosperity at home. The relatively high amount of waste created by concentrating on quantity and speed hardly seemed worth considering.

But as Japan and Germany recovered from the devastation of World War II, and as nations around the globe industrialized, competition increased. The Japanese, through the influence of W. Edwards Deming and others, radically improved standards of quality, captured large shares of many markets, and forced the consideration of quality as a major factor in productivity. George Labovitz sums up the new view:

The cost of quality is very simply defined as the price you pay for not being perfect. One of the great gurus, Dr. Deming, says that in manufacturing organizations the cost of quality can represent 25% of all costs, in service organizations 30% of gross sales. If you add up the waste, the scrap, the lost customers, God forbid, the explosion in your refinery, the law suits, if you add it all up, in any business that you are in, it's an enormous number.

Quality can be defined in various ways (see Lesson 9), but in terms of competitiveness and profitability, none is more important than customer satisfaction. The standard which Japanese automakers and other companies have taught American competitors is that, beyond just selling a product, it's critical to create products that customers will buy, enjoy, tell their friends about, and buy again.

A Brief Look at American Productivity

The bind in which American companies find themselves can be gauged by pressures from two different directions.

America is still the most productive country in the world, but Germany and Japan are gaining and improving their productivity at far faster rates. Reasons for their gains include faster adaptation to new products and manufacturing processes, greater investment per capita in capital equipment and other aids to productivity, and higher rates of savings among citizens. Indebtedness – whether personal, corporate, or national – reduces leverage to buy or invest.

From another standpoint, America, Germany, and Japan have much higher labor costs than developing nations, and labor costs are one of the major inputs needed for productivity. The contrast is particularly ironic for America, since the low-cost products associated with mass production once enabled it to dominate world markets. The question becomes, how other than by reducing wages and standard of living can America compete? Sanford Jacoby points to a possible answer – and the "or else" factor if it fails:

One thing that American companies are discovering is that we have an edge in the knowledge area, and in the quality area. It's that human capital rather than the physical capital that will hopefully give American companies an edge in the years to come. Otherwise, we're going to be sunk in the global marketplace, because we can't compete any longer on the basis of cost.

Factors that Affect Productivity

Before turning to the central question of how management can improve productivity, several other influences need to be considered.

First, government influence is vast and far-reaching. Tax policies can attract business or drive it away. Capital spending on infrastructure (roads, bridges, power plants, etc.) creates support conditions vital to many businesses. Regulatory policies, although necessary to benefit citizens and protect the environment, can impose burdens that cause companies to move operations abroad. And a large federal deficit tends to push interest rates higher than in competing nations and make it difficult for businesses to borrow funds.

Another major influence on productivity is exerted by unions. For the decades when America had little real competition abroad, unions played an active role in winning workers a fair share of profits, but in some cases they've become locked into inflexible positions and adversarial relations with management. World competition makes it crucial for unions and management to learn to act more as partners, sharing strategic decisions and cooperating in efforts to enable workers to become more productive.

A third major influence on productivity is the quality of the workforce. Few factors will attract business to a country or region as readily as the availability of educated, skilled workers. The Educational Testing Service points out that American 13-year-olds rate below Asian, European, and Canadian children in math and science. In some ways this challenge resounds back to government to improve the educational system, but responsibility also falls on individuals. The day when an unskilled worker could punch in at the same plant for 40 years and accumulate raises and job security is past. Today's workers, if they want to rise beyond flipping hamburgers at fast-food restaurants, need to come to work able and willing to take on complex challenges.

In early 1992, two high-ranking Japanese officials raised a storm of protest by criticizing American workers as lazy and illiterate. While the educational challenge is ongoing and the average American worker does put in somewhat fewer hours than the average Japanese (44 per week, versus 52), American workers have generally proven themselves capable of rising to challenges. For instance, Japanese auto and other plants in America have achieved almost the same level of performance as those in Japan. George Labovitz reports another sobering message to management that goes back to Dr. Deming:

Deming argues that only five percent or so of all the systems problems in organizations, very generally, are caused by people making mistakes, people doing the right thing wrong. The trouble is they are doing the wrong thing. Seventy, eighty percent of most of the problems in organizations are systems problems. That's another big `ah ha' in total quality. The culprits are not people making mistakes. The culprits are us, the management. We're responsible for the processes and the systems that drive behavior.

Managing for Productivity

If the cause behind many of America's productivity problems is outdated processes and systems, then managers must become committed to changing them. Commitment involves flexibility and willingness to break old habits. Managers need to learn the messages that have come via Japan to empower and involve workers, and to improve efficiency, effectiveness, and time-management to bring higher quality products to market faster.

Commitment also involves swallowing the bitter pill of costs, particularly in long-term investment. William Lareau points out the Achilles heel of American management:

> *American business is in trouble because we have an almost fanatic obsession with short-term results. Everything has to be better next week, next month, next quarter, next six months. We never take the long view, and consequently what we've done is, for the last forty years, we've sold our future away to look good next month.*

The first major area of long-term investment necessary to productivity is training. Even the best educated employees will see their capabilities wither in an organization that doesn't provide the means for them to increase and adapt their skills to meet new challenges. Gurminder Bedi, Director of Quality at Ford Motor Company, observes: "Training is absolutely the fundamental point of getting more productivity. The only way you could really improve anybody, other than improving the method of how they do the work, is to train them."

The second major area of long-term investment is research and development. From research projects come new materials, machines, methods, technologies, and products. Robert Galvin, Chairman of Motorola's Executive Committee, describes the benefit in contemporary terms: "Research and development in telecommunications or in biotechnology or whatever it is, represents the multiplier that causes all of us to be able to do more business and thus create more wealth." America has a distinguished tradition of funding research and development, beginning with Thomas Edison and expanding through unparalleled government support of university research. But in recent decades America's investment in research and development, measured as a percentage of Gross Domestic Product, has fallen behind that of nearly half a dozen other nations.

The third crucial area of long-term investment is in capital improvements. The message behind the Industrial Revolution – if not the Stone Age – is that productivity is a function of workers **and** tools. In 1989, for the first time, Japanese business outspent American businesses in capital improvements – a shocking statistic given that the Japanese economy is half the size of the American. We are well into an era of astonishing technological development. For the foreseeable future the rate of change appears likely only to accelerate. For any company, updating its equipment and facilities to keep abreast of technological breakthroughs is an expensive game to play . . . but the alternative is to move to the sidelines.

ASSIGNMENTS

- Read the Overview, familiarize yourself with the Learning Objectives, and peruse the Key Terms below. Then turn to Plunkett & Attner, *Introduction to Management*, and read Chapter 3, "Management's Commitment to Quality and Productivity," pages 62–89.

- Next, scan the Video Viewing Questions and watch the video program for Lesson 22, "Above and Beyond: Managing for Productivity."

- After watching the video, answer the viewing questions and assess your learning with the Self-Test.

- Familiarize yourself with the Review Questions, Discussion Questions for Critical Thinking, and Skill Building Exercises on pages 89–90 of Plunkett & Attner.

- Strengthen your understanding of the lesson's ideas and issues by undertaking the Expanded Analysis.

KEY TERMS

<u>benchmark</u> A standard by which something can be measured or judged; the level to match or exceed in design, manufacture, performance, and service.

<u>continuous-improvement process (kaizen)</u> The ongoing search for incremental betterment.

<u>process improvement team</u> A group of people assigned to cooperatively assess a process and make is better.

<u>productivity</u> The determination of how much input is needed to produce an amount of output, usually expressed as a ratio.

<u>project improvement team</u> A group of people engaged in executing a project whose purpose is to make the subject project better.

<u>quality</u> The totality of features and characteristics of a product, service, or process that bear on its ability to satisfy stated or implied goals or requirements of producers and users of the outcomes. For a compelling analysis of quality, see Robert Pirsig's *Zen and the Art of Motorcycle Maintenance* (New York: William Morrow, 1974).

quality audit A determination of how well customer or consumer requirements are being met by an organization, product, service, or process; may include recommendations and actual implementation of corrections to discrepancies.

quality circle A small group of employees who meet, as part of their jobs, to improve their unit's processes, products, and services.

quality control (QC) A system of production methods which economically produces quality goods or services meeting the requirements of customers; uses statistical measures and methods and is often called statistical quality control (SQC).

quality control audit A check on an organization's and its systems' quality control efforts; two questions are asked and answered: "How are we doing?" and "What are the problems?"

quality function deployment A disciplined approach to solving quality problems before the design phase of a product; research discovers and ranks customer needs for translation into design specifications.

quality improvement team A team composed of people from all functional areas of a company who meet regularly to assess progress toward goals, identify and work to solve common problems, and cooperate to plan for the future.

research and development (R&D) Resources invested to guarantee an organization's future by discovering, acquiring, and providing the processes, materials, and products to be funded over the short- and long-term.

statistical process control (SPC) The application to processes of statistical tools and methods to measure and predict variations; establishes boundaries to determine if a process is in control (predictable) or out of control (unpredictable).

statistical quality control (SQC) The use of statistical tools and methods to determine the quality of a product or service.

VIDEO VIEWING QUESTIONS

1. How did Edison's "invention factory" (research laboratory) start a revolution in productivity?

2. How are a nation's schools vital to its long-term productivity?

3. What is the relationship between quality and productivity at Domaine Chandon?

4. How has W. Edwards Deming promoted understanding of the relationship between quality and productivity?

5. How did Henry Ford's mass production assembly line revolutionize standards of productivity in its day?

6. How has Ford Motor Company used Deming's "systems" approach to increase productivity?

7. How does employee involvement contribute to productivity at Ford? At Domaine Chandon?

S E L F - T E S T

1. If any productivity plan is going to succeed over the long term, it must possess several essential characteristics. Which of the following is **not** among them? The plan must

   a. be modeled on an existing plan that's been tried and proven effective.
   b. have the support of all the staff who will implement it.
   c. be part of an ongoing long-range plan that's reflected in the corporate budget.
   d. feature a built-in provision to reward those who help it succeed.

2. The relationship between quality and productivity

   a. is powerful and immediate, because a decline in either one cripples the other.
   b. cannot be known because each phenomenon is essentially unmeasurable.
   c. is insignificant.
   d. is only marginally significant.

3. Decreasing the amount of input required to generate a fixed amount of output results in improved

   a. employee morale.
   b. quality.
   c. productivity.
   d. quality and productivity. The two are inseparable.

4. Joseph Juran cautioned that moving toward improvement means change and change breeds resistance and fear. He suggests **all but one** of the following to minimize the resistance to change:

   a. provide participation
   b. establish new leadership
   c. treat people with dignity
   d. look at the alternatives

5. If any productivity/quality improvement plan is going to succeed for the long term, it must have several critical characteristics. Which of the following is **not** one of them? The plan must

   a. be modeled on an existing plan that's been tried and proven effective.
   b. have the support of all staff who will implement it.
   c. be part of an ongoing long-range plan that's reflected in the corporate budget.
   d. feature a built-in provision to reward those who help it succeed.

6. Designing quality into a product is an approach called

   a. quality function deployment (QFD).
   b. statistical quality control (SCQ).
   c. total quality management (TQM).
   d. none of the above.

Match each of the following terms with correct definition below:
   a. Kaisen
   b. Benchmark
   c. Productivity
   d. Quality

7. The product to meet or beat in terms of design, manufacture, performance, and service.

8. The relationship between the amount of input needed to produce a given amount of output and the output itself.

9. An approach to improvement that calls for gradual but continual efforts.

10. The ability of a product to meet or exceed customer expectations and needs

E X P A N D E D   A N A L Y S I S

1. Many commentators suggest that the most important single weakness in U.S. productivity, both now and for the future, is the troubled state of American education, particularly at the kindergarten through 12th grade level. Education is normally assumed to be a responsibility of the public sector, and business primarily a function of the private sector. What role should private companies play in education? Suggest specific steps individual companies and business at large might undertake to improve American education, particularly as it relates to business.

23 World of Opportunity: Managing in a Global Environment

Upon completing this lesson, you should be familiar with the facts, ideas, and processes contained in this lesson, and be able to:

- Discuss the impact of globalization of business and mounting economic interdependency of nations on business management.

- Describe today's international management environment and identify some management attitudes and practices needed to operate successfully in this environment.

- Suggest the variety of international business ventures now underway and likely to be developed soon.

- Describe defining characteristics of multinational firms.

- Selecting one country or region as the location for a multinational business venture, suggest what an American manager must learn about each of these elements in the host location in order to accomplish the assignment:

  a. the country's political, economic, and legal systems.
  b. culture and social customs.
  c. workforce expectations and technological sophistication.

- Compare the risks and rewards of multinational business operations.

- Discuss ways in which managers can "protect" stakeholder interests in international environments they cannot control.

O V E R V I E W

Globalization and its Impact

In recent decades, international trade and investment have multiplied many times over. Companies no longer just send goods and services to compete in global markets; they set up operations in each other's back yards. Giant U.S. firms such as Exxon, IBM, Mobil, Citicorp, and Xerox derive over half of their profits from foreign investments, and firms from Britain, Japan, and other countries have invested hundreds of billions of dollars in the United States. The fall of the Iron Curtain and of numerous trade barriers have opened vast new markets.

Globalization is an umbrella term that covers many different activities, including exporting products and services; locating operations outside one's national borders; using foreign partners to help in research and development and to sell products and services around the world; and tailoring strategies, management functions, and products and services to meet the needs of customers worldwide.

Before focusing on issues that companies face as they go global, it may be useful to put globalization in broad perspective. Prior to the Industrial Revolution, economies were largely local. Certain products might come from various distances (tea from China), but the crude state of transportation made it necessary to generate most goods and services locally. (The exception that proves the rule would be water transport, which did carry considerable long-distance trade.) With the Industrial Revolution came improvements in transportation – railroads, trucks, then airplanes, not to mention bigger, faster ships – that made it feasible to manufacture large quantities of goods in one place and distribute them regionally, nationally, and internationally. Goods that could be manufactured cheaper or better in one place or not at all in other places became logical candidates for transport. Globalization is just the extension of this process, with the power of transportation, communications, an other improving technologies enabling companies to move into wider and wider arenas.

A second perspective concerns the changing trade relationship between the United States and the rest of the world since the end of World War II. William Ouchi capsulizes it:

> *At the end of World War II, the factories in Japan, Europe, and the rest of the industrial world – for example, Singapore – had been destroyed, bombed flat. If you wanted to buy a ton of steel, a ship, an oscilloscope, or an airplane, you had to buy it here in the U.S. We, therefore, became the suppliers for the rest of the world, as they resupplied. We had no competitors. Now the rest of the world has*

recovered from the ravages of the war. They've rebuilt their univer-sities. They've rebuilt their research and development. They've re-built their companies. There no longer is the automatic extension of the major U.S. firm abroad, and our companies are having a more and more difficult time competing abroad.

One hard fact of global competition for workers in the United States and other developed nations is that third-world nations have a competi-tive advantage in labor costs – wages are a fraction of those here – and many companies respond by moving facilities to these nations.

Two benefits of global competition for consumers in the United States and elsewhere are that it serves both to hold down prices and to improve quality. Companies are forced to operate more efficiently and effectively and not to take even their local markets for granted. Virtually any company that wants to survive today needs to meet world-class standards, or competition will move in.

Cost and quality advantages undergird the major argument in favor of open trade: that a world economy operating at full throttle, without quotas, tariffs, and other restrictions, will produce the best goods at the lowest prices and also stimulate rapid innovation and development. The major argument against open trade is that even change which is benefi-cial in overview can wreak havoc as it goes (consider the local impact of a plant shut-down), and the problem is compounded by nations and corporations pursuing narrow self-interests.

The process of globalization, then, is fraught with implications for nations, for corporations, and for individuals as both workers and con-sumers. Balance of trade, currency rates, domestic investment abroad, foreign investment at home – these and many other topics bear colossal political and economic import. But with their existence only noted, let's narrow our focus down to issues that businesses face in the global arena.

The Multinational Corporation

The term multinational corporation describes companies that don't just export products or services, but operate facilities abroad. Many multina-tional corporations rival **countries** in economic might. As of 1991, 47 of the top 100 economies in the world were corporations, not countries, with General Motors the 20th-largest economic unit on the planet.

Multinational corporations tend to share a number of characteristics. They create foreign affiliates – either wholly owned or jointly held with foreign partners – which serve as arms of business. They tend to locate affiliates in developed countries and to view less-developed countries as sources for raw materials and cheap labor and as markets for low-end products. They operate with a global vision and strategy, seeing the world as their market. And they tend to concentrate in certain industries, mostly manufacturing but also petroleum, banking, agriculture, and public utilities.

The Environments of the International Manager

Although globalization is, in a sense, the other end of a continuum from local production and commerce (with inter-galactic transport yet to be developed), the change is one of kind as well as degree. As corporations move beyond the national, cultural, and language boundaries of their origins, they enter new realms of complexity, and the challenge of dealing with this complexity falls, first and foremost, on international managers.

In each country where we do or consider doing business, international managers need to assess and adjust to five different environments: political, legal, economic, technological, and sociocultural. The political environment may be friendly or unfriendly to outside investment. Government stability is also a major issue, since it doesn't pay to set up operations in a country that's about to crumble. Legal environments are thorny by nature, and a company will face a whole new set of rules in each country that it enters. The economic environment will present issues such as infrastructure, availability of raw materials and supplies, proximity to customers, stability of currency, and levels of inflation, wages, interest rates, and taxes. The technological environment can be compared to a plug and socket. The product or technology "plug" that the company brings needs to find a "stocket" of readiness in the host country – people wanting to buy its products and/or people capable of doing the jobs it needs done. Finally, and at a level of complexity all its own, comes the sociocultural environment. The success of an international manager in a host country will depend to a large extent on how well he or she comes to understand its traditions, language, customs, values, and religion. The task is complicated by the need for managers to sort out their own cultural biases.

Because of the complexity of adjusting to so many environments, many companies are moving away from sending expatriate managers abroad and toward hiring and developing nationals. Les Nishimura of Solectron expresses the current wisdom in describing how his company staffed its new facility in Panang, Malaysia:

> We see the advantage to hiring managers from the local economy or the local industry, because they're familiar with the way business is conducted. They're familiar with the laws. They're familiar with the customs surrounding employees' expectations, and all businesses are successful because of the human resource element.

Of course, even when an organization staffs its international operations largely with nationals, it still faces the task of integrating its overall operations, and this task involves all five management functions.

Planning and the International Manager

Planning on an international level involves the same elements as all corporate planning – assessing the environment, developing assumptions, and forecasting based on those assumptions – but many more variables need to be taken into account.

One planning decision involves how to go global. There are four options:

- export your product or service through foreign distributors;
- license others to act on your behalf;
- enter into joint ventures; and
- build or purchase your own facilities abroad.

Some or all of these options are often taken in sequence, as they allow a company to test the waters before risking greater degrees of investment.

For managers charged with assessing a company's possible entry into an international market, certain risks pose particular concern. These include: political and currency instability, competition or pressure from national governments, intense nationalism, the absence of patent and trademark protection, and – particularly in lucrative markets – intense competition from other companies.

Assessment of risks and opportunities leads to forecasts which managers then use to construct plans. Global corporate objectives need to be formulated to cover questions of profitability, marketing, production, finance, and other areas.

Organizing and the International Manager

As it extends its operations internationally and modifies its objectives, an organization must also adapt its structure. The structure of a company changing from a domestic to an international outlook generally evolves through three phases. The pre-international division phase involves adding an export manager to the present marketing department. The international division phase involves establishing marketing or production operations in the host country or countries, with the international division head often reporting directly to the CEO. Finally, as international operations achieve success, top management makes a greater commitment and shifts to a global structure with a total-company perspective.

As a company moves through these stages, it often moves from centralized authority with tight control over international facilities toward decentralization, giving those closest to problems and opportunities the authority needed to respond to them quickly. Vincent Kontny, President and COO of Fluor Daniel, describes the recent evolution of that giant engineering and construction firm:

> *Where we were ten years ago, I think we were in the hierarchical structure. Five years ago we were in a matrix. Today we're in a network. A network is really based on mutual trust and teamwork of all of our people, and what it is essentially is that all of our employees, regardless of their culture or their background or whatever the case may be, feel that they're empowered to make decisions within their sphere of influence.*

Staffing and the International Manager

Not surprisingly, as a company moves toward decentralization it usually increases the number of foreign nationals and staff. This process serves not only to provide managers who are familiar with the five environments but also to give the company access to new pools of talent. Increasingly, foreign nationals are rising through the ranks to head up headquarters staffs of American multinationals.

A separate set of staffing issues centers around compensation. Compensating host-country personnel in line with parent-company practices seldom works. Differing levels of taxes, inflation, and standards of living, host country customs, and a number of other factors bear on the most appropriate compensation. Also, the perks that are valued vary from culture to culture.

Directing and the International Manger

Directing – when managers interact most actively with employees to perform work – is the function in which cultural and other differences can stand out most glaringly. Communications problems can emerge not only from language but also from body language. An innocent gesture in one culture may be perceived as an insult in another.

Also, employee attitudes vary widely from culture to culture. A manager steeped in rugged individualism will have to adjust to a more collective, group oriented approach in many countries; a manager focused on doing and getting results through rewards may conflict with employees in a culture that favors being and valuing a process, and taking delight in doing it better; and a manager concerned about time may run head-on into *mañana*.

Controlling and the International Manager

As a rule, controlling benefits from proximity and frequent contact, both of which are made more difficult by international distances. Also, the potential of control systems to be misunderstood is multiplied across cultures and languages.

To deal with these problems, most international companies rely on (1) regular reporting procedures and communications between affiliates and their headquarters; (2) progress toward goals that have been established with the input of affiliates; (3) regular screening of reported data by area and functional experts, and (4) regular on-site inspections by various corporate personnel. Satellite linkups, teleconferencing, and telecommunications links by phone, fax, and computer also help companies to overcome the problems of distance.

A S S I G N M E N T S

- Read the Overview, familiarize yourself with the Learning Objectives, and peruse the Key Terms below. Then turn to Plunkett & Attner, *Introduction to Management*, and read Chapter 20, "International Management," pages 608–641.

- Next, scan the Video Viewing Questions and watch the video program for Lesson 23, "World of Opportunity: Managing in a Global Environment."

- After watching the video, answer the viewing questions and assess your learning with the Self-Test.

- Familiarize yourself with the Review Questions, Discussion Questions for Critical Thinking, and Skill Building Exercises on page 642 of Plunkett & Attner.

- Strengthen your understanding of the lesson's ideas and issues by undertaking the Expanded Analysis.

K E Y   T E R M S

balance of trade The difference between the dollars flowing into a country and those flowing out.

cross-cultural management An emerging discipline focused on improving work in organizations with employee and client populations from several cultures.

direct investment The purchase of real property or other major assets by foreign nationals and foreign businesses in a country.

embargo A government regulation enacted to keep a product out of a country for a time or entirely; often used as a political sanction to enforce a nation's foreign policy.

global structure The arrangement of an organization's management decision making to efficiently and effectively operate in a multinational mode; form may contain functional, product, and geographic features based on worldwide product or area units.

globalization The aggregate processes of exporting products and services; locating operations outside one's national borders; using foreign partners to help in research and development and to sell products and services around the world; and tailoring strategies, management functions, and products and services to meet the needs of customers around the world; requires that managers think beyond national borders and see all world markets as part of one world economy.

international division A parent company's corporate unit, commonly a marketing or production operation, located in a host country offshore from the parent headquarters, and whose head reports directly to the CEO; common practice for companies in the early stages of international involvement.

international management The process of managing resources (people, funds, inventories, and technologies) across national boundaries and adapting management principles and functions to the demands of foreign competition and environments.

multinational corporation A company with operating facilities, not just sales offices, in one or more foreign countries; management favors a global vision and strategy, seeing the world as their market.

quota A national government regulation which limits the import of a product to a specified amount per year.

tariff A tax placed on imported goods in order to make them more expensive and less competitive in order to protect domestic producers.

V I D E O V I E W I N G Q U E S T I O N S

1. Why is it unrealistic to expect the United States to regain the economic dominance it experienced in the decades after World War II?

2. How has Northwest Airlines moved to increase its cultural sensitivity?

3. How does the training provided to international managers differ between Japanese and American companies?

4. Why have Northwest, Fluor, and Solectron all pursued a policy of hiring nationals in operations abroad?

5. How does Fluor use its global network?

6. How has global competition contributed to efficiency? Quality? Innovation?

7. How does Solectron improve its performance by participating in global markets?

S E L F - T E S T

1. The European Community

   a. is the principal European defense treaty organization.
   b. is a group of 15 European communities that have formed an economic union.
   c. is the informal term applied to all the Western European countries.
   d. is a trade group formed to protect European trade from excessive U.S. competition.

2. A multinational corporation is

   a. any corporation with significant operations in two or more countries.
   b. a corporation operating in the North American Free Trade Area.
   c. a company that manufactures in one country and sells in another
   d. a company that does business in the European Community.

Companies may no longer have a great deal of choice about going global. In general companies go global for reasons characterized as proactive or reactive. In the situations below, indicate which reason is most likely be the case. You may use either option as often as you like or not at all.

  a. Proactive
  b. Reactive
  c. A combination of both pro- and reactive.

3. BMW is building a new assembly plant in between Greenville and Spartanburg, South Carolina. The reasons, say chairman Eberhard von Kuenheim, are to strengthen the company's position in the U.S. market, to become more independent of fluctuations in international exchange rates or possible trade barriers, and because "to be successful in the world, a company has to be successful in the United States."

4. Joseph Lucas Company, the British manufacturer of electrical parts and equipment, long maintained parts distribution centers on both the East and West coasts of the United States in order to serve the aftermarket of parts for English cars sold in America.

5. The Allison Division of General Motors, a major builder of automatic transmissions for trucks, buses, and other heavy vehicles, maintained distribution centers in Japan, Europe, and Latin America, partly in an effort to market their transmissions to vehicle manufacturers in those countries.

6. The five elements of the environment which managers in an international company must understand are:

  a. political, legal, economic, sociocultural, and technological.
  b. material culture, social institutions, values and beliefs, aesthetics, and languages.
  c. individualism, informality, materialism, change, and time orientation.
  d. communication, currency, and culture are the only environmental issues with which a manager in an international company needs to concern him- or herself.

7. Managers operating in the international environment

  a. must be sensitive to the cultures of the countries in which they serve.
  b. should learn the language of their host country.
  c. should be open, patient, and flexible people.
  d. all of the above, and more.

Match the definition with the term.
a. Tariffs
b. Quotas
c. Embargo
d. ISO9000

8. a tax on imported goods.

9. a government regulation to keep a commodity out of a country for a specified period of time.

10. a government regulation that limits the import of a product to a specified amount per year.

11. a set of technical standards for determining whether organizations are following sound quality procedures.

EXPANDED ANALYSIS

1. Accepting the proposition that business is likely to continue on its track to complete internationalization, how might the American education system cooperate with American industry and commerce to improve the performance of American enterprise abroad? Suggest specific programs and recommend sources and process for funding, administration, and expected outcomes for your programs.

24

The Right Fit:
The Individual and the Organization

L E A R N I N G   O B J E C T I V E S

Upon completing this lesson, you should be familiar with the facts, ideas, and processes contained in this lesson, and be able to:

- Discuss the importance of a manager's knowledge of the organization and its existing internal power sources.

- Discuss the problems that arise when personal and organizational values conflict.

- Describe the abilities most often associated with managers who advance in organizations.

- In the organizational context, compare the kinds of individual actions (behaviors) likely to be rewarded with actions likely to be viewed less favorably.

- Discuss the kinds of stress managers typically encounter in the business environment.

- Differentiate between positive and negative aspects of stress.

- Suggest techniques available to managers that mitigate harmful effects of stress and avoid burn-out.

O V E R V I E W

Career Management

Career management is a difficult subject for many people. There's a human tendency to want to sit back and wait for good things to happen to you, or simply to expect to rise on your natural merits. The problem with being passive about career management is that, while strokes of good fortune may come your way, they seldom continue for years, much less the duration of a career. If you were starting a business enterprise, you would want to set goals and plans and be alert and responsive to the business environment. Your career **is** a business enterprise.

Another resistance that many people feel toward career management is that it strikes them as Machiavellian. Indeed, it can be conducted in a cold, calculating fashion, but it can also be conducted with high moral standards and still be clear and objective. The essence of empathy is to be able to see things from other people's points of view. **Career management** involves not just "doing your own thing" but appreciating the point of view and needs of the company and other individuals in the company.

If you're averse to assessing the company and looking out for your own interests, consider that the company will be continually assessing you and looking out for its interests. For every promotion and opportunity that comes along, higher managers will be looking for the person who can do the best job for the company and for them. They are far likelier to give the job to someone who has foreseen it and worked toward it than someone who has been blithely going along.

Assessment and Alignment

Career management begins with self-assessment, thinking deeply about your personal values, interests, and abilities. You're not likely to go far in a direction where you lack interest or ability or where you feel a conflict in values.

The second step is to analyze the organization you're in or are considering joining. What are the opportunities? What kinds of behaviors are valued and rewarded? What avenues can be pursued?

Your relationship with the company as an employee will go through several phases, which psychologist Edgar Schein has characterized as organizational socialization. First, you will form impressions and expectations of the company, then you will match your needs with those of the company, and finally you and the company will come to a state of mutual acceptance. This acceptance may include compromises, particularly on your part. John Young describes how employees become accepted and conforming members of the Four Seasons Hotel organization:

We each have our internal code, which is the value programming from our parents and other people around us as we're growing up. Then there are the ethics, the standards within the organization itself, which may be slightly different from those. We have to adapt to and internalize those, and behave in a manner consistent with those, while we're in that place of business.

Somewhere along the route of organizational socialization, you will move from assessing yourself and the organization and into aligning the two. How do your skills match those which the organization values? What paths in the organization are you capable of taking? What other preparation, education, or training might you need? Alignment, like assessment, is a process you will need to perform not once and for all but continuously throughout your career.

Strategies for Career Advancement

Career advancement depends not only on merit but visibility. One way to create visibility is to do good work, but good work alone will often go unnoticed. Barbara Lawrence points out a particular trap:

Frequently there are jobs in organizations that are seen as dead ends, or jobs in which people have never gone anywhere, and it's very risky to be put into a position like that, because they may tell you, `Well, we're going to change things,' but the fact is that perceptions about such jobs change very slowly and it's very risky to take a position like that.

One way to gain visibility if your job doesn't put you in the limelight is to volunteer for projects, tasks forces, and other high-profile assignments. Volunteering shows initiative, one of the traits that executives most seek in candidates. A well-chosen volunteer assignment can highlight talents your regular job may not give you the chance to show. It can also provide developmental opportunities and broaden your experience in the company, a vital part of reaching general-management responsibilities.

Critical questions to ask in choosing a volunteer assignment include: (1) What new experience or knowledge can be gained? (2) What will the impact be on your immediate boss and the boss's success? (3) What will the impact be on the organization? and (4) What will the exposure be to multi-level management?

As well as general exposure, a useful goal in gaining visibility can be to try to catch the attention of a sponsor, someone higher-up in the organization who will actively promote your talents and help to hook you up with opportunities.

A similar strategy is to find a mentor. **Mentors** are also higher-up in the organization, but their role is to act as guide, teacher, counselor, and coach. By and large, new employees have a lot to learn – the more substantial the profession, the more there is to learn – and mentors are people who can help teach them. In most cases, mentoring is a mutually rewarding process, with the senior employee gaining the satisfaction of both helping someone and passing along what he or she knows.

Many companies develop formal mentoring programs to link up employees at both ends of the career spectrum. They don't just do it to be supportive of employees – although that's part of it – but also to pursue the needs of the company. Ko Nishimura describes the advantages to Solectron:

> *A mentoring program is important for a rapidly growing company like ours, where you need executives to fill positions very rapidly. We'd like to grow our company from within whenever possible because it would be demotivating if you bring in too many people in the top positions.*

On a broader scale, a vital strategy for career advancement is to understand company power and politics. The term politics has a Machiavellian ring, but the essence of the matter is to gain advantage by being clear and objective about certain issues: Who are the people upon whom the leaders of the organization rely? What skills and knowledge do these people provide? Are you able to supply the same skills and knowledge? Could these people help you as sponsors or mentors?

There are several ways to obtain power. One is to develop expertise in areas critical to the company. Another is to develop a network of contacts who can provide information, support, and help in solving problems. A third is to acquire line responsibility. The organization sets up lines of authority and responsibility to get the job done; you want to have a place in those lines. Finally, help someone else solve his or her problems. The cynic might call this collecting favors, but the crux is to perform services of substance and value to other people.

Among the forms of helping other people solve their problems, none is more important than working cooperatively with your boss. Most of us tend to carry over from adolescence some degree of rebellion against people to whom we're expected to report. But again, empathy helps. Think of your boss as a person like yourself who is charged with a job to do. Does he or she need your help or your acrimony, your solutions or your complaints? There are situations when bosses are incompetent or act outrageously, and these may legitimately call on you to resist, but by and large it's not only the best career move but the best human policy to be supportive and help the boss succeed.

A final career-long strategy that's of great importance is learning to deal with stress. The pressures of business inevitably create stress. To a degree, stress can help people to perform. For example, the pressure to meet a deadline may spur people to work hard and efficiently. But extreme levels of stress cause performance to decline and can lead to physical problems and psychological burnout.

The first step in dealing with stress is to learn to recognize it. Often a physical symptom – anxiety, headaches, insomnia, etc. – may serve as a warning. More preventively, people can learn to recognize situations that put them under stress. There are many such situations and they vary with each job and person, but obvious examples would include ones that cause you to feel helpless, trapped, violated, bored, or overworked.

Individuals and companies need to develop techniques to manage stress. Research has validated what mother knew all along: relaxation, good nutrition, and exercise are major tools for combatting stress. Companies can provide facilities and support systems in all of these areas. Individuals and companies can also look carefully at situations and environments that are producing stress and find ways to change them.

Organizational Dilemmas

In career management, certain organizational dilemmas can put people in binds that they would be well-advised to address and resolve.

One is a conflict between personal and organizational values. You may be asked to do things that you don't believe are right, or you may find, say, that your job is requiring more travel and creating problems in your home life. Whatever the source of conflict, it's best to come to grips with it, and whatever course you choose – accepting a compromise or making a change – you will function better for having dealt with the issues.

Loyalty demands can also put people in binds. A boss who's saying, "Don't make me look bad," may be asking you to help cover up. Someone who is saying, "Trust me," may be asking you to violate another trust. In these situations it's important not to get drawn in. You don't have to assume a confrontational style, but when your conscience says no, it can be very psychologically damaging to say yes.

Advancement decisions can also put a person between a rock and a hard place. A job may be offered that doesn't fit into your career plans or causes other problems. For example, job transfers frequently raise questions of whether the position offered is worth the disruption to you and your family. On the other hand, failure to receive advancements opportunities can push even the most patient managers to decisions about whether it would be better to seek their futures elsewhere. For both types of advancement decisions, there's no easy answer. The best approach is a complete analysis of costs and benefits.

Finally, the issue of independence versus sponsorship can create conflicts. As clearly beneficial as having a sponsor can be to a career, it can also carry a price tag, either in the independence you are asked to give up or the risk of the sponsor leaving the organization or being fired and taking you down with him or her. A possible solution to the dilemma is to build relationships with many people in the organization.

In overview, two aspects of career management stand out. One is the importance of understanding who you are at the start, so that you will set out in a direction that can lead to satisfaction. People can work harder and longer from love than from ambition or obligation. The other is the importance of flexibility. Over the course of your career, situations will change in ways that you could never have foreseen. You will change in ways that surprise you. At each stage of the way your chances of career satisfaction will depend on your ability to keep assessing where you are, how you feel about where you are, where you can go, and where you want to go.

ASSIGNMENTS

- Read the Overview, familiarize yourself with the Learning Objectives, and peruse the Key Terms below. Then turn to Plunkett & Attner, *Introduction to Management*, and read Chapter 21, "Succeeding in Your Organization," pages 658–675.

- Next, scan the Video Viewing Questions and watch the video program for Lesson 24, "The Right Fit: The Individual and The Organization."

- After watching the video, answer the viewing questions and assess your learning with the Self-Test.

- Familiarize yourself with the Review Questions, Discussion Questions for Critical Thinking, and Skill Building Exercises on page 676 of Plunkett & Attner.

- Strengthen your understanding of the lesson's ideas and issues by undertaking the Expanded Analysis.

KEY TERMS

authority The formal legitimate right of a manager to make decisions, give orders, and allocate resources.

burnout A state of emotional exhaustion as a result of overexposure to stress.

career The sequence of jobs a person holds over a lifetime and the person's attitude toward the involvement in those job experiences; involves a long-term perspective, a sequence of positions, and a psychological involvement.

career management The planning, strategy, activities, and behaviors involved in executing a career.

career perspective A proactive strategy that involves a global view of career progress or growth over time.

job A specific position a person holds in an organization.

mentor A senior employee who acts as guide, teacher, counselor, and coach for a less experienced person in the organization.

norms Any standard of conduct, code, or pattern of behavior perceived by a group to be important for its members to honor or to conform to.

organizational socialization A process through which new members of an organization gain exposure to its values, norms, policies, and procedures.

organizational visibility A strategy for career advancement that involves highlighting a person's abilities, talents, and contributions for those people in the organization who influence promotions and advancements.

power A person's ability to exert influence.

psychological contract The unspoken contract that marks the end product of the organizational socialization process and defines what people are expected to give to the organization and what they can expect to receive in return.

responsibility The obligation to carry out one's assigned duties to the best of one's ability.

sponsor A person in the organization who will promote a person's talents and look out for his or her organizational welfare.

stress The physiological and psychological reaction of the body as a result of demands made on it.

V I D E O   V I E W I N G   Q U E S T I O N S

1. How is the Four Seasons' determination to provide world-class service reflected in the traits and values it seeks in employees?

2. In what ways can initiative be a particularly valuable trait for career advancement?

3. How does Solectron's mentoring program reflect a broad philosophy of helping employees develop their careers?

4. How are some companies loosening up so that they can fit better with different employees?

5. How does the idea of "band widths" enable Apple to make a good fit with creative individuals?

6. Why does it take "passion" to fit with Patagonia?

S E L F - T E S T

1. Which of the following is probably the best definition of stress? Stress is

   a. tension.
   b. the body's reaction to demands placed upon it.
   c. mental fatigue.
   d. any negative response to a stimulus.

2. The Fortune 500 interviews about actions likely to be rewarded in today's organizations included four. The one **not** included is

   a. hard work.
   b. team player.
   c. risk taking.
   d. make contributions.
   e. be independent.

3. Which practice on the list below is **not** one of the four ways in which people obtain power for career advancement?

   a. Developing a network of contacts.
   b. Developing expertise in areas significant to the company.
   c. Solving others' problems.
   d. Making sure that all credit due for good work is received.

4. The practice of mentoring

   a. is an extraordinarily useful practice highly recommended by career counselors.
   b. is a luxury few managers ever experience.
   c. is largely a matter of luck.
   d. is predominantly a learning device recommended by feminists for women to combat the glass ceiling phenomenon.

5. Organizational politics

   a. are a distasteful element to be avoided.
   b. a necessary evil.
   c. merely the unwritten rules of work life and informal methods of gaining power or advantage.
   d. the primary path to advancement in most organizations.

6. Ms. Jean Brodie is doing a comparative analysis of 10 careers she rates moderately interesting to very appealing. she has made extensive notes n the disadvantages and advantages implicit in each and compared these to her personal goals and needs. Unfortunately, there's not a perfect match in the lot. What is most likely to be the problem here?

   a. There is no problem; the "perfect match" doesn't exist.
   b. Jean needs to do a broader search; the best match for her apparently isn't within the 10 careers she's focusing on.
   c. Jean doesn't know herself as well as she thought.
   d. The information Jean is using isn't comprehensive enough; she needs a Spark of inspiration.

7. An indidvidual in the organization who will promote a person's talents and look out for his or her organizational welfare:

   a. Mentor
   b. Sponsor

Match the term below with the correct definition that follows:

   a. Networking
   b. Organizational politics
   c. Organizational visibility

8. Highlighting of a persons's abilities, talents, and contributions for those people in the organization who influence promotions and advancements.

9. The unwritten rules of work life and informal methods of gaining power and advantage

10. Building long-term two-way interaction based on shared ideas, personal relationships, and commmon experiences.

E X P A N D E D   A N A L Y S I S

1. In the March 29, 1993, *Time Magazine*, the cover story called "The Tempting of America," senior editor Lance Morrow wrote:

   "America has entered the age of the contingent or temporary worker, of the consultant and subcontractor; of the just-in-time work force — fluid, flexible, disposable. This is the future. Its message is this: You are on your own. For good (sometimes) and ill (often), the workers of the future will constantly have to sell their skills, invent new relationships with employers who must, themselves, change and adapt constantly in order to survive in a ruthless global market.

   How should such a view affect your career planning?

25 Making Choices: Managerial Ethics

Upon completing this lesson, you should be familiar with the facts, ideas, and processes contained in this lesson, and be able to:

- Define managerial ethics and social responsibility and differentiate between the two.

- Recognize the diverse ethical dilemmas that a manager may face in today's business environment.

- Compare legal standards with ethical standards.

- Explain how a manager's values affect his or her actions; his or her organization.

- Explain how outside factors may influence a manager's decisions in which considerations of ethics apply.

━━━━━━━━━━━━━━

O V E R V I E W

Ethics in the Management Context

Whether we choose to treat ethics as a set of principles governing conduct or as the study of human values, moral duty and obligation, we come to the central question of what constitutes ethical behavior. In asking that question of managers, we find that answers in their universe differ little from those valued in the world at large. James R. Wilburn, dean of Pepperdine University's School of Business and Management, says "Ethics isn't a way of looking at certain things. Ethics is a certain way of looking at everything." The dean's observation provides a part of every manager's answer to the question of appropriate conduct. Managers by definition make a primary ethical choice to act and not to remain indifferent to problems.

During this course of study we have explored the thoroughfare of contemporary management, and glimpsed its primary destinations, major intersections, and noisy traffic. In the process, working managers have shown that management itself is a powerful tool for acting on many of the challenges humankind faces. With competence and determination, and with limited resources, managers balance the diverse and conflicting demands of their multiple stakeholders – employees, owners, customers, suppliers, and their communities. And in the process of providing a framework for the world's work, and making things happen, good managers ensure that the question of right conduct in management is no theoretical inquiry, but a factor in each decision they make. For them, as with Dean Wilburn, ethics is a certain way of looking at everything.

Managing Ethically

One modern survey found that, "Ethical managers and ethical businesses tend to be more trusted and better treated and to suffer less resentment, inefficiency, litigation, and government interference. Ethics is just good business." Accompanying this notion lingers the belief among the general populace that products and services should be safe and reliable, that business leaders should care about the public welfare, and that business practices should be equitable and just. Of course, there is often a sizeable chasm between the idealism of what should be and the reality of what is.

One possible explanation for ethical lapses is that we live in troubled times – competition, economic turbulence, downsizing, retrenching, outsourcing, massive lay-offs. At Santa Clara University, Manuel Velasquez says, "I think that most instances of unethical behavior are not due to people's characters, but are due to the pressures and the situations in which they find themselves. In most businesses, the unethical behavior that you find very decent people engaging in is behavior that they're driven to because of the pressures that are put upon them, pressures to cut corners, pressures to produce, pressures to get a product out the door, pressures to cut costs." Many of those remaining in the workplace, it has been suggested, feel threatened and insecure, fear losing their jobs or are anxious to gain some benefit for their companies. "The `moral dilemma' comes at crunch time," says one academic, "when there is a seeming choice between ethical actions and profits."

Organizational Controls and Ethics

Any organization that's serious about implementing uniform standards of ethics must first secure the commitment of top management. Says Peter Madsen, "You have to have strong leadership at the top that does a good job of communicating with vision about the notion of ethics, and the values of an organization." Another technique is publication of codes of ethical conduct that specify the ethical standards a company expects of its people. According to the Center for Business Ethics at Bentley College, such codes of conduct have increased dramatically in the last ten to fifteen years: more than half the Fortune 500 companies use them.

Some firms mount coordinated compliance programs, including recurrent training in ethics. Academic efforts such as Carnegie Mellon University's Center for the Advancement of Applied Ethics have proven that ethics training can be most effective. Such training principles and methods for managers and organizations may strengthen and deepen their personal and institutional capacity to act in an ethical and socially responsible manner. They can also be exceedingly practical. The Arthur Andersen & Co. ethics program is designed not so much to shore up employee morals as it is to provide them with the tools needed to make difficult choices.

Peter Madsen's advocacy of ethics training is compelling on general grounds: "If [managers] they have some background in moral reasoning, some background in critical thinking about these ethical dilemmas, they become much more like moral philosophers. It would be my argument that they become much better managers as well."

Legal Constraints

Able managers ensure that their people are familiar with laws that apply to their organizational and individual conduct. But, as Madsen points out, statutory and case law provide only a beginning: "But the law is a moral minimum. . . . The best ethics training goes beyond legal compliance."

If we act without a moral and ethical base to our decision making, we are adrift and may rely solely on self-interest and economics. People and organizations lacking a moral point of view and reference can put themselves, their organizations, and others at great risk.

When managers choose to pursue an ethical course for themselves and for their organization, the benefits are impossible to ignore. The evidence suggests that both the company and its people reap positive results. Equally significant is the evidence of so many companies whose dealings are honest

and forthright, both internally and with the general public: such companies tend to truly succeed, not only in terms of their own profitability, but in the contributions they make to the betterment of all.

ASSIGNMENTS

■ Read the Overview, familiarize yourself with the Learning Objectives, and peruse the Key Terms below. Then turn to Plunkett & Attner, *Introduction to Management*, and read Chapter 22, "Management Ethics and Social Responsibility," pages 678–691.

■ Next, scan the Video Viewing Questions and watch the video program for Lesson 25, "Making Choices: Managerial Ethics."

■ After watching the video, answer the viewing questions and assess your learning with the Self-Test.

■ Familiarize yourself with the Review Questions, Discussion Questions for Critical Thinking, and Skill Building Exercises on page 704 of Plunkett & Attner.

■ Strengthen your understanding of the lesson's ideas and issues by undertaking the Expanded Analysis.

KEY TERMS

<u>business ethics</u> The rules or standards governing the conduct of persons or members of organizations in the commerce.

<u>dilemma</u> A situation that requires a choice between options that are or seem equally unfavorable or mutually exclusive.

<u>ethical dilemma</u> A situation that arises when all courses of action open to a decision maker are judged to be unethical.

ethics　Study of the general nature of morals and of the specific moral choices to be made by a person; concerned with what constitutes good and bad human conduct, including actions and values.

green products　Those manufactures that reduce the amount of energy and pollution connected with their manufacture and disposal.

social responsibility　The notion that, in addition to their business interests, individuals and organizations bear certain obligations (duties) to protect and to benefit other individuals and society, and to avoid actions that could harm them.

VIDEO VIEWING QUESTIONS

1. USC's Jay Galbraith and others contrast views of ethical business practices among major industrialized nations. Provide an example of such a contrast and suggest how an American manager might deal with the problem if it arises.

2. How does the question of privacy become an ethical issue for the manager?

3. What are some of the arguments in favor of ethical codes of conduct? Against?

4. Suggest the place of communication in the matter of ethics in the organization.

5. Patricia Werhane of Loyola University – Chicago suggests that the loss of the space shuttle "Challenger" occurred as a result of decisions about performance of the rocket's O-rings, but she does not elaborate. How might questions of ethics affect such an event?

6. Suggest four reasons for the Arthur Andersen group's extraordinary emphasis on the matter of ethics.

S E L F - T E S T

1. Business ethics

   a. are specific rules of corporate conduct distinct from general moral questions.
   b. are general moral principles applied to the world of business.
   c. should be carefully codified in each corporation's company procedures manual.
   d. have been essentially outmoded by today's highly competitive environment.

2. A dilemma is

   a. any perplexing management decision.
   b. an insoluble problem.
   c. a situation that requires a choice between two equally unfavorable or exclusive solutions.
   d. any situation requiring unethical action.

3. Codes of Ethics

   a. should provide guidance for all business-related moral questions likely to be encountered at the particular company.
   b. are generally unsuitable for very large companies.
   c. are an unchallengeable basis for firing an unethical employee.
   d. are seldom used by large American firms.

4. Comparing ethics and the role of law in organizational and individual conduct, which statement is most accurate?

   a. Law provides the maximum protection in matters of moral question; it generally covers most situations.
   b. The law can be considered an adequate standard of moral conduct.
   c. Laws for mboundaries for human and corporate conduct; laws and ethics together define acceptable behavior.
   d. The law, in general, compromises more than ethics.

5. A rationalization is

   a. a carefully constructed solution to any managerial problem.
   b. a self-satisfying but incorrect reason for behavior.
   c. a belief in the power of thought to solve a problem.
   d. a complex answer to an essentially simple question.

6. Which of the following is **not** among the three primary ways that businesses can promote ethical conduct?

   a. The commitment of top management
   b. Codes of ethics
   c. Compliance programs
   d. Swift, severe, public punishment of offenders

7. The **least likely** motivation for unethical conduct in the workplace, according to many experts, is

   a. management not conspicuously committed to ethical behavior.
   b. unspoken pressure to perform regardless of method.
   c. some people's basic underlying nature.
   d. ignorance of what constitutes acceptable conduct.

8. Which two powerful factors imperil a manager's ability to balance the demands of stakeholders while managing and allocating limited resources?

   a. government takeover of corporate decision-making and economic hardship
   b. the globalization of business operations and the scarcity of resources
   c. the magnitude of the conflicting demands manager face, and the unprecedented impact of management decisions on people and environments
   d. the privatization of many public "institutions" and the lack of qualified workers

9. The relationship between personal ethics and organizational ethics is best characterized by which of the following statements?

   a. The two are completely independent.
   b. The individual's ethics should be determined by the company's.
   c. The company shouldn't care about an individual's ethics as long as they don't directly affect the company.
   d. The two are related and interdependent in many ways.

10. Professor Saul Gellerman points out that organizations can encourage unethical behavior in employees in several ways. Which item is **not** included in his list?

   a. Offering unusually high rewards for success
   b. Drawing a clear line between the behavior the company will tolerate and behavior that will be punished
   c. Threatening unusually severe punishments
   d. Emphasizing results with minimal concern for the means employed to achieve those results

EXPANDED ANALYSIS

1. Make a strong case for this proposition: "So long as no one is hurt and no laws are broken, corporate managers should do whatever is needed to advance the best interests of the corporation."

2. Make a strong case opposing the above proposition.

26 For the Common Good: Social Responsibility and Management

Upon completing this lesson, you should be familiar with the facts, ideas, and processes contained in this lesson, and be able to:

- Describe how expectations regarding the social responsiveness of business organizations are changing.

- Compare proactive and reactive responses to customer/social demands upon organizations.

- Discuss a manager's responsibility to stakeholders (stockholders, employees, customers, suppliers, the community) and how such responsibility may come into conflict with social or environmental interests.

- State the case for government regulation of business; state the case against government regulation.

- Discuss the particular skills and abilities today's managers must have in order to respond to the conflicting pressures with which they are faced.

O V E R V I E W

The Nature of Social Responsibility

As we explore the modern corporation's relationship to stakeholders and the larger community, we turn (for the last time in these pages) to the insight of Peter Drucker's *Management: Tasks, Responsibilities, Practices*:

> *Social responsibilities — whether of a business, a hospital, or a university — may arise in two areas. They may emerge out of the social impacts of the institution. Or they may arise as problems of the society itself. Both are of concern to management because the institution which managers manage lives of necessity in society and the community. But otherwise the two areas are different. The first deals with what an institution does to society. The second is concerned with what an institution can do for society.*

The distinctions are important to managers because they influence a company's choice of approaches when responding to matters of social responsibility.

Only in relatively recent times has much detailed attention been paid to the nature of corporate responsibility beyond its role as an economic unit. The modern corporation has generally been held legally accountable within an economic context as well. But increasingly in the last two decades, industrialized nations have taken a far broader view of the obligations of individuals and organizations in commerce.

The Current View of Corporate Obligation

The contemporary view of **social responsibility** focuses on each organization's obligations to protect and to benefit other individuals and society, and to avoid actions that might cause harm. This broadened view stems in part from the recognition that businesses have gained tremendous power in the world order. Their operations generate direct benefits and costs for their societies. All through the industrialized world, the public increasingly recognizes its dependence upon businesses to meet a large number and variety of individual and societal needs. From organized pressure on legislatures and other elected officials to boycotts and class action lawsuits, public citizens are enforcing their demands that businesses join in the urgent tasks of solving societies' problems.

Before the issue of social responsibility can be addressed by a company, a threshold of ethical awareness must exist within its culture. That awareness and the capability to act ethically occurs when corporations nourish cultures that promote ethical conduct, and their owners and employees act with an ethical perspective. The commitment of top management, including the allocation of adequate time and funding, is necessary to make organizations socially responsible.

A number of companies promote social responsibility through written policies that acknowledge and dynamically advocate a concern for ethics in general and social responsibility in particular. Employee training emphasizes and specifies how employees can contribute. As at Patagonia and Esprit, management urges people to involve themselves in their communities by granting time off and other incentives.

Approaches to Social Responsibility

Not unexpectedly, the responses of American businesses to the demands that society is now placing upon them differ markedly – from eager acceptance to obdurate defiance. Most fall somewhere in between, and most choose from among three primary strategies in confronting the issue of social responsibility: to resist, to react, and to anticipate.

Companies adopt the resistance approach when they actively fight to eliminate, delay, or fend off the demands being made on them. In the early days of modern business, corporations behaved largely as their owners and senior managers chose. Governments had not yet begun to regulate business matters, and the business community resisted what efforts there were to interfere with their conduct, no matter what the source. The public mood changed with the times, and especially during the Great Depression of the 1930s and the World War II years of 1941–1945, a substantial regulatory framework was built up. From stringent rules for banks and airlines to detailed tariffs for truck lines and railroads, industry felt the web of regulation.

Social activism in the 1960s ushered in the current era of public concern with corporate conduct. Rachel Carson's book, *Silent Spring* (1962) compellingly the nation's wholesale use of deadly insecticides, launched the current environmentalism movement, and led to the National Environmental Protection Act of 1970 in the United States. The message of Miss Carson's book was fiercely resisted by the chemical and agriculture industries.

Corporate resistance to demands for social responsibility continues almost as a policy of default by large corporations even today. The *Exxon Valdez* oil spill of 1989 released 10 million gallons of oil into Alaska's Prince William Sound. The Exxon Corporation's preparation and response to the disaster provided a classic case of corporate denial and avoidance. One might have expected the incident to influence industry to improve its conduct, to change its strategy about environmental safety. Yet even with tighter regulations, five of the world's 15 biggest oil spills have occurred in the 1990s, according to Joel Havemann writing in the *Los Angeles Times* of March 26, 1993. "Three and a half years after the *Exxon Valdez* spill," the Natural Resources Defense Council reported in December 1992, "key prevention and response measures have not been implemented. . . . As a result, the public still faces serious risks of oil spills." Numerous other examples suggest that companies still resist the notion of social responsibility.

Businesses that adopt the **reactive approach** wait for demands to be made and then react to them, choosing a response by evaluating alternatives. Instances of such corporate responses are many, from chemical companies belatedly cleaning up hazardous waste dump sites to the automotive industry's development of fuel efficient engines only after regulatory pressure from state and federal regulators. Hundreds of "citizen suits" since 1980 have forced industrial polluters to clean up their acts all across the country.

Companies that choose the **proactive approach** pay close attention to constituents' needs and actively pursue ways to serve stakeholders and improve corporate financial performance in the process. Companies like Patagonia and Esprit represent the outer edge of this approach. They preempt public concerns and turn them into a primary marketing advantage. In Patagonia's case, founder Yvon Chouinard asserts that accomplishing social change is his company's literal and only reason for existence. California has produced many examples of proactive corporate strategies toward social responsibility. Pacific Bell in San Francisco pioneered a cost-effective program for protecting and caring for employees with AIDS. Southern California Edison's conservation policies allowed it to simultaneously improve return on investment while lowering pollution. ARCO pioneered in developing cleaner burning gasolines.

Responsibilities to Stakeholders

The people who have an interest in or who are affected by how a business conducts its operations comprise its **stakeholders** – a firm's owners and stockholders, employees, customers, suppliers, and communities. Very large and influential companies, whose actions affect people and environments beyond its physical location may properly regard society as a whole as a stakeholder. The genuinely socially responsible corporation will take the interests of each of these groups into account in making its various decisions and implementing its plans.

Government Regulation

Recent history suggests that most regulatory statutes were developed and imposed in response to genuine or perceived abuse of the public interest. U.S. antitrust laws were passed in the wake of scandalous abuses by monopolistic "octopuses" – the railroads and oil companies. Principal labor legislation sought to redress flagrant exploitation of workers; mining safety laws were passed after thousands of men died: Child labor,

Environmental Protection, Endangered Species, Civil Rights – all were responses to public outcry for redress or protection or equity.

A Future of Responsibility

In recent decades, there seems to be a growing recognition among academicians, politicians, pundits, and people of good will and common sense that government and the law, no matter how beneficent and well-intended, cannot be the primary agents for achieving the public good. For one thing, government regulation is costly and unproductive. For another, regulations are believed by some to have made the United States less competitive around the world. Increasingly, the private sector is seen as a powerful and capable agent for improvement. It is time, many intelligent and caring people argue, for business to assume its full and proper social responsibility. At the same time, more corporations are accepting that challenge, assuming a proactive approach and accepting greater socially responsibility.

David Logan, of Corporate Community Relations International, summarizes the matter of corporate social responsibility this way:

> *Corporations need to have an ongoing system for assessing the social and ethical impacts of its business activity, and do internal managing. If you do that and get it wrong, people will forgive you. What they won't forgive you for is blind greed, selfishness, and insensitivity. Anybody can forgive a mistake, particularly when you've tried hard. But what the customer and the employer and the voter won't forgive is deliberate choice to ignore the social and moral dimension. It's not acceptable in the 1990s and into the next millennium. Corporations are a major force in our global civilization. They need to act like it.*

A S S I G N M E N T S

- Read the Overview, familiarize yourself with the Learning Objectives, and peruse the Key Terms below. Then turn to Plunkett & Attner, *Introduction to Management*, and read Chapter 22, "Management Ethics and Social Responsibility," pages 691–703.

- Next, scan the Video Viewing Questions and watch the video program for Lesson 26, "For the Common Good: Social Responsibility and Management."

- After watching the video, answer the viewing questions and assess your learning with the Self-Test.

- Familiarize yourself with the Review Questions, Discussion Questions for Critical Thinking, and Skill Building Exercises on page 704.

- Strengthen your understanding of the lesson's ideas and issues by undertaking the Expanded Analysis.

K E Y   T E R M S

dilemma A situation that requires a choice between options that are or seem equally unfavorable or mutually exclusive.

ethical dilemma A situation that arises when all courses of action open to a decision maker are judged to be unethical.

green products Those manufactures that reduce the amount of energy and pollution connected with their manufacture and disposal.

proactive approach A strategy toward social responsibility in which businesses continually look to the needs of constituents and try to find ways to meet those needs.

reactive approach A social responsibility strategy in which businesses wait for demands to be made and then react to them, choosing a response by evaluating alternatives.

resistance approach A social responsibility strategy in which businesses actively fight to eliminate, delay, or fend off demands being made on them.

social audit A report on the social performance of a business.

social responsibility The notion that, in addition to their business interests, individuals and organizations bear certain obligations (duties) to protect and to benefit other individuals and society, and to avoid actions that could harm them.

V I D E O   V I E W I N G   Q U E S T I O N S

1. What are the principal methods by which a community may influence the behavior of a corporation?

2. Dennis Hayes of Green Seal identifies the social activism of the 1960s as an important period of government involvement. What legislation followed?

3. Steven Cerri says there are two reasons why companies may become environmentally sensitive. What are they?

4. What is Patagonia CEO Yvon Chouinard's view of the recent trend of corporate emphasis on "green marketing"?

5. Describe Susie Tompkins' apparent corporate vision for Esprit. Compare that vision with the corresponding views of Yvon Chouinard and Kris McDivitt at Patagonia.

S E L F - T E S T

In facing various challenges of social responsibility, organizations may adopt any of several approaches. For each of the following situations, select the approach from the list that most nearly characterizes the organization's choice. You may use an approach once, more than once, or not at all.

    a. Resistive Approach
    b. Reactive Approach
    c. Proactive Approach

1. In the Spring of 1993, protesters staged demonstrations, including a hunger strike, on the campus of the University of California at Los Angeles to force university administrators to create a department of Chicano Studies in place of a related interdisciplinary program that had long been in place. The chancellor compromised by announcing the formation of a center with less than full department status.

2. In June 1993, syringe needles were found in several cans of Pepsi-Cola. No injuries were reported, and the company announced an investigation into the matter, assured the public that there was no apparent danger, and suggested that people shake Pepsi cans gently before opening them, and pour the soda into glasses before drinking the soda.

3. For many months, reports of fires following side impact collisions with certain models of GM pickup trucks circulated. Many lawsuits were brought against GM charging negligence, with a number of them resulting in large awards for the plaintiffs. Consumer advocate groups called for a manufacturers recall of the suspect vehicles. Damaging video footage showing a GM pickup bursting into flame in a side collision were shown on national TV and later proven to be faked. GM maintained the design was safe and steadfastly refused to recall the trucks.

4. A company assists local schools by creating a "talent account" of services they will provide on an as-needed basis. Srvices range from tutoring to facilities repair.

5. The concept of social responsibility requires that managers

   a. donate a reasonable portion of their profits to worthy social causes.
   b. must meet the legitimate social demands of all their stakeholders.
   c. must act with an ethical perspective and devote some of their resources to solving social problems they have in part caused.
   d. maintain adequate health insurance coverage for all their employees.

6. Which of the following least qualifies to be listed among corporate social responsibilities.

   a. Management's duty to maximize return on invested capital.
   b. Consumers' rights to know of a product's potential hazards in use.
   c. Suppliers' privilege to be informed of a company's needs sufficiently in advance to deliver on time.
   d. A local charity's anticipation of an annual donation.

7. Compliance with governmental regulation of industry is

   a. usually discretionary.
   b. almost always left largely to the regulated industry or its individual companies.
   c. almost always meticulously enforced by inspectors from the appropriate agency.
   d. seldom complied with because firms know there is little chance of their being inspected.

8. The costs of rectifying environmental problems caused by businesses after the fact

   a. are generally borne by the offending companies through fines.
   b. are often passed along to the public in the form of higher taxes.
   c. should be written off and forgotten because many of the offending companies either didn't know their practices were damaging to the environment or are no longer in business.
   d. are, by common agreement, shared by all the businesses that produce a similar product or service.

9. Corporate donations that support specific efforts and provide a return to the giver are termed

   a. a proactive approach to social responsibility.
   b. corporate responsibility.
   c. strategic philanthropy.
   d. social audit.

10. A social audit refers to

   a. a year-end review of monies expended to encourage comradery among employees.
   b. a popular vote in the community which reveals which business is most admired.
   c. a review of the benefit package and educational programs a comany offers its employees.
   d. a report that summarizes the social performance of a business.

EXPANDED ANALYSIS

1. Economist Milton Friedman asserts that the primary duty of managers is to run their companies profitably, and that additional responsibilities jeopardize the efficiency of profit making. Kris McDivitt of Patagonia says: "One of the things that we're after is to act as a tool for social change. We will use this company for that." Are these two positions ethically compatible? Take the side of the person with whom you least agree – Friedman or McDivitt – and try to construct a detailed argument to support their position.

2. Esprit and Patagonia appear to equate social responsibility with a concern about environmental protection. Suggest two other significant issues relating to social responsibility and recommend specific courses of action corporations might take to address them.

Appendix A:
Recommended Reading

B O O K S

Ansoff, H. Igor, *The New Corporate Strategy*, New York, NY: John Wiley & Sons, 1987.

In this updated version of the landmark book, *Corporate Strategy*, Ansoff broadens his original concept of strategic planning to include strategic management and its two key ingredients: transforming a firm to meet new strategies, and managing resistance to change.

Asman, David, *The Wall Street Journal on Managing: Adding Value through Synergy*, New York, NY: Doubleday, 1990.

From the regular "Manager's Journal" columns in *The Wall Street Journal*, these articles describe how to build bridges between departments, people, and products to create synergy with foreign markets, within an industry, and between service providers and customers.

Badaracco, Joseph. Jr., and Richard R. Ellsworth, *Leadership and the Quest for Integrity*, Boston, MA: Harvard Business School Press, 1989.

Managers who excel do so through the ways in which they resolve dilemmas. The authors argue that managers are more likely to excel if they approach dilemmas with certain prejudices, that is, preconceived biases toward handling problems in certain ways.

Bowles, Jerry, and Joshua Hammond, *Beyond Quality: New Standards of Total Performance That Can Change the Future of Corporate America*, New York, NY: Berkley Books, 1992.

The authors provide an energetic and concise assessment of the current quality trend, with ample illustrations, but an excellent review of the historic development of the movment in the U.S. and Japan. Their compact summaries of the contributions of the quality pioneers are excellent, and their bibliography provides an excellent survey of the essential material about this vitaly significant topic.

Bradford, David L. and Allan R. Cohen, *Managing for Excellence*, New York, NY: John Wiley & Sons, 1974.

Aimed at middle managers, this book presents a leadership model to turn a company's strategic plan into a personal commitment on the part of individuals in a department. The ideas were fine-tuned by consulting with more than 200 managers from leading corporations and government agencies.

Carlzon, Jan, *Moments of Truth*, Cambridge, MA: Ballinger Publishing Company, subsidiary of Harper & Row, 1987.

In one year, Carlzon led the turnaround of Scandinavian Airlines System (SAS) from a loss to the most profitable of Europe's airlines by managing the moments of truth (the moments at which a customer forms an opinion about a company). He shifted focus to the customer, empowered frontline people, cut costs, and transferred autonomy to the field. Although this is the story of an extraordinary turnaround in the airline industry, it's full of practical advice that has general applicability.

Collins, Eliza G.C., *The Executive Dilemma: Handling People Problems at Work*, New York, NY: John Wiley & sons, 1985.

This book is a collection of articles from the Harvard Business Review describing the many different kinds of challenges managers face when the must deal with personal issues involving their employees. Authors of the articles are practicing managers and university researchers.

Collins, Eliza G.C., and Mary Anne Devanna, *The Portable MBA*, New York, NY: John Wiley & Sons, 1992.

While there's no substitute for completing a full MBA program, this book covers management of people, quantitative tools, managerial economics, marketing management, strategic management, and more. The chapters are written by experts from leading business schools.

Davidow, William H. and Bro Uttal, *Total Customer Service: The Ultimate Weapon*, New York, NY: Harper & Row, 1989.

Drawing on case histories, this book presents a six-point plan for turning exceptional customer service into a competitive edge, including turning employees into customer service fanatics, designing products and services that make good customer service possible, and monitoring achievement of customer service goals.

Deal, Terrence E. and Allen A. Kennedy. *Corporate Cultures: The Rites and Rituals of Corporate Life*, Reading, MA: Addison-Wesley, 1982.

Every business has a culture – values, heroes, rituals and rites, and networks. The authors say that people at all stages of their careers need to understand culture and how it works because it likely has a powerful effect on their work lives. Also covered: how to assess a firm's culture and how to manage cultural change.

Deming, W. Edwards, *Out of the Crisis*, Cambridge, MA: Massachusetts Institute of Technology Center for Advanced Engineering Studies, 1986.

In this most famous of his books, the distinguished dean of the American quality reformation advances his central thesis that has become gospel for many U.S. managers: "Management will in time be judged not by the quarterly dividend, but by plans and innovation with the aim to stay in business, to protect investment, to ensure future dividends, and to provide jobs and more jobs through improvement of product and service for the future." Deming writes with blunt clarity and plenty of passion. His many first-hand examples and practical bibliography make this an especially useful book for students.

Drucker, Peter F., *The Practice of Management*, New York, NY: HarperBusiness, a division of HarperCollins Publishers, 1993.

Peter Drucker is know to millions in American business and economics circles as the preeminent business and management writer of our time. Because it fairly states the case, we cite the cover blurb of this recent paperback reprint: "A classic since its publication in 1954, [this book] has been a continuing international bestseller for nearly forty years. It was the first book to look at management as a whole, the first to depict management as a distinct function, managing as specific work, and being a manager as a separate responsibility. The Practice of Management created the discipline of modern management practices and principles. Comprehensive yet concise, clearly presented and readable, fundamental and basic, it remains an essential book for students, aspiring managers, and seasoned practitioners."

_____, *Managing for the Future: The 1990s and Beyond*, New York, NY: Truman Talley Books/Dutton, 1992.

Drucker here looks at how changes in the social and economic environments will affect businesses. Also examined: the end of the blue collar era, lessons non-profits offer businesses, multinationals, and the changing roles of middle managers.

_____, *Management: Tasks, Responsibilities, Practices*. New York, NY: HarperBusiness, 1993 (1973).

This may be the most "teaching oriented" of Drucker's books, a solid and practically organized work. In his introduction to the 1985 edition, Drucker said, "The book therefore tries to include what every manager needs to know – but which is also accessible to people who themselves have not yet worked as managers or even as employees in managed institutions. The user of this book can therefore be sure of two things: everything in the book has been developed in management practice and found to be effective in it and central to it; and everything has been tested by students of management and found to be meaningful to them, as well as easily accessible." Many of the highly readable chapters correspond closely to the major issues covered in this course.

Fisher, Roger, and William Ury, *Getting to Yes*, Boston, MA: Houghton Mifflin, 1981.

This book on negotiating gives readers a strategy, called "principled negotiation," for pursuing their own interests while getting along with those whose interests conflict with theirs.

George, Stephen, *The Baldridge Quality System*, New York, NY: John Wiley & Sons, 1992.

This book shows how the criteria for the prestigious Malcolm Baldridge National Quality Award can be a model for developing total quality management. It is also an insider's guide to putting together a winning Baldridge application and explains how applications are reviewed, site visits conducted, and winners chosen.

Hamermesh, Richard G. *Making Strategy Work: How Senior Managers Produce Results*, New York, NY: John Wiley & Sons, 1986.

Drawing on interviews with ten Fortune 500 CEOs who have introduced major strategic plans to their companies, this book presents a guide to the practices and problems involved in putting strategy to work. Detailed case studies of General Electric, Memorex, and Dexter Corporation are included.

Heskett, James L., *Managing in the Service Economy*, Boston, MA: Harvard Business School Press, 1986.

> Heskett has identified management strategies that have given leading service companies a competitive advantage. He presents them in a four-point "strategic service vision" for service managers, supported with many examples across a range of service industries.

Kanter, Rosabeth Moss, *When Giants Learn to Dance*, New York, NY: Touchstone Books, 1989.

> For businesses to survive in today's environment where technology, suppliers, customers, employees, corporate and industry structures are in motion, corporations must evolve flatter organizations, stressing greater responsiveness to change, and an openness to developing strategic alliances. Based on a five-year study, Kanter's book details how companies can be masters, not victims, of change. Also by Kanter, *The Change Masters*.

Noble, Sarah P., *301 Great Management Ideas from America's Most Innovative Small Companies*, Boston, MA: Goldhirsh Group, 1991.

> The ideas here come from a monthly department in *Inc.* magazine called "Hands On, A Manager's Notebook." It's quick reading (with one idea per page) and is divided into 36 chapters, including Managing People, Motivation, Incentives, Customer Relations, Meetings, Strategic Planning, and cost control.

Peters, Thomas J. and Robert H. Waterman, Jr., *In Search of Excellence: Lessons from America's Best-Run Companies*, New York, NY: Harper & Row, 1982.

> One of the best-selling business books of all time (despite being panned by many academics and professional managers), this volume is filled with stories of impassioned leaders. Peters and Waterman identify eight basic practices they say characterize successful companies. In later books, Peters revises many of the views espoused here. "We got a lot wrong in Search," said Peters later, "but in the real world, it was the right advice for the time. In fact," wrote commentator Daniel Akst in the Los Angeles Times (when reviewing the book below), the characteristics Peters and Waterman attributed to successful companies – "close to the customer, autonomy and entrepreneurship, a bias for action, and others – remain perfectly sound."

_____, *Liberation Management: Necessary Disorganization for the Nanosecond Nineties*, New York, NY: Alfred A. Knopf, 1992.

About Peters' fourth book, Daniel Akst says, "Studded with exclamation points, parenthetical asides and buzzwords like marketization, *Liberation Management* is an exasperating work proving that if companies are better off disorganized, books surely are not. . . . On the other hand, [the book] is full of interesting case studies to which clever readers will skip. Moreover, the basic message is probably sound: things are changing so fast and business is so competitive that firms must demolish their bureaucracies. form smaller units and let workers take charge of their jobs."

_____, *Thriving on Chaos; Handbook for a Management Revolution*, New York, NY: Alfred A. Knopf, 1987.

About this volume (actually arranged in handbook format) commentator Paul Weaver said in the Wall Street Journal, "Mr. Peters is saying that effective management is management that delivers more value to customers and more opportunity for service, creativity and growth to workers. He is saying that the decent thing to do is also the smart and effective thing, and he backs this assertion up with dozens of examples and studies."

Tichy, Noel, and Mary Anne Devanna, *The Transformational Leader*, New York, NY: John Wiley & Sons, 1990.

The key to global competitiveness is a company's ability to transform continuously. The authors believe transformation leadership is needed at all levels of an organization, and this book dissects the process of transformational leadership, giving managers specific ideas for transforming their own firms.

Townsend, Patrick L., *Commit to Quality*, New York, NY: John Wiley & Sons, 1990.

The author here describes how he developed and implemented a quality improvement at Paul Revere Insurance Group that saved the company $16 million. It is the first book to discuss the philosophy and detailed "how-to" steps of the quality process within a service business.

Walter, Russ, *The Secret Guide to Computers*, Somerville, MA: Russell Walter Publishing, 1990.

This offbeat book by "Boston's computer guru" covers everything you need to know about computers – history, programming languages, hardware and software. It also has industry gossip, buying advice, and tutorials, all written with humor and irreverence. Walter, a cult hero in the computer world, provides free phone consultation day or night.

White, Ron, *How Computers Work*, Emeryville, CA.: Ziff-Davis Press, 1993.

Inspired by the popular "How it Works" series in *PC/Computing* magazine, this pleasing volume provides lucid narratives of basic computer processes. Elegant illustrations by Timothy Edward Downs graphically dismantle the personal computer and show in vivid, full-color detail what goes on inside the machines.

PERIODICALS

Business Week. McGraw-Hill, Inc. 1221 Avenue of the Americas, New York, NY 10020. Weekly.

This magazine gives readers a comprehensive look at the week's business news. Features, profiles, and articles cover major news stories, international business, economic analysis, government, people, science and technology, social issues, information processing, finance, the workplace, and personal business. The Business Week Index charts the leading economic indicators over the week, and an index to companies listed in the issue is provided in the back.

Forbes. Forbes, Inc., 60 Fifth Avenue, New York, NY 10011. Biweekly.

Regular departments cover careers, investing, law, marketing, computers and communications, science and technology, and features about companies and business executives. Each issue also features a commentary by the publisher and a look at what's ahead – economically, legislatively, etc. – for business. A listing with page numbers in the front of each edition called "Companies In This Issue" provides an easy reference for those seeking information about a particular firm or industry. While some business publications strive for at least the illusion of disinterested journalism, Forbes makes no apology for its vividly capitalistic bias.

Fortune. Time, Inc. Time & Life Building, Rockefeller Center, New York, NY 10020. Biweekly.

This magazine features a broad spectrum of business reporting covering the "big story" as well as the human side of business. Departments include stories on general management, entrepreneurs, technology, corporate performance, news trends, and books. Each year, an April issue presents the magazine's renowned list of the Fortune 500. This prestigious roster of the largest U.S. firms includes wide ranging data about each company. Other lists include the "most admired" companies.

Harvard Business Review. Harvard University, Boston, MA 02163.

> This publication of highly readable and educational articles is considered must reading for serious managers. One outstanding feature in each issue is the case study. A significant and interesting situation is presented, with relevant history and current background, and readers are invited to recommend appropriate action to resolve applicable issues. Following are recommendations by a variety of authorities – professors, writers, psychiatrists, and others. Regular items include briefs on international topics, personal lessons from experienced managers, and perspectives on business issues-in-progress. At the back are pithy executive summaries of each article.

HRM: Magazine on Human Resource Management. Society for Human Resource Management, 606 N. Washington St., Alexandria, VA 22314. Monthly.

> This publication is devoted completely to the management of people, and focuses on topics such as productivity, awards and incentives, recruitment and hiring practices, and training. Other sections provide executive briefings on government affairs, legal trends, HRM seminars, book reviews, and new products.

Inc.: The Magazine for Growing Companies. 38 Commercial Wharf, Boston, MA 02110. Monthly.

> Aimed specifically at managers of small businesses, this magazine features a variety of short, readable articles on managing people; sales and marketing; and financial strategies. A special feature is the Inc. Network, in which readers request information and help on specific topics: the answers are intended to help others with similar questions. Another feature, FaxPoll, gives readers the opportunity to provide the editors with instant feedback on the issue and to make suggestions for future articles. General-interest stories cover topics like child care, insurance, and performance measurement.

International Management: The Voice of European Business. 151 Wardorn Street, London, England W1V 4BN. Monthly.

> Focusing exclusively on Europe, departments cover European trends, "EC Dateline," profiles of industries, plus news on travel and health matters, and news bits on profits, losses, cutbacks, and expansions of major European companies.

Journal of General Management. Braybrooke Press, Henley-on-Thames, Oxfordshire, England R9G 3AU. Quarterly.

This journal contains concise, well-written explanations to help managers understand the main economic, social, political, and technological issues that affect organizations. It focuses on an exchange of information between academics and policy makers on an international basis. Special attention is given to issues that confront managers dealing internationally, including involvement of governments in business affairs, changing technology, protectionism, terrorism, and environmental concerns as well as efficient marketing, financial and operations management in increasingly interdependent markets.

Journal of Systems Management. Association for Systems Management, 1433 W. Bagley Road, Berea, OH 44017. Monthly.

Articles, guest columns, and case studies focus on technology and techniques for successful information systems management. This journal recently increased its coverage of members' information and news to facilitate an exchange of ideas in the belief that reading about what other members have done well will give readers ideas to improve their own careers. A listing of ASM seminars is included in each issue.

Management Review. American Management Association, 135 W. 50th St., New York, NY 10020. Monthly.

This publication by the AMA offers articles on general management with attention to the Washington and legal perspectives and developments that affect businesses. The magazine also features a section on AMA-sponsored courses and seminars, members' activities, and news of special interest to members. The AMA also is producing a special report series, "Management in the '90s," which looks at critical issues facing managers such as the shrinking labor force, mergers, and AIDS. The editors promise "how-to," solution-oriented strategies for dealing with these issues.

Management Today. Management Publications, Ltd., Lithospeed Ltd., 5-25 Scrutton St., London, England EC2. Monthly.

This oversize, glossy magazine circulates to members of the British Institute of Management, and focuses on management and business issues in Britain and Europe. It includes profiles and features on management techniques, perspectives on economics and industry. It also runs book reviews, and an extensive section in the back of the magazine spotlights conferences, degree programs, plus training and management research services.

Management World. Administrative Management Society, 4622 Street
Road, Trevose, PA 19047. Bimonthly.

This publication focuses on timely managerial issues, with regular
columns on trends, human resources, entrepreneurs, resources
(book reviews, etc.) and general issues related to the workplace.

The Office: Management of Information Systems and Management. Office
Publications, 1600 Summer St., Stamford, CT 06905. Monthly.

This magazine will keep managers abreast of developments in
information systems management. Topics covered include telecommunications, computer software and hardware, and ergonom-
ics. General management issues receive a secondary focus: recent
articles dealt with actual employee grievances and how they were
handled by management.

Personnel Journal: The Business Magazine for Leaders in Human Resources.
ABC Communications, 245 Fischer Avenue, B-2, Costa Mesa,
CA 92626. Monthly.

A helpful feature in this publication is the Managers Newsfront, a
symbiosis of recent court decisions and legislation affecting managers and their management of people. General-interest features
cover topics like employee relocation, health costs, retraining,
and day care. Companies who overcame specific human resource
management problems are profiled.

Sloan Management Review. Sloan Management Review Association of the
MIT Sloan School of Management, 292 Main St., E 38-120,
Cambridge, MA 02139. Quarterly.

This academic journal is written by management academics, consultants, and practicing managers for professional managers. The
focus is general management theory and practice, with special
attention on organizational change, management of technology,
and international management.

The Wall Street Journal. Dow Jones & Company, 200 Liberty Street, New
York, NY 10281. Daily, weekdays.

The best daily dose of business news available. Features and articles cover major news stories, marketing, money, and investing.
An index of all companies mentioned in the issue allows readers
to scan quickly for news on particular firms or industries.

Appendix B
Self-Test Question Key

All page references are to the 6th edition of *Introduction to Management* by Plunkett & Attner.

Lesson 1 – Management at Work: The Managerial World

1. c   p. 6
2. c   p. 13
3. c   p. 18
4. b   p. 21–22
5. c   p. 22–24
6. b   p. 6
7. d   p. 8
8. a   p. 24
9. c   p. 20
10. b   p. 18–20

Lesson 2 – In Transition:
The Changing, Challenging Environment of Management

1. c   p. 35–57
2. b   p. 36–43
3. c   p. 41–42
4. b   p. 42
5. d   p. 38–39
6. c   p. 44–45
7. d   p. 44
8. c   p. 108–110
9. g   p. 43
10. b   p. 41
11. d   p. 44
12. f   p. 39
13. a   p. 38
14. e   p. 41
15. c   p. 39

Lesson 3 – Setting the Stage: The Planning Process

1. d   p. 117–118
2. b   p. 123
3. c   p. 128
4. d   p. 141
5. a   p. 124
6. c   p. 140
7. d   p. 135
8. c   Fig. 5.3, p. 121

Lesson 3 – Setting the Stage (continued)

9. c	p. 126–128	15. f	p. 127
10. h	p. 128	16. i	p. 117
11. e	p. 128	17. d	p. 138–139
12. c	p. 127	18. j	p. 128
13. b	p. 129	19. a	p. 121
14. b	p. 128		

Lesson 4 – The Game Plan: Strategic-, Business-, and Department-level Planning

1. a	p. 155–156	6. a	p. 167–170
2. d	p. 150–151	7. d	p. 160–164
3. c	p. 153–154	8. d	p. 170–172
4. d	p. 164	9. b	p. 160–163
5. c	p. 165–166	10. d	p. 164

Lesson 5 – Calling the Shots: Decision Making

1. d	p. 179	6. c	p. 183–189
2. c	p. 179–180	7. b	p. 179
3. d	p. 191	8. c	p. 200
4. b	p. 195–197	9. d	p. 205–206
5. a	p. 183–189	10. d	p. 203–205

Lesson 6 – Putting It Together: The Principles of Organizing

1. b	p. 215–217	6. h	p. 231
2. a	video	7. b	p. 228
3. c	p. 213	8. a	p. 231
4. f	p. 231	9. e	p. 226
5. d	p. 215	10. g	p. 230–231

Lesson 7 – Laying the Groundwork: Organizational Design

1. b	p. 251	6. d	p. 262–263
2. c	p. 254	7. b	p. 254
3. d	p. 254	8. a	p. 262
4. a	p. 255	9. c	p. 266–268
5. c	p. 258–259	10. d	p. 251

Lesson 8 – Running the Show: Influence, Power, and Authority

1. c	p. 229, 439	6. d	p. 241–242
2. b	p. 229, 440	7. d	p. 242–243
3. e	p. 230–231	8. c	p. 240
4. c	p. 230–231	9. L	p. 225–227
5. c	p. 236	10. S	p. 225–227

Lesson 8 – Running the Show (continued)

11. S   p. 225–227   14. S   p. 225–227
12. L   p. 225–227   15. L   p. 225–227
13. L   p. 225–227   16. S   p. 225–227

Lesson 9 – Heart of the Matter: Organizational Climate

1. d   p. 286   6. b   p. 280
2. c   p. 279   7. c   p. 78
3. d   p. 279   8. b   p. 73
4. d   p. 67–69   9. b   p. 278
5. d   p. 67–69   10. c   p. 80–81

Lesson 10 – Shifting Gears: Managing Organizational Change

1. c   p. 296   6. a   p. 303
2. b   p. 293–294   7. d   p. 304
3. a   p. 293–294   8. d   p. 304–5
4. b   p. 298–300   9. c   p. 307
5. b   p. 298–300   10. d   p. 307–310

Lesson 11 – Help Wanted: Recruitment and Selection of Employees

1. c   p. 316   6. c   p. 327–329
2. a   p. 317–318   7. d   p. 334–335
3. a   p. 317–318, 327   8. b   p. 319
4. d   p. 322, 335–336   9. a   p. 320–322
5. b   p. 535–536   10. d   p. 333

Lesson 12 – High Performance: Staff Development and Maintenance

1. c   p. 337   6. c   p. 342
2. d   p. 337   7. d   p. 338
3. b   p. 338–339   8. c   p. 339
4. a   p. 340–341   9. c   p. 341–342
5. d   p. 341   10. b   p. 346

Lesson 13 – Keeping in Touch:
Interpersonal and Organizational Communication

1. d   p. 359   6. c   p. 370
2. a   p. 373   7. b   p. 379–380
3. a   p. 373   8. c   p. 361
4. c   p. 370   9. a   p. 375–379
5. b   p. 371–372   10. d   p. 371–372

Lesson 14 – All Systems Go: Motivating for Excellence

1. d p. 390
2. b p. 391
3. a p. 394
4. c p. 395–396
5. c p. 402–403
6. b p. 402–404
7. d p. 398–399
8. a p. 400–401
9. a p. 409–411
10. c p. 413–424

Lesson 15 – Pulling Together: Building Morale and Commitment

1. c p. 416
2. c p. 419
3. d p. 417–419
4. a p. 420–422
5. d p. 420
6. b p. 421–422
7. c p. 420–422
8. d p. 422
9. d p. 420–422
10. a p. 467–480

Lesson 16 – At the Helm: Styles of Leadership

1. b p. 430
2. d p. 454–455
3. a p. 433–437
4. b p. 433–437
5. a p. 433–437
6. a p. 433–437
7. a p. 433–437
8. b p. 433–437
9. b p. 442–443
10. d p. 453
11. b p. 441–442
12. b p. 449–450

Lesson 17 – Working It Out: Managing Organizational Conflict

1. a p. 482
2. b p. 482–483
3. a p. 484–486
4. d p. 486–487
5. d p. 486
6. b p. 483
7. b p. 488
8. d p. 488–489
9. a p. 483
10. a p. 487

Lesson 18 – Keeping Track: Management and Control

1. a p. 496
2. b p. 498–499
3. d p. 499–502
4. c p. 506–507
5. d p. 507
6. b p. 508–512
7. a p. 508–511
8. b p. 502
9. a p. 508–511
10. a p. 514

Lesson 19 – It All Adds Up: Financial Methods of Control

1. a p. 533
2. d p. 533
3. b p. 533–535
4. a p. 530–532
5. b p. 524–525
6. b p. 524–525
7. d p. 524–525
8. a p. 524–525
9. c p. 524–525
10. b p. 524–525
11. b p. 527

Lesson 20 – Taking Stock: Production/Operations Management

1. c	p. 554–555	6. a	p. 573–574
2. b	p. 556–557	7. d	p. 573–574
3. e	p. 559–561	8. a	p. 556–557
4. b	p. 559–561	9. b	p. 570
5. c	p. 575–576	10. b	p. 555

Lesson 21 – Point of Information: Information Systems Management

1. a	p. 587	6. c	p. 596
2. c	p. 588	7. b	p. 599
3. c	p. 589	8. b	p. 599–604
4. d	p. 589–590	9. d	p. 602–603
5. b	p. 597	10. a	p. 594–595

Lesson 22 – Above and Beyond: Managing for Productivity

1. a	p. 72–83	6. a	p. 65
2. a	p. 71	7. b	p. 70
3. c	p. 71	8. c	p. 74
4. b	p. 73	9. a	p. 66
5. a	p. 72–83	10. d	p. 64

Lesson 23 – World of Opportunity: Managing in a Global Environment

1. b	p. 611	7. d	p. 632–637
2. a	p. 613–614	8. a	617, 622
3. a	p. 611–612	9. c	617, 622
4. b	p. 611–612	10. b	617, 622
5. a	p. 611–612	11. d	617, 622
6. a	p. 615–620		

Lesson 24 – The Right Fit: The Individual and the Organization

1. b	p. 668	6. a	p. 671
2. e	p. 660–661	7. b	p. 663
3. d	p. 666	8. c	p. 663
4. a	p. 664	9. b	p. 665
5. c	p. 665	10. a	p. 665

Lesson 25 – Making Choices: Managerial Ethics

1. b	p. 680	6. d	p. 684–685
2. c	p. 689	7. c	p. 683
3. c	p. 685	8. c	p. 681
4. c	p. 687–688	9. d	p. 681–683
5. b	p. 682	10. b	p. 684–685

Lesson 26 – For the Common Good: Social Responsibility and Management

1.	b	p. 692–693	6. d	p. 701
2.	b	p. 692–693	7. b	p. 698–699
3.	a	p. 692–693	8. b	p. 699
4.	c	p. 692–693	9. c	p. 693
5.	c	p. 700–701	10. d	p. 700–701